Florence Kinrade

Lizzie Borden
of the North

Florence Kinrade

Lizzie Borden
of the North

Frank Jones

DURVILE IMPRINT OF DURVILE AND UPROUTE BOOKS
CALGARY, ALBERTA, CANADA

Durvile Publications Ltd.

DURVILE IMPRINT OF DURVILE AND UPROUTE BOOKS

Calgary, Alberta, Canada
www.durvile.com

LIBRARY AND ARCHIVES CATALOGUING IN PUBLICATIONS DATA

Florence Kinrade: Lizzie Borden of the North
Jones, Frank, author
Book Five in the True Cases Series

1. True Crimes | 2. Theatre
3. Canadian Law | 4. Canadian History

ISBN: 978-1-988824-35-2 (print pbk) | ISBN: 978-0-9952322-8-0 (e-book)
ISBN: 978-1-988824-31-4 (audiobook)

Design and art direction, Lorene Shyba
Photos and illustrations are those of the author, unless otherwise described.

Alberta

We would like to acknowledge the support of the Alberta Government through the Alberta Book Fund.

Durvile is a member of the Book Publishers Association of Alberta (BPAA)
and Association of Canadian Publishers (ACP).

Printed in Canada

First edition, first printing. 2019

To the memory of George Edward Hart
1914 – 2018,
neighbour and friend.

Contents

PART THREE
FINDING FLORENCE

Florence Kinrade. On the back of the photo, in Florence's own handwriting are the words, "18 yrs old. How could *anyone* fall for me ???

Do You Think I Did It?

In Florence's own hand, an expression of her teenage romantic insecurities.

THE FLORENCE KINRADE CASE has been on my mind for a long time. Since January 1987, in fact, when I picked up the phone to call her nephew, Ken Kinrade, who was wintering in Clearwater, Florida.

"Ken Kinrade?"

"Yeah, that's me," came back a harsh, raspy voice. I half-expected Kinrade, then in his seventies, to rebuff me. People, I've found, are generally not eager to discuss a murder in the family, even a long-ago one. But the voice was deceptive. Kinrade, I found when I met him on his return to Hamilton, Ontario in the spring, was a kindly, even timid man, happy to share what he knew about that shocking 1909 crime that had made the family's name notorious.

Now it's been thirty years since I made that phone call. Ken is long dead, as are several of the people who helped me reconstruct the lives of Florence, her sister, Ethel, and their well-to-do parents. The Rev. Graham Cotter, a nephew of Florence's fiancé, Monty Wright, and a long-retired

Anglican clergyman whose letter to me led me to the most important revelations of all, has been unfailingly patient as he waited for the story to be finally told. My manuscript languished on a shelf at the University of Toronto Press for several years. And then, like so many neglected projects, it continued languishing.

But the murder of Ethel Kinrade that snowy day in Hamilton, Ontario, Canada in 1909 deserves our attention because it uncovers a rich vein of social history. It tells us a lot about the obstacles an ambitious young singer from an upper-class family faced in seeking a career in – horrors! – vaudeville. It tells us about a forgotten underclass – the thousands of tramps who rode the rails of North America in that era and who were often the first to be suspected when a crime occurred. It tells too of the sometimes-odd practices of the psychiatric profession in that pre-Freudian time. And it also tells the story of a formidable woman who was as resilient as she was devious and was, quite simply Canada's Lizzie Borden.

The parallels with the notorious 1892 Fall River, Massachusetts case in which Lizzie was suspected of the axe murder of her father and step-mother, are uncanny. In giving her testimony at the inquest into the death of her parents, Lizzie has been described as, "circling, evading, contradicting, revising her story as she went along, scorning the badgering of District Attorney Hosea Knowlton."

The description could just as easily have applied to Florence who, from the first hours after she ran into the street crying that Ethel had been shot – six times – told different and contradictory versions of the murder of her sister. Ultimately, the newspaper-reading public followed with fascination her epic duel with one of the great counsel of the day, George T. Blackstock Q.C. at an inquest which was described by Coroner Dr. James Anderson, as, "unparalleled in the history of Canada, not only for the interest it has aroused throughout the whole country, but by reason of the legal points raised." Dr. Charles Kirk (C.K.) Clarke 'the father of Canadian psychiatry,' who watched Florence throughout and interviewed her several times, said of her testimony, "a more startling and complex psychological study has rarely been offered."

Edmund Lester Pearson, America's pre-eminent crime essayist of his era, wrote that the Lizzie Borden case "is without parallel in the criminal history of America. It is the most interesting, and perhaps the most puzzling murder which has occurred in this country." The same can be said of the Kinrade mystery – up north in Canada.

Pearson suggested that the Borden case had retained its fascination because it involved a class of people not normally involved in bloody crime, because it was purely a problem of murder, uncomplicated by sexual passion, and because it divided national opinion on the guilt or innocence of Lizzie Borden (who was subsequently but never convincingly judged innocent at her trial). The parallels hold. The Kinrade case too involved a well-off family; it was a 'pure' murder and one of shocking violence; it was, and remains, a mystery as to motivation, and it divided the public on the question of Florence Kinrade's guilt or innocence.

So why hasn't the Kinrade case caught the public's imagination until now – say on a Lizzie Borden scale? Of course, there was a coroner's inquest that went on for many weeks that was reported verbatim in the newspapers. Day after day, Florence was tested ruthlessly in the witness box by Blackstock, the Crown's lawyer. In addition, reporters interviewed everyone with the remotest connection with the case in Canada and in Virginia, where Florence led a clandestine existence. Without a transcript of the inquest, I compared the multiple newspaper accounts of the coroner's inquest. Particularly in the moments of high courtroom drama, I found Kit Coleman, Canada's first female war correspondent, an invaluable mood and scene-setter whose reports I have made generous use of. By a stroke of luck, we also have the detailed psychiatric notes of Dr. C.K. Clarke.

The facts were laid shockingly bare. But Florence was never charged with murder. The inquest did not lead to a trial, meaning there was no official transcript to frame an account. And while she was still alive (she died in 1977), any careless accusation of guilt might have invited a civil suit.

All that the Kinrade mystery seems to have lacked in securing its place in history is the nursery rhyme factor: Lizzie Borden's fame was enshrined with a rhyme chanted by generations of American children:

Lizzie Borden took an axe,
And gave her mother forty whacks.
When she saw what she had done,
She gave her father forty-one.

Nevertheless, Florence's life following that period of high notoriety in 1909 was full of interest and surprises. Against all odds, she did achieve a career in vaudeville, endured years of misfortune and then, still singing the songs of her golden years, died at an advanced age and was buried in the Hollywood Cemetery alongside some of the film capital's greats. A puzzle was Florence Kinrade; an enigma, larger-than-life woman who in her last encounter with her daughter asked provocatively, "Do you think I did it?"

— Frank Jones, 2019

— Part One —

A SHOOTING ON HERKIMER STREET

Ethel Kinrade

Chapter One
HE SHOT POOR ETHEL

Florence Kinrade

Ethel and Florence Kinrade 1904 in the Centenary Methodist Church Choir.
Ethel is fifth from the left, second row. Florence is second from the right, second row.

FEBRUARY 25, 1909. The city of Hamilton, Ontario, Canada is wrapped in silence. Only the clanking of cars shunting in the Toronto, Hamilton & Buffalo Railway yards, the occasional steam train whistle, and the regular clang of a passing streetcar intrude on the hush of Herkimer Street. Falling snow muffles footsteps and the sound of hooves. It is ten degrees Fahrenheit below freezing.

Shortly after lunch, Thomas L. Kinrade, a tall, heavily built man, emerges from number 105, closing the bevelled glass door behind him, careful not to slip on the fresh snow. At this time, Hamilton, a steel town at the western end of Lake Ontario, bills itself, 'the ambitious city.' It is a seething boomtown, the working class East End one vast construction site in the frantic race to build houses for immigrant workers flocking to the metals industries. Kinrade, a prominent educator, also has an eye to business: he has constructed some thirty houses, the rents from which are collected weekly by his daughters, Ethel and Florence.

He turns in the direction of the Cannon Street public school, one of four schools over which he is principal. A few minutes later, the Kinrades' youngest daughter, Gertrude, sixteen, leaves for school. She turns the corner, and Herkimer Street is once again empty and silent. For the next two hours, as far as anyone is aware, nobody comes or goes. In a front upstairs room across the street from the Kinrade house, Mrs. Frank Hickey is busy sewing for her little ones. She notices nothing. Next door to the Kinrades, Mrs. William Acres sits in the front room, reading a novel. Perhaps it is exciting, because she too notices nothing.

At around 3:25 *p.m.*, by her own count, the front door of number 105 opens and Mrs. Thomas Kinrade (whose first name was Isabelle, or 'Bella'), snug in her fur coat, emerges and waddles off down the street in the direction of downtown Hamilton like a rotund beaver, going about her business. Time passes, measured by the slow progress up and down the street of a carriage driven by Henry Woodridge. Waiting for his mistress, who is making a social call, Woodridge, wrapped in a blanket, is keeping the horse moving so that it doesn't get cold.

It is exactly 3:57 *p.m.* – he is quite sure he is on time – when Ernie Stone, driving his electric streetcar along Herkimer Street at a stately five or six miles an hour, sees a young woman run down the steps of number 105. He is preparing to stop, thinking she is trying to catch a ride, but she doesn't seem to notice the streetcar, and runs right in front of it. He brakes hard. The steel wheels screech and luckily he manages to avoid hitting her. All he can do is shake his head and wonder at 'the recklessness of young women today.' She runs across the tracks and through the side gate of the house opposite. Tom Roach, the streetcar conductor whose responsibility it is to keep the stove alight and the interior snug, also sees the young woman. He notices that she is dressed for the outdoors, wearing a broad-brimmed hat. A moment later, Mrs. Hickey, busy sewing, hears her name called from downstairs. "Mrs. Hickey! Mrs. Hickey!" Florence Kinrade is lying sobbing at the foot of the stairs. "Mrs. Hickey, Ethel is shot!"

"Oh, surely not!" the woman says, hurrying down the stairs and lifting the prostrate girl.

"It's true! Ethel is shot six times." A tramp, she insists, has burst into the house and shot her older sister, Ethel. Mrs. Hickey notices there is foam around Florence's mouth and her voice sounds thick.

"Stay here, dear," says Mrs. Hickey, "I'll run next door and have them telephone the police station."

At police headquarters, Mrs. Hickey's frantic message that a vagrant has shot a young woman, Ethel Kinrade, on Herkimer Street is transmitted immediately to Inspector of Detective Bernard McMahon. In his many

Ethel Kinrade

Florence and Ethel's mother, Bella Kinrade

years of service, the Irish-born cop has rarely heard anything so surprising. Because, shortly before, he was taking a complaint from Mrs. Kinrade that tramps had been bothering the family night and day. Something, she had insisted, had to be done to stop them. They were dangerous.

After leaving the police station, Mrs. Kinrade crosses the street to the Bethel Mission where some seventy-five men, many of them tramps, sleep each night. She is sitting in the mission parlour, talking to the proprietor when he notices the police patrol wagon leave the station on an emergency call – to Herkimer Street, it turns out. After appealing to the proprietor to be more circumspect in the tramps he directs to her door, Mrs. Kinrade leaves with a book of meal and bed tickets to hand out to transients.

Back on Herkimer Street, while Mrs. Hickey is calling the police, Florence, who is twenty-three and a gifted soprano popular at concerts throughout the region, again emerges, and hurries down the street to the corner grocery and butcher shop. "There's a man in our house," she tells the proprietor, L.M. Brown, between sobs, "and he's shot poor Ethel. He's acting like a maniac. Poor Ethel!"

Meanwhile, Dr. W.J. McNichol, a coroner and general practitioner, is about to leave his office at Herkimer and Bay Streets on calls when he receives a telephone message to go to the Kinrade house where Ethel Kinrade has been shot. His buggy is at the door, he jumps in and is at the Kinrade door in minutes.

Brown, prudently armed with two meat cleavers, encounters Dr.

McNichol at the house. The two men, the grocer brandishing his cleavers, step gingerly through the double front doors, both of which are open to the frigid winter air. The parlour window, opening on the side of the house, is half open, and snow drifts in. "Miss Kinrade!" the doctor calls. There is no sound. In the dining room, at the foot of the servants' back stairway leading up to the second floor, the doctor finds Ethel's body. A woman of twenty-five, she is dressed for the outdoors in her coat, hat and veil; her ermine stole is on the table, which is pushed to one side, and her mink muff is on the floor. There is, Dr. McNichol will say later, a strong smell of powder fumes and smoke in the room. He can find no pulse, and notes that Ethel's hands are cool to the touch. The doctor also notices two bullet wounds in her lower lip. Opening her coat, he finds three more bullet wounds on the left side of her chest. The clothing is burned to the skin; the shots, he conjectures, were fired at close range. He would say that Ethel had been dead anywhere from fifteen minutes to possibly an hour-and-a-half. "No medical man can say for sure," is his opinion. Informed by Mrs. Hickey that Florence is across the street at her home, Dr. McNichol finds Florence nervous and distraught on a sofa in the back room and his observation is that,

> … she was helpless and seemed to be unable to think let alone talk about the terrible affair. I gave her some sedatives, and shortly after she became calmer, and I asked her to tell me about it and to give me a description of the one who did the crime. I wanted to get this for the police so that they might get to work as she alone could describe the man who had murdered her sister.

"It was a tramp," she tells him. "He was wearing a slouch hat. He forced his way into the house. He had a gun. He shot Ethel."

"Did you see him do it?"

"Yes, I was there. I saw him."

Across the street, the police wagon arrives with Detective John W. Bleakley, a slim Irishman with a brush moustache and military bearing, and his colleague, Detective Coulter. The call to the police station had mentioned the tramp was still in the house. Bleakley and Coulter search the home from cellar to attic without finding anybody. There is no sign of the murder weapon. The place is chilly from several sashes being left open, and the policemen also notice a smell of smoke. Turning his attention to the body on the dining room floor, Bleakley (apparently aware that Dr.

McNichol has already ascertained that Ethel is dead) is surprised to see no blood at all.

A horse-drawn ambulance pulls up in front of 105 Herkimer Street, and a stretcher is brought in to remove the body. Then Bleakley gets his explanation for the apparent lack of blood. As attendants lift the body and place it on the stretcher, a large pool of blood measuring about eighteen inches by six or seven inches is revealed. It corresponds to the small of Ethel's back although, curiously, no bullets penetrated at that point. Studying the crime scene, the careful detective notes a dining room chair beside the body. If Ethel had been sitting in the chair when she was shot in the head, he decides, she would have tumbled forward, her head ending up where the blood had collected on the floor. The conclusion is unavoidable: the body has been moved.

Stooping down, his face almost touching the floor, Bleakley picks up two small items from the pool of congealing blood: a small-calibre bullet and a broken tooth. It confirms his belief that when Ethel was shot in the mouth, her head had fallen where the blood was found. He finds another flattened bullet at her feet along with a piece of bone or tooth.

It is 4:30 in the afternoon. A hackney carriage arrives carrying Tom Kinrade. He had been leaving for home at 4:10 when one of the teachers, Miss Simpson, called to him from the steps of the school. There was an urgent phone call for him. When he picked up the receiver, Brown, the grocer, told him, "A tramp has broken into your house and shot your daughter and she is dead."

When he arrives home there is a crowd outside the house. He hands the school caretaker, who has accompanied him, a dollar bill, walks up the steps into the house and throws himself into an armchair in the parlour.

"Oh, my God! This is awful!" he exclaims. "Why should this happen in our home?"

Detective Bleakley is surprised at the father's first words to him: "I have just expected something like this would happen."

Kinrade follows the policeman into the dining room where the body remains on a stretcher. The father gets down on his knees and lifts back the oilcloth covering her face. She is still wearing her hat, her veil drawn across her forehead. "It's Ethel!" he remarks in surprise. He kisses her.

As he steps back, the two ambulance attendants, one at the head, one at the feet, pick up the stretcher carrying Ethel's body and make to carry it out of the back door.

"Where are you going with her?" demands the father. "What are you going to do?" They ignore him and carry Ethel away. In response to his query, he is told that his wife and Florence are across the street at Mrs. Hickey's. It was supposedly at her husband's prompting that Bella Kinrade that afternoon had walked the mile down the hill to the police station. She had been in a state of nerves. Tramps had rung their doorbell after dark the previous evening, and that morning the family had noticed a chip hacked out of the windowsill near the front door. Mrs. Kinrade, busy telling the charity people only to send the most respectable-seeming tramps to her door, did not notice the police wagon leave following the call from Herkimer Street. It is only as she is going home on the streetcar that she notices a crowd of people in front of her door and asks to be let off on the spot. Mistaking the ambulance for a hearse, she cries, "Oh, Earl's dead, and they've brought his body home!" Her nineteen-year-old son had sent a message from Montreal, where he works in a bank, to say he was quite ill. Mrs. Hickey heads her off at the front door of 105, and urges her to come across the street, where the mother swoons into the arms of Daniel Lawlor, a *Hamilton Herald* reporter. He carries her into the Hickey house and lays her on a couch.

The sequence that follows demands our close attention: Tom Kinrade finds Florence at Mrs. Hickey's. His wife, he is told, is in a faint in the front room and he had best leave her there. Florence's first words when he put his arm around her shoulder were, her father later testified, "Oh, Papa, you must keep up. I will keep up if you will, Papa. And, you know it could have been worse. He said he would shoot me too." He thanked God, Kinrade would say, that he had not lost both daughters.

Do father and daughter exchange further words out of the hearing of reporters as he leads her back across the street to be interviewed by the police? Or is a suspicion forming in Thomas Kinrade's mind? At any rate, he is obviously feeling put out when Detective Bleakley insists on interviewing Florence alone.

In her first account to police of the afternoon's tragedy, she tells the detective that she and Ethel had been upstairs getting ready to go out for a walk when the doorbell rang. A man she describes as a tramp was at the door asking for something to eat. She turned to fetch some food when he pushed open the door, saying if she had any money, he would take that too. She ran upstairs to fetch ten dollars she had saved and, passing the door of Ethel's room, called to her to lock her door. She received no reply. She

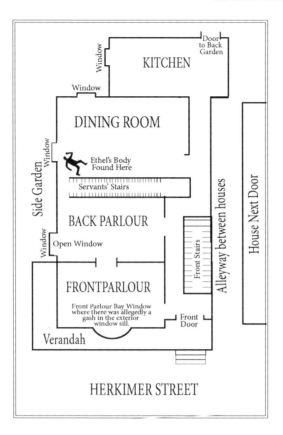

Floor plan of the Kinrade home at 105 Herkimer Street.

opened her bedroom window intending to step out on the balcony and give the alarm, she says, but then changed her mind. At that point, she says, she heard a scream and "bang, bang, bang." She got the ten dollars, went down the front stairs, and gave the man the money. She ran through into the kitchen, apparently not noticing Ethel's body in the dining room, and out into the back yard. She had intended climbing the fence, but then changed her mind and returned to the house. The man, still there, pointed a gun at her and said, "If you make any noise, I will shoot you too." She threw up her arm to try to grab the revolver, and then fled through the front door to Mrs. Hickey's. The man, she tells Bleakley, is about thirty-five years of age, height five-foot-seven or -eight, with a medium dark complexion and a long, droopy dark brown moustache. He was wearing a dark suit, dark overcoat and black slouch hat pulled down over his eyes.

Florence is visibly upset and any further questions Bleakley might have are cut short by the intervention of her father. He does not wish his daughter interviewed in this manner, he declares. His own words would be: "I bolted up and I said, 'I won't let her stay alone with you nor any other man.'" With his daughter's blood still staining the dining room floor, it seems an odd moment for Kinrade to insist on the social proprieties, but Bleakley, conscious of Tom Kinrade's prestige in the community, meekly surrenders his witness. He would not resume his interview until the following day.

Police put a watch on the railway stations for anyone leaving town who might match Florence's description of the murderer. Acting on the description of the tramp-murderer, police from Buffalo, across the American border, to Toronto and out into the hinterland for hundreds of miles around are soon hunting for the tramp with the droopy moustache. *The Toronto World* reports on February 26 that police have interviewed everyone in the neighborhood and no one reports seeing a tramp of that description.

But there is more to Florence's tramp story. And, oddly enough, Tom Kinrade evidently sees nothing wrong with his daughter sharing the details with a reporter from *The Toronto Daily Star* at Mrs. Hickey's shortly afterwards.

It was not the first time she had seen the intruder, she relates. He had first appeared the previous Sunday when the Kinrades had just returned from church. "We noticed him peeping through the dining room window," she says. When his eyes met theirs, he disappeared. The night before the murder, Wednesday, he had turned up at the door again asking for a meal ticket. Because of the lateness of the hour and his suspicious appearance, she says, her mother had told him to go away. Hearing his wife's concerns, her father had armed himself with a poker, says Florence, and walked down the road to meet her and Ethel as they came home from a birthday party at their brother, Ernest's house.

During the night, Florence relates, "I was awakened by a grating noise."

Chapter Two

Tramp Panic

An affront to Hamilton, Ontario middle-class values, tramps and vagrants were
an unforeseen consequence of the railway age.

T HE EDITOR OF *The Hamilton Spectator* could be forgiven if, as details
of the murder on Herkimer Street trickled into his office that afternoon of February 25, 1909, he experienced not just feelings of sadness and
shock, but also the thrill of vindication. In the depths of the winter season,
with Hamilton experiencing its usual seasonal influx of vagrants or 'vags,'
as they were called, he had, the week before, assigned a reporter to write a
major series of articles on the tramp menace. The articles were already written and ready for the presses when the Kinrade murder seemed to provide
proof absolute of the seriousness of the threat. In the following days, *The
Spectator* pounded home its advantage in what is a textbook example of a
media attempt to inspire panic.

It was a time when Hamilton was at the very pinnacle of its success.
"The decades preceding and following the turn of the century," according to
a local history, *Steel City*, "were the most exciting in the history of Hamilton
because they marked a remarkable outpouring of human energy and
innovative initiatives." The city's population doubled to 100,000 between

1906 and 1913 providing a wonderful opportunity for entrepreneurs like Kinrade. His little rental empire would crumble in the wake of the murder, but his name lives on in Kinrade Avenue, an undistinguished street in the East End.

But while thousands of immigrants flocked to Hamilton seeking work principally in the steel industry, the city was also a Mecca for men of a different sort. They arrived each winter looking simply for a cozy billet and free meals, most of them with no intention of working at all. The tramps or hobos were an unforeseen consequence of the railway age. As the railroad companies spread their cobweb of tracks across the continent in the nineteenth century, suddenly young men with an itch to travel – or a simple aversion to work – were free to roam; jumping boxcars, riding the rails from town to town, sleeping rough and cooking their meals over campfires in hobo jungles on the fringes of town. The tramps tended to see themselves as rebels and rugged individualists, outlaws who often fought rearguard battles against railway and city police forces. Instead of waiting on street corners, they canvassed the best neighborhoods, knocking on doors and leaving their own secret marks on fences or gates to indicate a good touch or a house to be avoided.

According to a hobo interviewed by a *Toronto Globe* reporter in 1881, tramping was an enjoyable experience in the summer. He slept outdoors in fine weather and in barns or empty houses when it rained. It was safer in Canada than the United States. As he put it, "There's no shooting or anything of that kind." He continued:

> Last night, I slept out in a ravine behind Rosedale (the city's poshest neighborhood), me and another man lookin' for work. He had a chicken which a storekeeper had given him – so he said – an' I got half a loaf at a house nearby an' we built a roaring fire an' were as jolly as sandboys.

Winter was a different matter, and Hamilton, served by two railways and strategically located at the western end of Lake Ontario not far from the American border, was a natural magnet for the travelling clan. "It is a well-known fact among men engaged in charity work here," reported *The Hamilton Times*, that

> Hamilton is the headquarters in winter of hobos from all over the country. Some of these characters have frankly confessed

to Relief Officer McMenemy and officers of charitable societies that this city is the softest place they ever struck, that they voice the fact abroad and that many flock here year after year when the cold weather comes.

While some householders felt vulnerable and intimidated by these scruffy men knocking at their doors, others were sympathetic and responded generously. Even policemen, charged with arresting tramps for vagrancy often showed sympathy, especially in getting them into a shelter or a cell in the coldest weather.

But tramps, with their easy-going ways, were a profound affront to middle class values, a view expressed in extreme form by the Reverend Francis Wayland, Dean of the Yale Law School, in an 1877 speech:

> And as we utter the word 'tramp,' there arises straightaway before us the spectacle of the lazy, shiftless, sauntering or swaggering, ill-conditioned, irreclaimable, incorrigible, cowardly, utterly depraved savage. He fears not God, neither regards man. Indeed he seems to have lost all the better instincts and attitudes of manhood. He will outrage an unprotected female, or rob a defenseless child, or burn an isolated barn, or girdle fruit trees, or wreck a railway train, or set fire to a railway bridge, or murder a cripple, or pilfer an umbrella with equal indifference, if reasonably sure of equal impunity. Having no moral sense, he knows no gradation of crime…. Practically he has come to consider himself at war with society and all social institutions.

Between murdering cripples and pilfering umbrellas, there really wasn't much your average tramp wasn't capable of, according to this less-than-charitable Christian gentleman. Not surprisingly, starting in the 1880s, both the U.S. and Canada experienced periodic tramp panics, usually in the aftermath of some spectacular crime – whether or not a man of the road was ultimately found to blame.

In southern Ontario, conditions were already ripe for a panic. In Stratford, 65 miles west of Hamilton, five months before the Kinrade murder a farmer, William Peah, returning home from work, found the farmhouse silent and with no sign of his wife. He discovered her bloodied body in the basement where she had been raped and murdered. Beside her, drunk and asleep, lay "a Negro tramp named Frank Roughmond, 32, his hands, face and clothing spattered with blood." Neighbouring farmers were considering lynching Roughmond when he was saved by the arrival of a constable and the local police chief.

Two weeks later, under a headline, "Assailed by a Tramp" *The Toronto World* reported that Mrs. William Charlton had been choked and beaten by a tramp in her home near Brockville, Ontario. She had agreed to give the man breakfast, but when she brought him into the kitchen, he demanded money, then attacked her, leaving her unconscious before making his escape.

Hamilton newspapers were quick to pick up the cue. "No crime in recent years," *The Hamilton Times* reported on February 26, 1909, the day after the Kinrade murder,

> … has created such a tremendous sensation as this brutal murder… The affair instilled fear into the hearts of many who have been troubled by tramps and who have been in the habit of meeting their demands for assistance. Many of these shiftless characters who appealed last night for help had the doors rudely slammed in their faces.

Later in the same *Times* article, the writer speaks of the need "to rid the city of this class of leaches."

But it was *The Spectator* that really went to town. A huge black streamer headline across the top of the front page asked: "Who Shot Ethel Kinrade?" Tucked beneath it on the left side of the page was the story of the murder, on the other another large headline: "A Rendezvous for Tramps and Bums" with a deck headline, "Undesirable Characters Flock to Hamilton From Other Places Where Authorities Are More Active." The theme of *The Spectator* campaign would be that the Hamilton authorities were soft on tramps and bums, leaving citizens open to being cheated, assaulted, or even murdered. "Many professional bums have found Hamilton a safe retreat," editorialized *The Spec*, and the newspaper's research only strengthened local belief that Ethel Kinrade had been murdered by a tramp.

The reporter had visited three out of a number of lodging houses that, in addition to a police shelter, catered to transients: the Bethel Mission, where Bella Kinrade had called the afternoon of the murder, the People's Lodging House, and the Workman's Home. He found conditions varying from the decent to the deplorable. Of more interest to the citizenry, the reporter discovered that the proprietors of the lodging houses conspired with their clients to work a racket on unsuspecting householders.

The proprietors supplied tramps with blank meal tickets, an idea that appealed to the public because, ostensibly, the tickets could only be used for food or a bed rather than booze. The People's Lodging House ticket, for instance, was headed, "Help those who cannot help themselves," and mentioned prices of five cents for a bowl of soup, ten cents for a full meal (usually hash), and fifteen cents for a bed. Householders were encouraged to fill in an amount and sign the ticket, the money being collected from them later by the lodging house proprietor. At the bottom is a biblical text about good works, and the promise, "This cannot be sold, commuted or transferred."

What donors were not aware of, according to *The Spec* story, was that tramps, after being directed to the better sections of town, including Herkimer Street, by the lodging house keepers, would go door to door getting a number of coupons signed. As they had no need for more than one meal and bed a night, the proprietors would turn a deceitful penny by buying back surplus coupons at a discount – providing the transients with spending money for the saloon – then charge the householders full face price.

By the second day of *The Spectator* campaign, Edward Leonard, proprietor of the People's Lodging House, had been charged with keeping his several premises "in a filthy and unsanitary condition," and one of them, at 72 York Street, was ordered closed by the city board of health.

But it was the tramps, and not the people making a tidy living from them, that attracted the newspaper's attention. "Clear Them Out" was the headline on an editorial the first day:

> In the presence of so horrible an outrage as occurred yesterday afternoon at the home of T.L. Kinrade, the citizens of Hamilton may well stand aghast. That an unknown tramp should be able to enter a residence on a thickly populated and constantly traveled street in mid-afternoon, rob one young woman and foully slay another, getting away from the place without anyone being the wiser, seems inconceivable…. That the murder was committed by one of the hundreds of roaming tramps who have during the whole winter infested the city, making their living easily by

begging from the citizens, there seems little reason to doubt. Herkimer Street homes have for weeks been regarded as easy pickings by these men…. For many reasons Hamilton has long been regarded as an 'easy' town by the idle and shiftless population of the country. Hamilton citizens are notoriously sympathetic, and a distress cry at the door seldom goes unheeded…. The kitchen door that has in the past been freely opened to admit the wandering beggar for a hot meal will in future be barred…. The appeal for assistance will go unheeded…. Moreover, the police authorities would be well-advised if they undertook a roundup of the inhabitants of the cheap lodging houses and ordered out of the city, every man whose excuse for his presence here is regarded as flimsy. This is a section of our population that we can well afford to be rid of, and the sooner the better.

Big *Spectator* headlines continued to hammer home the attack: "How Down and Outs Impose on the Public" appeared in the February 27, 1909 issue, and on March 1, "Ways of Getting Rid of the Tramp Nuisance" with columns of type devoted to the issue. The Monday after the murder, *The Spectator* could report with satisfaction:

> According to information from police headquarters, there has been a great shift the last couple of days among the hundreds of tramps in the city, and one officer stated yesterday that the bums were leaving the city in bunches as a result of the feeling aroused by the Kinrade murder and the tramp articles in the Spectator…. There has been a general exodus since Friday, and at the present rate, followed by a little action by the police, a good part of this element will be cleaned out for the time being.

It couldn't happen too fast for *The Spectator*. When, later that week, a policeman and a citizen were wounded by a gun-toting burglar caught red-handed, even though there was nothing to suggest the assailant was a tramp, the newspaper was at it again next day with an editorial headed, "Round Them Up."

> And why, if the invitation to move along is not accepted instanter should (the police) not arrest every man of them?

> Better that the jails should be filled up and that we should
> have to pay for the keep of these birds of passage in custody
> than that we should be terrorized by them roaming at large, a
> daily and nightly terror and menace to both life and property.

Kit Watkins, columnist for *The Toronto Mail and Empire* and Canada's
most famous woman journalist of the time, tried to throw a cloak of warm
sentimentality over the issue:

> It is hardly to be wondered at that the whole City of Hamilton
> became hysterical in the matter of the Kinrade murder mys-
> tery. The thought of the place, the hour, the victim – poor
> young girl! – of the tragedy, the first wild outcry against the
> tramps, set every woman locking her doors and refusing to
> answer a ring or knock. To many an unfortunate man or boy
> during the winter you had handed out meat and money. Few,
> if any, were refused. It does not appear seemly for you in
> your warm house, after your pleasant meal, to refuse to help
> some poor wanderer standing shivering in thin clothes on
> your doorstep. Perhaps your tramp may smell of drink, but if
> your heart is bigger than a walnut shell, you will excuse him,
> remembering that five cents will buy him a warming drink,
> but very little beyond a dry loaf in the way of food; remem-
> bering, too, that misery seems uplifting or oblivion, that we
> are humans, not angels, and that to a miserable outcast, a
> drop of whiskey seems a foretaste of Heaven.

Her words seem to have melted few hearts in Hamilton. The same
day, *The Spectator* reported that the city's mayor, John Inglis McLaren, was
asking the police for a roundup of vagrants. A *Toronto Daily Star* reporter,
walking the streets at one *a.m.*, found that two thirds of the houses in the
Queen and Herkimer Streets area had their living room lights blazing to
frighten away intruders.

On March 10, 1909 *The Spectator*, under a front page headline, "Vags
Sentenced to Three Months," reported that two tramps, Gladstone Davies
and Fred Thompson, picked up while begging, were sentenced to three
months in jail by the magistrate. Davies, when searched, had clasp knives
and a dinner knife on him – the requisite tools, one would have thought, for
eating on the wild side.

But if the Hamilton authorities were hustling the tramps out of town, where were they to go? The tramp panic in the wake of the Kinrade murder stretched far and wide. In Toronto, in the days following the murder, the police were receiving many calls from worried householders about suspicious characters, and a roundup of the unemployed was being considered. An unfortunate Polish transient named Michael Steffin was picked up by the Buffalo police on suspicion of being the Kinrade murderer the day after the killing, even though an officer admitted he bore no resemblance to the man Florence had described. Steffin, described as a professional tramp, said he had walked from Chicago via Hamilton and when arrested on the International Bridge was wearing two overcoats, the pockets of each stuffed with food and toilet articles. *The Hamilton Herald* reported ominously, "He is being put through the third degree this morning in the expectation that, if he is the guilty man, the Buffalo police will know it by noon." The paper was able to report later that Steffin had come through the grilling "with flying colours," and had been released. Tramps were similarly arrested in several other communities in southwestern Ontario, but were soon released. And no wonder. Because almost from the beginning, police detectives were voicing doubts about Florence Kinrade's tramp story.

Chapter Three

THE KINRADES

Ernest   Earl   Ethel   Mrs. Kinrade   T.L Kinrade
Gertrude   (105 Herkimer St.

The Kinrade family home at 105 Herkimer Street, Hamilton, Ontario.
It was here that Ethel Kinrade was shot and killed.

B LUNDERS WERE MADE. Any modern-day homicide detective review-ing the methods of the Hamilton police force in the Kinrade murder would be driven to despair. No effort had been made to secure the crime scene. Policemen and neighbours stomped around the back yard compro-mising the evidence of the footprints in the snow. There was only one brief cursory search made of the house to discover if an intruder was present, but no thorough search for the murder weapon or any other evidence.

The body was removed almost immediately from the Kinrade house and Thomas and Florence, and perhaps other members of the Kinrade family, had been allowed back into the house right after the murder. Worst of all, the Kinrades were allowed to return to take up residence at

105 Herkimer Street that very evening. Whatever evidence still existed, it was within their power to remove or destroy. Because the tramp account was initially so plausible, no effort was made to examine Florence's hands or her mother's to determine whether they had recently fired a gun, and no search was made in case they had discarded any blood-stained clothing. Such an intrusion in the first hours of the family tragedy was considered unthinkable.

In Detroit, Chief of Detectives James McDonnell, one of the most famous police detectives of his time, took a harsher line. If the murder had occurred in his city, he would say later, Florence Kinrade and her mother would have been taken to police headquarters immediately, questioned closely, and their statements taken down by a stenographer. He declared, "There should have been no opportunity given the principal characters connected with the mystery to get together until after their statements had been taken."

It was more than a case of police sloppiness. If the murder had occurred in one of Tom Kinrade's working men's cottages in the city's East End, the results might have been different. A Florence in humbler circumstances would, at the very least, have been taken to the police station and questioned closely out of reach of her family. As it was, Tom Kinrade had used his authority and social position to cut short Detective Bleakley's interrogation at the scene. Indeed, throughout the investigation the police seemed to regard themselves as intruders, and to a great degree Tom Kinrade's social position as an educator and man of property protected Florence from proper questioning. The second obstacle the police faced was that Florence was a member of the 'delicate gender' and therefore helpless and prone to tears and vapours.

In Victorian and Edwardian times, the words female and hysteria were frequently uttered in the same breath. "Women, because they were female, were at risk," writes Canadian historian Wendy Mitchison. "Lack of control over the emotions was the predominant characteristic of hysteria." So when Bleakley returned to 105 Herkimer Street the next morning to interview Florence again and try to repair the damage, he did not seem surprised that, when he sat down with her in the room where the murder occurred (certainly not to a setting congenial to calm interrogation) he found her tearful, confused and apparently close to breakdown.

"Of course, we must allow for hysteria," he told a reporter afterwards. The night before, said Bleakley, Florence had told her now-familiar story of a man pushing his way in and demanding money, which she had gone upstairs to retrieve. She said she called to Ethel to lock herself in her room, but received no reply. She heard a shot, followed by a scream, and then four shots. Bleakley consulted his notes from the previous day:

> She went downstairs and into the dining room where she met the man and handed him the ten dollars. She went through the dining room and kitchen and out into the back yard to the rear fence. I tracked her footsteps in the snow. The snow showed she dragged her feet and evidently ran back into the house, judging by the footmarks.

In that first account, said the officer, she had described encountering the man in the dining room when he turned his revolver on her and told her if she shouted or made noise he would shoot her. "She tried to wrest the gun from him," said Bleakley, "but she was not successful and ran out of the front door. During all this time," he said, shaking his head, "she says she never saw her sister – who was found at the bottom of the back stairs." And he said dryly, "She had to pass through the room both going and coming."

That morning though, said Bleakley, Florence had changed her story. When she had come downstairs, she now insisted she had met the man in the hallway, not the dining room, and had turned away from him towards the rear parlour, where she had opened the window. "The window was open when we arrived," said Bleakley, and a woman's tracks were to be seen in the snow. They didn't go anywhere, and he surmised she had climbed back through the window. "Miss Kinrade declared she did not get out of the window, although she thought of doing that, and changed her mind." In this version, Florence now said she ran back through the house from the kitchen and out into the street to give the alarm without ever encountering the man.

"I called her attention to the fact that she told me last night she had a tussle with the man the second time," said Bleakley in his best witness box manner. That was right, she'd added hurriedly, she'd forgotten that. She was also not as certain as she had been about the colour of the man's moustache, whether it was dark or brown. But she was quite sure that, although she had never seen him before, she would recognize him again.

Detective Bleakley had several other crumbs to offer: Ethel, who, according to her father, had neither a boyfriend nor an enemy in the world, had in fact been shot seven times. "She may have received the first shot standing up," said Bleakley, "but she received most of the shots lying down."

Two reporters who accompanied Bleakley to the Kinrade house had seen for themselves the peculiar nature of the footprints in the backyard. The prints leading from the back door and still quite clear were large and the footwear had been dragged, never quite coming clear from the snow. They had stopped several feet from the fence and there were no footprints in the alleyway beyond the fence to suggest an intruder had escaped that way. Rather, there was a pattern of footsteps returning to the house, these much smaller, the toes making deep indents, the heels not touching the ground, and clearly made by a woman's footwear. "Could the heavy, dragging footsteps have been made by someone wearing men's rubber overshoes too large for them?" one reporter asked. "It was possible," replied Bleakley.

At noon, Bleakley was summoned to the office of Mayor John Inglis McLaren, where he told his story again to the mayor, two aldermen and the police chief. In any normal murder investigation, the assistance of the Provincial Criminal Investigation Branch in Toronto, the provincial capital, would not be requested until the local police force had hit a brick wall in its inquiries. In this case, however, the mayor proposed that a provincial detective should be called in immediately.

Why the rush? This would be a high-profile case. A prominent Hamilton family was involved, the case was baffling, and the government would be questioned in the Legislature later that day on its proposed course of action. A telegram was duly fired off to the Hon. John S. Hendrie, a former mayor of Hamilton and now a Member of the Legislature, who contacted the attorney general's department with the request.

Even before the telegram arrived though, you sense, the wheels were turning. In Toronto, Provincial Detective Inspector John Miller had left a wife just about to go into labour and caught a train to Hamilton that Friday morning. Miller, who received his training with the Hamilton force and still numbered many friends among officers there, was officially assigned to the case that evening.

Next morning, with Detectives Bleakley and Coulter, he went to 105 Herkimer Street with the intention of interviewing Florence Kinrade, but was told Florence was too upset to talk to the officers. After examining the scene of the crime, Detective Inspector Miller was ready to give

Florence's brother Ernest, who was not always highly exacting
in his real-estate business transactions, according to his father, Thomas.

a surprisingly frank assessment of the case to local reporters: "There are many peculiar features to this case which I am at a loss to account for," he declared.

> Everybody has a theory, and I have mine, but I do not believe it is safe to uncover it just yet. So far we are unable to do a thing. Our hands are tied. There is absolutely no beginning to the case. In the first place, we have not found a motive for the crime. I am satisfied that the motive for the murder was not robbery. Why should a man stand there and pump lead into her (Florence's) sister while he was getting everything he wanted without the slightest trouble? It does not appear reasonable.

Why, he wondered, would Florence, hearing shots downstairs, have come down and given the man money? As if rehearsing the arguments in his own mind, he went on:

> Why should any man remain in a place after committing a murder for five minutes after, as this man must have done, according to the newspaper reports? That girl (meaning Florence) passed that man three times, which must have taken over five minutes. In the first place, she says she came downstairs and handed him the money. She then ran into the back parlor, raised the window to get out, changed her mind, ran into the dining room where he was shooting her sister, went out to the back yard—

As he numbered the inconsistencies he punctuated his points with a chop of his hand, continuing,

> … walked east on the path, then south to the back fence, stood there for a while, we do not know how long, and then returned to the house. Passed the man again and then ran out by the front door.

Miller looked from one to another, eyebrows raised skeptically. "That," he said at last, "does not appear reasonable. Unless—" he added quickly, "the man was insane." A final thought. How, he wondered, could a man enter the house and then leave again in a busy neighbourhood without anyone having seen him. "That strikes me as almost incredible."

Both Miller and Bleakley had been surprisingly forthright in talking to the press about the case. That phase of the affair would now close. Whether they were warned to clam up or simply understood that self-restraint was politically expedient, they would not speak as plainly again.

Other wheels too were already turning. Within a couple of hours of the murder, Constable Robert Lentz was rousted from his bed by the arrival of a police patrol wagon. All the officers on duty being engaged in the hunt for Ethel Kinrade's murderer, Lentz was sent to round up a coroner's jury which assembled at 8.30 *p.m.* at the City Hospital morgue – not for the purpose of hearing testimony but simply to examine the body. Ethel was still decorously dressed and wearing her hat ready to go out, but the coroner, the same Dr. W.J. McNichol who had been first on the scene, showed the jurors where the flesh had been exposed by the burning of the clothing, set smoldering, he suggested, by the close proximity of the gun when it was fired. He indicated three wounds in the left breast, covering no more than the size of a fifty-cent piece. He speculated that at least two of the bullets, likely from a .38 calibre or larger weapon, had pierced the heart. The doctor also pointed to a wound on the left side of the head, in front of the ear. From the direction of the wound, he said, the ball was likely to have passed through the jawbone and into the neck or lower part of the skull.

As the fifteen jurymen – consisting of tradesmen and businessmen – dispersed to their homes that night, the coroner's words remained with them. "The crime," he said, "is a terrible one." They could only wonder at the savagery of the attack, clearly carried out with the intention of killing Ethel Kinrade. Why had it been so important to kill her?

At the morgue, two doctors worked on into the night performing an autopsy on the body.

On Sunday, three days after the murder, Ethel was buried amidst the scenes of melodrama that typically accompanied notorious murder cases a century ago. While a crowd estimated at three thousand people thronged the street outside, Bella Kinrade lay in her room oblivious and drugged (She had not been told of the murder: Ethel, her husband told her, met with an accident, was taken to the hospital to be operated on, and did not recover). Florence, making her way down the stairs for the private service, cried, "Ethel!" Then, walking over to the casket in the parlour, she screamed, "Ethel, lock your door!" She was taken back upstairs to be cared for by Loula Walker, a registered nurse who had been hired by Tom Kinrade to see them through these trying times.

Nurse Walker was one of two invaluable aides who had arrived at 105 Herkimer Street in the hours after the murder, and who would play important supporting roles in the drama to come. The other: Florence's fiancé, C. Montrose Wright, a slim, scholarly looking young man. Monty, as everyone called him, was the son of a clergyman in Palmerston, Ontario, and was taking postgraduate studies in theology at Victoria University in Toronto. Already preaching and conducting services, Monty had met the sisters at Centenary Methodist Church, where both sisters were in the choir.

In the parlour, with the bloodstain still marking the spot where Ethel died, the Reverend Richard Whiting, pastor at Centenary Methodist, delivered the peroration. He spoke of Ethel as "unaffected and unassuming." Visiting the Kinrade home in the past, he said, he had been struck by the atmosphere of affection, and had been particularly impressed by the devotion of one member of the family – clearly Florence – towards her older sister.

With the crowds pushing and jostling for a view of the family, six pallbearers, including Monty, carried the coffin down the path to the horse-drawn hearse. Fully one thousand people accompanied the funeral procession through the streets, and on arrival at the cemetery the crowds trampled graves in an effort to see inside the tent where the family was gathered for the last rites. The coffin sank out of sight – though not for long. Within days the body would be exhumed.

Back at the house, the crowds refused to leave, standing on lawns, blocking traffic, and forcing residents to elbow their way in and out of their homes. Finally Nurse Walker emerged, asking people to have a regard for Florence's sad condition. They were deaf to her appeal.

The following morning the three bowler-hatted detectives Miller, Bleakley, and Coulter, returned to interview Florence again, determined this time to get definitive answers. But, tearful and reclining among pillows on a drawing room couch, Florence proved as difficult as ever to pin down. Questioning proceeded only slowly. "Whenever the detectives led back to the only subject in which they were really interested," reported *The Toronto Evening Telegram*, "she instantly became agitated and semi-hysterical, covering her face with her hands and beginning to sob."

Why, on returning to her room and opening the window on to the verandah, had she not raised the alarm? "While I stood there I heard a number of explosions, and was frightened." Going downstairs, she met the intruder in the hallway and, after she gave him the money, he warned her, "Now don't you cause an alarm." The odd business of the parlour window? After she climbed out,

> I heard shots fired then. I came in again, I think because he pulled me in. I went into the dining room and didn't see him, so I tried to escape out of the back door, and, as I was running I heard shots. I think he was trying to shoot me. I couldn't climb the fence, but returned to the house and found the man in the dining room again. He tried to hit me with the revolver, but I warded it off with my arm, and as he was threatening me, I got past him and ran out of the front door as he was firing after me.

The house, according to Florence's account, had been a regular shooting range. Yet when the three detectives examined the walls, ceilings and furniture afterwards, they found no trace of bullets.

Florence's scholarly fiancé, Mr. C. Montrose Wright.

There were other inconsistencies. Unable to identify the intruder from photographs of possible suspects, Florence added, "He was not a tramp. He was too well-dressed." Had she and her sister ever quarreled? "No," she replied. But a few minutes later she had admitted that they had quarreled about a man she had met in Virginia and from whom she had been receiving letters. Ethel disapproved of him. "Did you ever possess a revolver?" she was asked. "No," she replied, she had never even closely examined one. The questioning was cut short when Florence had a fit of hysterics and returned to her room.

It was to be their last chance: when the three detectives returned to Herkimer Street the following afternoon to see Tom Kinrade, they were in for a shock. He told them the family, with the exception of the older son, Ernie, was packing up and leaving on the evening train for Toronto. The inquest was due to resume the following day with Florence expected to be the first witness. The detectives were incredulous. There was really nothing to stop them going, claimed Kinrade. The family physician, Dr.

James White, had recommended a change of scenery to improve the health of Florence and her mother. But when a *Herald* reporter asked Dr. White if he had recommended the trip, he denied it. "I merely agreed with them (the Kinrades) when they said it would be advisable to go away for a rest and a change," he said. He added that, in his view, neither the mother nor the daughter were in any condition to give evidence. He would provide them with medical certificates to excuse their attendance at the inquest, he said.

The Crown's lawyer, S.F. Washington said he had been informed of the family's intention to leave Hamilton, but he was clearly frustrated about the decision. Some of the detectives felt they shouldn't be allowed to leave, "But how can you hold them," said Washington. "This is not Russia." The delay would be costly, he insisted, but finally, with Dr. White's assurance that the two women were not fit to testify, he agreed to a delay.

Washington's impatience would be shared by members of the coroner's jury who assembled the following night only to be sent home and told to return in a week. "Does it not handicap the police to have to wait for this evidence?" inquired juryman John T. Wilson. "If they could go to Toronto," put in another, "why could they not come here and give evidence?"

Huge public sympathy had attached to the Kinrades in their loss and even if there were flaws in the story that Florence told of the tramp, most people likely felt there was still some rational explanation for the mystery, something that had not yet come to light. So it was perfectly natural that, following the terrifying events she had lived through, Flossie, as the family called her, would be in a state of shock. And the repeated attempts of the police to interview her could only seem cruel and inconsiderate. Tom Kinrade's desire as family patriarch to remove his family from the glare of publicity, the crowds walking up and down outside the house, and the harassment of detectives and newspaper reporters, was entirely understandable.

Yet, from another viewpoint, Tom Kinrade's actions can be seen as part of a shrewd plan to frustrate the police investigation, win valuable time to prepare family members before they were required to testify, and – in modern terms – to put his own public relations spin on difficult issues just about to come to public attention. In the larger game, Kinrade had scored a major point by removing his family to Toronto, keeping the police and the coroner at bay. But the family was no sooner established in the Arlington Hotel in Toronto than Kinrade had to resort to further damage control.

"Flossie Kinrade was on the Stage in Virginia," read the main front-page headline in *The Toronto Daily Star* the day after they arrived.

The subject about which the detectives had really wanted to talk to Florence that previous Monday morning – and which had probably sent her into hysterics again – was, it turned out, her double life. Unbeknownst to her friends and possibly her family in Canada, Florence, the very proper church choir soloist, had gone into vaudeville in Virginia the previous year under the name 'Mildred Dale.' Police were now working on the theory that Ethel's murderer, perhaps a jealous boyfriend, may have come from Virginia, and inquiries were made in the South.

Looking tired, the besieged Tom Kinrade came down to the hotel lobby to give reporters his version. "My daughter had a position singing in the Manchester Presbyterian Church in Richmond, Virginia," he said in slow, measured terms,

> … she was a good musician and was always fond of music. One night she was sitting at the window playing and the manager of an amateur theatrical company heard her. He offered her twenty dollars a week to come and sing a couple of songs. As her duties in the choir were not onerous, she was pleased with the opportunity of supplementing her income of seven or eight dollars a week, which was paid by the church. We were fully informed of what she was doing. There happened to be some people she knew in the amateur company which made the work all the more agreeable.

Confirming Tom Kinrade's account, *The Hamilton Times* had on May 16, 1908, reprinted a report from a Virginia newspaper stating,

> Miss Florence Kinrade, who recently accepted an engagement at Richmond, Va., has already established herself as a prime favourite, not only there, but in a number of places around where she has sung. Her services are in great demand.

It went on to describe an anniversary concert at the First Presbyterian Church in Warren, Va., the climax of which was

> Miss Kinrade's high soprano voice soaring above the entire assemblage until a final B flat was reached and maintained

without the slightest effort, but with a distinctness and power that truly stamped her as a singer of merit.

Praise indeed, and soon the authorship would be brought into question. It was illness, explained the father, that had brought Florence home.

> Some people never get acclimatized, and her southern doctor told her to come home. She came back to Hamilton in July, remained a few months, and returned to Virginia in November. She came home again just before Christmas.

The two sisters, he insisted, were very close.

> They were always together, they could not have been more affectionate. I never remember them having any serious quarrel in their lives. In her delirium (Florence) has started up and cried, 'Lock the door, Ethel!' as she said she did at the time of the tragedy.

The father could not resist taking a swipe at the persistent detectives. "They interviewed her repeatedly and made her pass through those terrible scenes until she was practically out of her mind," he complained. "We have come away from home in order to secure rest for her." During one of the police interviews, he said Florence had started up and pointed at one of the detectives, crying, "There he is! There he is!" This, he said, illustrated her state of mind. As to the southern boyfriend, Kinrade insisted,

> I consider the report of my daughter's attachment to a Southerner absolutely without foundation. She may have had some friends down there and perhaps some of them were attracted by her. But she is and has been engaged to a student (Montrose Wright) with whom she has been in constant correspondence.

Tom Kinrade had done his very best to put questions about the Virginia episode to rest. Now, other members of the Kinrade entourage made their contributions: Monty Wright told newspapermen that, whether or not the murderer was a tramp, he was certainly an intruder who had broken into the house. Nurse Walker gave her view: "No wonder (Florence) gave different stories. It is surprising that she did not give more. She was not responsible for what she said half of the time owing to the state of her nerves." And

Florence's brother Earl, certainly with his father's approval, even wrote an article for *The Toronto Evening Telegram*, suggesting that the motive for the murder was "robbery or burglary, pure and simple."

The Kinrades had used the week's delay of the inquest to good effect in creating positive public opinion. Then, in rapid succession, two events put them once again on the defensive. The Attorney General, J.J. Foy, determined to show that the government meant business, appointed George T. Blackstock Q.C., a barrister with the reputation of a pit bull, to represent the Crown at the inquest. Foy also proposed that Florence and members of the family should be interviewed in Toronto by two psychiatrists, Dr. Bruce Smith, provincial inspector of asylums, and Dr. C.K. Clarke.

Then, two days before the inquest was to resume, a large headline in *The Hamilton Herald* announced: "Twenty Minutes Between the Firing of the Shots." The two pathologists who had conducted the autopsy on Ethel Kinrade, the newspaper claimed, had determined there was a fifteen or twenty minute interval between the first shots to the head and the final three shots to the heart that killed her. It seemed unlikely that a tramp would shoot someone in the head and then hang around for a quarter of an hour or more before finishing the job.

To say that the people of the ambitious city awaited the resumption of the Ethel Kinrade inquest with eagerness and curiosity is an understatement.

— Part Two —

THE INQUEST

Chapter Four

STARTING THE INQUEST ALL OVER AGAIN

The Hamilton Spectator of Friday, February 24, 1909 puzzles, "Who Shot Ethel Kinrade?"
The story about 'Tramps and Bums' a column over is conveniently positioned as a response.

SOME FIFTY NEWSPAPERMEN, as they were always referred to, jostled for places in the dreary green courtroom over Hamilton's number three police station on the night of Wednesday, March 10, 1909, two weeks after the murder. But our attention is confined to one, and she a woman. 'Kit of the Mail,' certainly the best-known Canadian woman journalist of her time, was there to attend the inquest into the death of Ethel Kinrade. Kit Watkins, born Catherine Ferguson near Galway, Ireland in 1856, was billed as, "the world's first accredited woman war correspondent," on the strength of having covered the Spanish American War in Cuba for *The Toronto Mail and Empire* in 1898. She was known for her red hair, her cinnamon brown eyes and her dramatic, if occasionally shabby, outfits. And wherever great

39

events were taking place, Kit was to be found – events like the Chicago World Fair, and Queen Victoria's Jubilee in London – and her series on the disappearing London of Charles Dickens was popular years later.

Inventing a new name for herself, Kathleen Blake, and subtracting eight years from her true age, Kit had immigrated to Winnipeg, Manitoba as a young widow in 1884. She made her start in journalism submitting an article to *Saturday Night* in 1889 when she was thirty-three. Immediately after her triumph as a war correspondent ("Kit Reaches Cuba's Shores," *The Daily Mail and Empire* headlined her first dispatch), she married Dr. Theobold Coleman, a mining company doctor, and moved to northern Ontario where she worked alongside him, fighting a smallpox epidemic. The couple later lived in Hamilton for several years.

She was not a great writer, but an observant reporter, and her descriptions of the Kinrade affair are invaluable. She noted when she arrived for the inquest that first evening a fine drizzle icing the sidewalk outside number three police station, the greystone building where Bella Kinrade had come to complain about tramps. It was obvious the authorities had picked the small police station courtroom, rather than the more commodious quarters at City Hall, to keep crowds to a minimum. Reporters and a few newspaper artists occupied three-quarters of the space while the remaining seats and the space around the walls were occupied by those – almost exclusively men – lucky enough to secure a ticket from the police chief. The upper windows were open to the mild winter night and gas jets cast a thin light over the room, which was dominated by a large lion and unicorn royal crest.

The first surprise was the presence of Dr. James Anderson, a slight man watching events with a kindly but keen expression from the elevated coroner's 'throne.' Coroner Dr. Anderson had been called in at the last moment to replace Coroner Dr. McNichol, ostensibly so that McNichol would be free to give testimony. Dr. McNichol was as surprised as anyone by the switch: he had intended having a deputy cover for him while he testified. In fact, the switch seems to have been a deliberate ploy by the Attorney General to cover up earlier ineptitude.

The substitution of a new coroner was given as the excuse for starting the inquest all over again, re-swearing the jury – and here was the point – exhuming Ethel's body so that, according to the law, it could be examined by the jury. In fact, there was serious concern about the thoroughness of the original post-mortem, and the exhumation provided the excuse for doing a more thorough second examination.

A letter addressed to Ontario Premier Sir James Whitney from an obviously in-the-know 'W.J. Wells, Ontario People's Detective,' writing from Victoria, British Columbia, and published in the press makes the point: "Why was this girl's body allowed to be buried without a complete post-mortem examination having been made? Who is responsible for this error?" The writer pointed out that the bodies of no fewer than three murder victims had recently been exhumed in Ontario. "Who has again been asleep at the wheel?" inquired the writer.

If there had been initial failures, the presence of George Tate Blackstock Q.C. at the front of the courtroom showed that the Whitney government now took the Kinrade case very seriously indeed. Blackstock, related to the Gooderham booze dynasty, made his reputation defending Reginald Birchall in perhaps the greatest murder trial of the era at Woodstock Assizes in 1890. Birchall, an English confidence man, duped well-to-do British fathers into paying large sums to have their sons trained and set up at Birchall's (non-existent) Canadian farming estate. When his scheme began to unravel, Birchall, who called himself Lord Somerset, shot and killed one of his victims, Frederick C. Benwell. In spite of Blackstock's widely admired defence, Birchall was found guilty of murder and hanged. (As he awaited his appointment with the hangman, Birchall earned pocket money selling his ink drawings, one of which decorates the desk of this writer.)

Crucially, the journalists and citizens gathered that night were not attending any sort of trial, but one of the most ancient investigative procedures of all. Inquests date back to tenth century Europe, their purpose to establish the facts where a suspicious death or one of public concern (like an industrial accident) has occurred. Inquest juries can certainly ascribe blame for an untoward death, but it is up to the Crown to lay charges.

At 8:10 *p.m.*, in line with its long traditions, the inquest commenced with the ancient cry, "*Oyez, Oyez, Oyez!*" The names of the jurymen – the foreman R.B. Spera, a small businessman, the others ranging in occupation from fruiterer, to barber, to street violinist – were called. Despite strong speculation that Florence would be the first witness, this, after all, was the era of patriarchal power in the middle-class household, Constable Lentz announced, "Mr. Kinrade."

"A big, broad-shouldered man walked slowly across behind the coroner and took the stand," recorded Kit.

> His rugged features were seamed with grief… his very bigness made him look all the more helpless. And, standing opposite him was that man of amazing personality and magnetism, Mr. George Tate Blackstock. Tall, slender, a little worn with life… with his deep eyes and expressive hands… he gives an impression of ability and power that is almost uncanny… Personally, I may say that I think that I would swear to anything Mr. Blackstock wanted if he asked me in those deep, resonant tones of his.

The first exchanges were anticlimactic: Thomas Kinrade could not recall if Ethel was twenty-four or twenty-five. Ill health? "Well, she complained a little of indigestion … she took little tablets and one thing and another for indigestion."

Blackstock: "Apart from trifling ailments of that kind, she was of fairly good health and robust constitution?"

Thomas Kinrade: "Yes, I think so. Not so very robust, a kind of slight build."

Blackstock had his witness go through a family roll call: Ethel, the eldest daughter, in fact twenty-five, Florence, twenty-three, Gertrude, sixteen, son Earl, nineteen, working for the Bank of Commerce in Montreal, and the oldest sibling, Ernie, twenty-six, a builder contractor living in the east end with his wife and three children. Tom Kinrade said he was fifty-seven, his wife, "is perhaps the same age." He then mentioned that she had been adopted as a child.

Isabella (Bella) was a church organist, and he was singing in the choir when they met and married in 1877. He was now principal of the Cannon Street School as well as head master of the Cannon Street school district, comprising four schools.

Kinrade was vague again about his real estate holdings. Ernest, who lived in a house provided by his father, had built "ten or twelve houses for me altogether … I have thirty houses now …" he looked thoughtful "… or maybe more." Rents, he explained, were collected the first Monday of each month by his wife and two oldest daughters with Florence taking the west part of the city, Ethel the centre part, and his wife the east end. "And I paid them," he added, "three per cent or fifteen dollars or so." While Florence was away in Virginia in 1908, Ethel and her mother shared the collecting duties.

Was theirs a household where there were many visitors?

"Not many visitors, except on my wife's calling day, Thursday. We hadn't many visitors, we hadn't many at-homes or things of that sort."

"Then in the family," said Blackstock, probing ever-so courteously,

> … may I ask, Mr. Kinrade, what was the relationship between the various members of the family? I hope that you will forgive my asking the question. All I want to know is what your representation would be as to whether there were any estrangements at the fireside, or whether everything was affection.

Kinrade replied with Pickwickian geniality: "We lived, the most affectionate family, my dear sir. The children wanted for nothing, and I kept nothing back from them, and my wife could spend what money she liked."

The question was not really about affection measured in money terms, but Blackstock let it pass.

"So that, inside the house, your representation to the coroner and the jury is that of an affectionate household?"

"Very much so."

"Any exceptions?"

"No exceptions at all. I never heard one say a cross word to the other." Blackstock left the jurors with the image of this quite remarkably amicable family while he moved on to ask about Mrs. Kinrade's health.

"My wife wasn't in the best of health. She was a little nervous. I wanted her to go to the doctor, but she was afraid of an operation."

"Was there any time when these illnesses of hers took the form of lapses from consciousness?"

"Well, through her life… especially in the younger part of her married life, especially if she was worried or nervous, she would become very weak and faint. It would be simply like a sleep or a swoon for a short time."

The switch was abrupt: "Was Florence living at home at the time of the murder?"

"Florence has been home since a week or so before Christmas. She came from Portsmouth (Virginia)." A note of hesitancy: "At least I suppose so."

"How long had she been away from home?"

"She went away about this time last year, in March sometime I think. She was offered a position in a church to sing as soprano soloist."

"Whereabouts?"

"That was in Richmond."

"Richmond, Virginia?"

> Yes… and then she wrote home to us. She always wrote to her mother, and about June, I think it was, she had symptoms of malaria and she was advised to go north at once, so she came home, I think perhaps the end of June and stayed with us all July. And then I think the two girls and myself went to Chautauqua (scene of an annual arts festival in Upstate New York) in the month of August… she stayed at home in September and she spoke of going away the first of October. But we kept her home to hear (American opera singer) Nordica on 8 October. Then she went away, I think, immediately after that.

"Where did she go then?"

> I understood she was going to Portsmouth (Virginia). My wife went as far as Buffalo with her, and saw her take a sleeper to Philadelphia; that was in the evening, and she wrote from Philadelphia (to say) she had missed the morning train by about five or ten minutes, and so she had to stay in Philadelphia all that day until the evening and then went south.

"Your daughter was going then to Portsmouth, was she?"

"Yes."

"Did you know what for?"

"Yes, I knew she was singing there and getting about fifteen or twenty dollars a week."

"What was the difference in the employment at Portsmouth from what it had been at Richmond?"

"Very much different. I think she sang songs on the stage."

"As I understood, you learned that for the first time during the time she was home in the summer?"

"No, she wrote, I think, before she came home."

"So that, before she returned in the summer, you found out from her letters?"

"I'm not so sure about that. I think it must have been in July, or very late in June, if I knew at that date. I knew it when she came home, and she persuaded me to let her go back, as she thought she had a talent in that direction."

"But it came as a surprise to you to find, without consulting you, she had gone into singing on the stage?"

"Of course I didn't know until after she did so."

"When she went back to Portsmouth, she went with the knowledge of yourself and your family that she was going to sing on the stage?"

"The manager wrote to her a letter while she was home and she prevailed upon me to let her go, although her mother was always opposed to it."

"Did you know anything of the character of the place where she was to sing? The theatre?"

"Nothing more than just what the manager of the theatre wrote – that he wanted her to come and that he would increase her salary."

"Perhaps you would tell us, what salary did you understand that she was getting after she went back in the autumn?"

"When she went back, we expected she would get twenty dollars or twenty-five dollars a week."

"And in point of fact, what did she get?"

"When she went back I don't think they raised her salary."

Tom Kinrade was not the kind Blackstock could bully. So when he had a point to make, he often came at it backwards, sideways, any way but up front: "What I was concerned about asking for the moment, Mr. Kinrade, was whether you knew anything of the character of the theatre. I mean to say, as I understand it, it was not a theatre at which plays were enacted, more of what we call…" as if the word left a disagreeable taste in his mouth, "a vaudeville performance?"

Vaudeville was the leading popular entertainment of the day. Yet to suggest that a respectably brought-up young woman from the professional classes would perform in vaudeville was next to saying she was aspiring to a career as a burlesque stripper. So Kinrade hastened to throw a mantle of respectability over Florence's activities:

> I understood when she went to sing, (that) the manager wanted to put on some little, what he called, sketches. She told me she took the part of a 'school marm' in a little play called School Days, and then she took a part in a piece called

> The Musician, and she went over those plays with me, and
> they were very humorous and nothing in them that was any-
> thing wrong that I could see.

Blackstock wasn't having it! A 'school marm' maybe, but he wanted to make clear that the 'little plays' were being performed in less-than-re-spectable surroundings: "What I meant, rather, was that it was the cheap, popular form of entertainment?"

"There was not anything dramatic about it, nothing that way."

"And the prices of admission would be comparatively small and trifling?"

"I never heard nor asked about that. It was coming on October and November when we made up our minds for her to come home."

"Then you say that your daughter prevailed upon you to allow her to go back; but that she never succeeded in gaining over her mother to that view?"

"Her mother was strongly opposed to anything of the kind."

"And I suppose that you yourself yielded with some reluctance to the idea of her going back?"

"She said that she had discovered that she was good at these sketches and singing, and got so much applause that she discovered she had that talent. And on that account I thought that I would let her try for a little while anyhow."

"Did she voluntarily give the matter up, or was it as a result of your adverse decision that she ultimately abandoned the idea?" Kinrade answered:

> Well, she wrote us a letter that there was a person there that
> was paying her attention, and wanting to see her home and
> back and forward; and we know she was engaged (to be mar-
> ried). She wrote that he thought a great deal of her, but she
> had told him she was engaged, and her mother and I became
> nervous about it, and thought she had better come home.
> So her mother wrote her a letter to that effect, and if she was
> not going to come, we were all going down there Christmas
> time, anyway, to see what it was like and get acquainted with
> the people.

"Did she tell you who the young man was?"

"Yes, she mentioned his name."

"Do you recollect who it was?"

The name did not come easily from Kinrade's lips: "Quite well."

"What was the name?'

"She gave me the name of James Gordon Baum."

"Did she tell you what his occupation was?"

"Yes, she said he was an actor."

Blackstock was making valuable points: an actor boyfriend and Florence under pressure at home. Now he could fill in more of the picture. His daughter Florence, Kinrade agreed, was engaged at the time to Claire Montrose Wright, of Victoria University. While Monty studied and lived in Toronto, he had met both Florence and Ethel when he sang for a time in the Centenary Church choir, of which both sisters were members. He would take the two girls out to concerts, said the father. "That was at the beginning, before he was engaged (to younger sister Florence)."

"And you say in the early stages of the acquaintanceship he was accustomed to take them both out?"

"If they went any place, they would go together."

"But later on he showed some preference for Miss Florence and ultimately became engaged to her?"

"Yes." They had been engaged about a year and a half, although Kinrade could not recollect Monty coming to see Florence when she was home in the summer or even in the fall, after the family returned from Chautauqua.

"He sent flowers frequently, but in July and August, as I understood it," he explained, "he was engaged as a fire ranger away up in the north somewhere for his health."

"Was there anything in the attentions of Baum, as reported to you by Florence, which excited any alarm in you, or was it just that you didn't care for anybody paying her attention at a time when she was engaged to Mr. Wright?"

"It seemed to occur to me that he was an actor without means and that he was getting very much in love with her, and going so far as, perhaps, to propose to her."

"Did she so report?"

"It seems to me she did say he proposed to her, or was about to propose to her, and she said she was engaged."

"She mentioned Baum's name… in such a way as to make you infer he was a person of not very much consequence?"

The father smiled: "Oh, very much so that way, laughed about him and gave the impression that he was a very inferior kind of man."

"You didn't gather from her letters that there was any change in her attitude towards him after she returned in the autumn to Portsmouth?"

"Her letters towards winter indicated he was paying her attention and acting a little differently in his manner and courtesy and his habits."

"How so?"

"I understood that the man had been accustomed to drink, but that he was living a different life to try and get her."

"Did she report that her own feelings were undergoing some change towards him?"

"No, nothing that way that I know. She simply said that she told him she was engaged to Mr. Wright, that (he) was a young minister; and I understood that she wrote to the minister and told him all about it."

"Well if she didn't care for this young man, and if she told him that she was engaged to somebody else, there was nothing that would occasion you any alarm at all!" Blackstock waited for Kinrade's response.

"I didn't get alarmed! But I thought she had spent enough time in that way anyway as she was not advancing in the profession in any way."

He had regarded the 'adventure in Portsmouth' as an experiment, insisted Kinrade, one which might lead to a career in opera in New York.

"These hopes at that time appeared to you not to be likely to be realized?"

"Yes."

"So you put an end to the discussion by deciding that she must remain at home?"

Tom Kinrade did not want to appear the tyrant: "Not determinedly."

"You gave that opinion?"

"I felt that, and she didn't urge it at all."

But now Blackstock brought the spotlight back to Herkimer Street: "What was Ethel's attitude towards this stage venture of Florence's?"

"Oh, I don't think she liked it. She, being the eldest girl, was more in touch with the mother during the time Florence was away; I don't think she liked it at all."

"That is the way she expressed herself on the subject?"

Kinrade answered

> I don't remember her expressing herself to me personally, but
> I would get things from her mother when we talked together.
> They were in harmony with each other, the mother and Ethel,
> and the mother was strictly opposed to any life of that kind.
> We didn't expect she would continue that if she got married,

but we thought if ever she needed, she would have some way
to fall back upon making a living for herself."

"So that Ethel supported your wife in her opposition to this stage venture of Florence's?"

Kinrade sensed he was slipping into a trap. "It wasn't anything of determined opposition."

"You have already told us that your wife was strongly opposed to the
stage work."

"Yes, she expressed herself strongly to me. She never gave her consent."

"And your daughter Ethel took the same view?"

"Not like her mother in any way. She didn't have much to say about it,
or anything that I know of."

The lawyer was not going to let him off the hook. He said:

> I am only using an expression used by yourself, but you
> may put it any way you like… But I understood you to say
> a few minutes ago that your daughter, Ethel, was opposed to
> Florence's stage venture, and took the side or views of your
> wife in opposing it. Is that true?

Grudgingly Kinrade answered: "To a certain extent that is true."

"Then the subject of Florence returning to the stage would, of course,
be discussed in the summer, when she was at home?"

"Yes."

"And that was the time when you say that your wife expressed her
opposition, which she never yielded upon, and in which she was supported
by Ethel; but you took the side of Florence and ultimately gave your consent to her going."

"Yes."

The wind gusted through the open windows, causing the gaslights
to flare and brighten. Kit Watkins observed, "The big, uneasy figure" of
Tom Kinrade, squeezed into the witness box and later, fidgeting on the
stool brought for him, "suggested strength brought to low ebb indeed."
Questioned minutely, persistently, recorded Kit.

> He was at once infinitely patient and extremely sharp and
> sudden. His voice, in his patient moods, was low, halting,
> careful – almost intimate, as though talking to a friend. But
> when the moment for the important query came, it rose, it

became incisive, almost thunderous and heavily weighted with meaning.

Quite remarkably, in the first hour of questioning, there had not been a single mention of the murder or of tramps. It might have been an inquest into Florence's musical ambitions in Virginia.

But now Blackstock, like a doctor probing a wound for the infection, turned to Kinrade's relationship with the elder son, Ernie, establishing that, except when he came to the house to collect cheques from his father in connection with their building activity, he and Tom Kinrade had little contact.

Blackstock: "Then apart from that, was there any intercourse between his household and your household?"

"Oh yes, his wife and little ones would be asked up frequently of late, and the girls were down there the night before the tragedy to a birthday party."

"Whose birthday party was that?"

"I suppose my son's. I don't know: I didn't enquire. They called it a birthday party."

"You know your son's birthday, don't you?"

"No, I don't exactly. There are five of them and they come around." It was not surprising that, with five children, Tom Kinrade did not know the date of his elder son's birthday. What was surprising – and indicative of his attitude towards Ernie – was that he did not know if the birthday party was for Ernie. Didn't he even ask? With mother and sisters at odds and father and son, as we shall see, maintaining a wall of hostility, it was beginning to seem an odd notion of 'a most affectionate family.'

"When did you see him last before this occurrence?"

Kinrade had difficulty remembering. Then it came to him: "I am positive I saw him the afternoon we went to see *The Merry Widow*. I took my two daughters and wife, and I coaxed him to go also. (But) he couldn't get a seat, so he came as far as the opera house and went home." That, they established, would have been about a month earlier.

Then back to the daughters: "If I may ask you as to the temperament, what would you say with reference to Miss Florence and Miss Ethel? Were they girls of what we would call a sweet disposition? Or were they persons who were given to exhibitions of temper?"

The father seemed shocked:

Never! Not in all the days of my life did I ever see a cross look from one of them. They were always together as twins. We dressed them as twins because Florence was two years younger, but she grew faster; and Ethel was slight; and soon they came head to head, and we dressed them in white and kept them as twins for years. They were most affectionate and devoted.

"How would you represent Ernest in that regard?"

"Ernest is a very sweet-tempered man, never saw him angry, never could get him angry. He was a quiet, nice boy."

"And there never was at any time any complaint by you that your son, Ernest, had used you badly in business transactions?" The cracks were beginning to show.

Oh, nothing that way. Of course, the frame houses (Ernie had built about twenty houses for his father), I thought he might have finished them up a little better, but I suppose he didn't get enough money for them (selling them). I think it was a thousand dollars apiece or something, but I wasn't anxious, and he was my own son… If it had been a stranger I would have been more exacting.

"What I was asking, Mr. Kinrade, was whether you had expressed yourself from time to time as being very strongly dissatisfied with your son in his business dealings with yourself."

"No, I don't think so—"

"But you never could have used so strong an expression as that he swindled you?" Blackstock looked all innocence.

"Never, never! I wouldn't say that about any of my children."

"Or that he cheated you?"

"No."

Blackstock was relentless: "Or that he had deceived you?"

"No, I don't think so."

"Or that he was constantly getting the better of you and not doing his work as he promised he would do it?"

"I felt it a little on the last five frame houses that he might have done better."

"You had angry words with him on that subject?"

"Not that I remember at all."

"Will you say you didn't?"

"There wasn't much anger on my part, I can assure you."

"You reproached him on the subject, found fault with him, did you not?"

"I have no recollection of doing so. I may have done so."

What possible connection could a row between father and son have with Ethel's murder? None, directly. But the lawyer was trying to break through that shell of patrician benevolence and show that, within the Kinrade family, ran deep and largely uncharted currents of anger and resentment. And with his hesitations and evasions it was quite clear that Tom Kinrade's word could not be relied upon.

Taking him back now to the birthday party, Blackstock asked if Kinrade recalled the two girls attending it?

"Yes, they telephoned for me to meet them at the corner that night… They were afraid to come home because they had been frightened two or three weeks before that." He had met them off the street railway, and brought them home. There had though been two tramp alarms earlier that evening:

> About 6:30 there was a man came to my door, as usual, to get a ticket signed or something. My wife went to the door. They are glass doors, and when she opened the first door, he stood up closely to the second one and, contrary to what she had always been used to, she was afraid to open the outside door. So she sang through the door, 'I can't give you anything. Go next door or go somewhere else!'

About 8:30 *p.m.*, as he was reading the newspaper, the doorbell rang repeatedly. Kinrade said,

> My wife said, 'Papa, I am not going to the door tonight. We are pestered with these people, and I have turned all the lights out in the hall and verandah, and they can just consider we are out tonight.' But when he rang the seventh time, she thought it was a telegram from my son, Earl (in Montreal)… because he had been very sick. And with that thought, she took her youngest child, Gertrude (to the door with her) and in a few minutes, both of them gave a terrible shriek, and I thought the man had got in on them.

He rushed to the door and turned on the lights and told them not to be frightened. "And they said if I had heard the noise at the front window in the parlour, I would have shouted too." It was only at noon the next day, the day of the murder, that he noticed as he arrived home for dinner a gash made in the windowsill. "So that noon, that Thursday, I told my wife that she had better go and tell the police that somebody tried to get through that window the night before." He also told Bella to call at the lodging houses where the tramps slept and tell the proprietors to send only the most deserving cases to their door.

Two or three weeks earlier, Kinrade testified, Ethel had been coming home on a stormy Sunday night from church when she saw a man with an umbrella, walking up and down in front of their verandah. As she came up the front steps he was standing in front of the bay window, his back to her. Thoroughly rattled, she pressed the doorbell repeatedly, said Kinrade, only to find the door handle turned and opened to her touch.

Kinrade had not reported the incident to the police, although he had gone out to investigate. Did he go out to investigate the subsequent incident when his wife and Gertrude shrieked?

"I think I did. I know I did the night the man was walking around the verandah."

"No, no. Did you go out to investigate this night, Mr. Kinrade?"

"I turned the lights on the verandah. No, I don't think I did. No, my wife wouldn't let me go out."

"It is perfectly clear, I think, if you had gone out to investigate that important occurrence, you couldn't have forgotten it, and you didn't go, did you?"

"I don't think I did."

The politeness, the touch of obsequiousness at Kinrade's position had vanished now. Blackstock intended to show that Kinrade, for whatever reason, was blowing the tramp scares out of proportion.

"Then, alarmed, excited, only prevented from going out to investigate by the dissuasion of your wife, you still did not report that night to the police?"

"No, I did not."

"Didn't telephone?"

Testy now: "No, I did not."

"And you didn't communicate it to the police next morning?"

"No, sir."

"And nothing was done about this matter until you returned to dinner about 12:30 on the day of the tragedy?"

"Thursday noon, when I saw the window was broken (the gash in the windowsill)."

"Then you sent your wife to go down to the police station. What for?"

"I didn't send her to the police station. I first told her to go to the restaurants (the lodging houses used by the tramps)."

Kinrade said he had left to return to work at ten minutes past one, leaving his wife, Ethel, Florence, and Gertrude in the house. Gertrude would have left a few minutes later to be at school for two o'clock.

When had he learned of the tragedy?

He was leaving the school on the way home at ten minutes after four when a teacher, Miss Simpson called that there was an urgent phone message for him. Someone calling from the grocery store near his home told him, "A tramp has got into your house and shot your daughter and she is dead." A teacher suggested perhaps that it was not as bad as he thought. He replied, "But they say she is dead, and I don't know which one." The caretaker was sent for a hackney carriage to take him home. At the house he noticed an ambulance or patrol wagon driving away, and people lined up on both sides of the street.

> When I got into the house, I threw myself into the armchair in the parlour and said, 'Oh God, this is dreadful!' and I understood it was my second daughter and I knew that was Florence. Some detective got beside me and he said, 'There may be more in this than you think.' He said, 'Had your daughter a lover?'
>
> And I thought it was poor Florence that was gone, and I said, yes, she was engaged to a student at Victoria College. And he said, 'Had she any lover down South?' or something to that effect, and I said there was a man down there was paying attentions to her, but she told him she was engaged.'

At that point, he said, someone told him it was Ethel, not Florence, who was dead. "I said, 'Well, if it is poor Ethel, what I have said to you does not apply to Ethel. She had no lover."

Kinrade's testimony here is not credible. The forthcoming Detective Bleakley had told no one of such an exchange, and how could he possibly have known at that early stage that Florence had a boyfriend down South?

Perhaps, in some convoluted fashion, Kinrade was trying to explain away his odd statement that he had expected something like this to happen, and his apparent surprise when the body turned out to be that of Ethel.

Going into the dining room, he continued, "I saw a dreadful sight … a pool of blood and my daughter was lying all wrapped up…. I got down on my knees and I helped uncover her face and I found it was Ethel with her hat on and veil across her forehead."

"She was afterwards taken, I think, on a stretcher to the ambulance?"

"As soon as I saw who it was, one man went to her head and another to her feet and picked her up and walked out of the back door. I said to the men, 'Where are you going with her? What are you going to do?' And they never said anything, not even spoke to me."

Hearing that Florence and Bella, his wife, were across the street at Mrs. Hickey's, he went to find them. "When I went in the front door they said my wife was in a faint in the parlour and I better not go in."

In the dining room, he found Florence, along with sister Gertrude. "Florence said, 'Oh Papa, you must keep up. I will keep up if you will, Papa. And you know, it could have been worse. He said he would shoot me too.' Then I seemed to thank God they were not both gone." Taking Florence back across the street with his arm around her, said the father,

> I thought (that) what I had told the detective about her should not be made public. I thought it was a private matter… and we met the same detective (Bleakley), and I said, 'This is my daughter; she will tell you how it happened.' And he said, 'Oh, I don't want anything of that kind; if she has got anything to tell me, she has got to see me alone or tell it to me alone.' So I let her go down into the back dining room with him and I stood there and in a little while I heard her in hysterics. I bolted up and I said, 'I won't let her stay alone with you or any other man!' That is all there was. I asked her the story and she told me about it before she told it to him.

Thomas Kinrade repeated the familiar story of Florence going to the front door to be confronted by a man who asked, "Can I have something to eat?" and then pushing in and demanding money. He recalled asking her why, as she went upstairs, she didn't tell Ethel. Her reply: "Papa, I thought he was right at my back coming up the stairs." She had, anyway called to Ethel to lock her door, she said. Why hadn't she run out on the upstairs verandah? She had thought of it, she told him, "but I thought he would kill me, papa, and I thought I had better give him the ten dollars." She had come downstairs, according to this version, given him the money, upon which he had told her, "If you make any noise, I will shoot you too."

"You haven't told me about any shooting yet?"

"No, but that is all she told me."

"Did she tell you that she saw Ethel shot by the man?"

"I can't say that she did."

"Now then, answer me please. Did Florence tell you that she had seen the man shoot Ethel?"

"No sir, she didn't tell me that." Neither, he said in reply to further questions, had she told him about running out in the backyard or climbing out of the side bay window. "I didn't go into particulars at all about it."

"Did you ever hear her say that when she was in the States engaged in those theatrical employments that she had fired off a revolver sometimes?" The courtroom was still.

"Oh, never – never heard her say that," replied Kinrade, almost stumbling over the words.

"And as far as you knew, she was quite unfamiliar with the use of firearms?"

"Quite – all my children are."

Since Florence had first told him the abbreviated story of the shooting the first day, had he spoken to her again on the subject?

"No, too many others speaking to her. I never spoke to her on the subject since."

Had he been present when others had spoken to her?

"She had not spoken to me. There were three detectives out here, spieling to her—"

"Please don't say anything more about detectives. We all know your animus with respect to them."

"No sir!" Indignant.

"You have told us that a great number of times now. If you would like to say anything disparaging about the detective, I will give you a reasonable amount of time to do so," said Blackstock with heavy irony. "And then let us go on with the evidence."

"I have nothing to say. And I have not said anything in animosity against the detectives!"

In this telling exchange, all pretense was finally set aside: Blackstock was essentially acting the prosecutor while Kinrade was, at the very least, a hostile witness. And the lawyer could not possibly have anticipated the lengths the outraged father would go to thwart the investigation.

"I want you to be clear and specific about it," Blackstock insisted a moment later, "since this first conversation you had with your daughter, Florence... she has not spoken to you on the subject and you have not spoken to her, nor have you heard her discuss the subject in the presence of other people?"

"That is right, I have not."

The Kinrade family lawyer, Thomas Hobson, who had been closely following the interrogation, made his first interjection: "I don't know whether Mr. Kinrade understands that question or not. As I understand, Mr. Kinrade was present when she was discussing it with detectives."

The father, more sure of himself now, grabbed at the chance to give further testimony on the inhumane treatment Florence had received at the hands of the police:

> The detectives, I was going to remark, asked to see her alone, and they were granted the favour. And I went in afterwards and saw her on the (chaise) lounge in a delirious state, when she pointed to one of them and said, 'That is the man, kill him.' They had been questioning her for a considerable time. I was simply going to make that remark. I have not expressed any animosity towards the detectives, as I am as anxious as they are to find out.

Blackstock, a few minutes later, invited Kinrade to give his ideas on who the murderer might be.

"I certainly think he was insane. I don't think any sane human being could put seven shots into my dear child like that."

The lawyer finally broached the most puzzling feature of Kinrade's reported behaviour on returning home the day of the murder: "Did you, when you first came into your front hall, use the expression, 'I had expected this would happen for a long time?'"

"I have no recollection of saying such a thing."

"Will you say that you did not make use of an expression of that kind? You could not give me any reason for using it?"

"There are two reasons I could give. In the first place, if I said it, and thought it was Florence, as I did in the start, I might have said it thinking perhaps the fellow down South had been crazy enough to try to stop her from marrying another."

"Did that come into your mind?"

"It came into my mind when they phoned to me."

"Then you have no recollection of using that expression, but I understand that you are not able to say confidently that you did not use it?"

"I would feel like swearing positively that I did not, because I don't recall saying it."

"That is what I am asking you: whether you would undertake to swear positively that you did not use the expression?"

Blackstock's invitation hung in the air, bringing no response from the witness.

"Just as you like," said the lawyer, and then, almost curtly, "I won't trouble you for anything else just now, Mr. Kinrade."

It had been a game performance. Kinrade had been questioned for two-and-a-half hours, sometimes in a hostile fashion. He had dealt fairly convincingly with the two issues relating to his behaviour after he learned of the murder – his confusion over which daughter was dead, and his odd statement that he had expected something like this to happen.

Wrote Kit Watkins,

> For a moment the hum of voices filled the room. The 'copy devils' moved about, gathering up loose sheaves of written words and hurrying to the waiting wires…. The lawyers conferred, heads together. The coroner shifted in his seat and wiped his forehead. A general let-up of the tension was noticeable. Only for a moment. Then, as if stiffened by electricity, the whole room sat up as the name, "Miss Florence Kinrade" was called.

Chapter Five

FLORENCE'S TRIUMPH

Intrepid newspaperwomen Kit Watkins, known as the first accredited
woman foreign war correspondent, covered the Inquest.

IT WAS THE PUREST THEATRE. As the name, "Florence Kinrade" was
called, every eye in the room focused on the open door to the witness
room. For a few moments it remained empty. Then, in a church-like hush, a
trio emerged, at its centre, "a slender figure clad in somber black…. On one
side was the trained nurse, her white uniform contrasting sharply with the
garments of her patient. On the other side, Montrose Wright, her fiancé,
supported the drooping figure."

The three, like some religious procession, made their way slowly to the
front of the courtroom. Kit Watkins' version: "I saw a tall and graceful girl
dressed in black; a little bright-faced woman in neat nurse's uniform and a
small youth (Wright) with a shock of dark hair and an earnest anxious, face."

Florence, gloved in black, carrying a black ostrich purse and wearing
a black hat in which a jet ornament glittered amongst the ribbons, made
a striking appearance. She was, reported Watkins, "far, far more attractive

than her pictures make her out to be…. She looked very much like a girl in a dream… or like a perfect actress fitted very perfectly to a pathetic role." Later Kit Watkins would call her, "pretty, inconsequent butterfly," using words like, "feminine" and "womanly and refined," in describing her. But with an aquiline nose and dark complexion, Florence did not conform to contemporary notions of beauty. Rather, wrote the journalist, "she suggests the Spanish or South American type." Others would describe her as Creole in appearance.

The performance had only just begun. Answering Florence's whispered appeal for help, Montrose helped her into the seat hastily offered by a constable, while Nurse Walker placed a glass of cordial on the desk beside her before taking her place with a protective arm around her patient's shoulder.

George Blackstock, sensing that he and the court were being upstaged, immediately objected to the nurse's presence.

"As a medical man," interjected the Kinrade family lawyer, Tom Hobson, appealing directly to Coroner Dr. Anderson, "you will know the necessity of having the nurse in attendance."

"I am certainly not going on with the nurse present!" snapped Blackstock. "If she is wanted, she can be called." Nurse Walker whispered to Florence then made a discreet withdrawal.

Once again, Blackstock astonished. Instead of bearing down on the circumstances of the murder, or even Florence's relations with Ethel, he straightaway turned to the episode in Virginia. As if that was what it was all about.

Blackstock: "You went to take an engagement as a soloist in a church in Richmond?"

"Yes."

"How often would you sing in the choir?"

"On Sundays and at practices."

"Had you friends?"

"Just the person I went with."

"Did you go with a friend?"

"Yes."

"From Hamilton?"

"No."

"Where was that friend from?"

"From Montreal. Her home was in England."

"How long had you known her before you went to Richmond?"

"Oh, about eight or nine months."

"How had you formed her acquaintance?"

"She made herself known to me at McNab Church (Hamilton)."

"And were you at that time singing at McNab Church?"

"Yes."

"Did she stay in Hamilton long after she introduced herself to you?"

"No, not very long. I went away with her some little time after… up to Goderich and Stratford (towns in southwestern Ontario) and around that way."

"What did you go with her for?"

"To sing at some concert engagements."

"How long did that trip last?"

"Oh, about two weeks. She then went to the old country."

"She was an English person, was she?"

"Yes."

"A married woman?"

"Not then."

"Of what age?"

"About thirty-five."

"With whom was she living?"

"Her sister."

"Whereabouts?"

"She had a summer residence at Goderich."

"What was the name, if you please?"

"Robinson."

"You don't remember what her Christian name was?"

"I think her sister called her Mabel."

"And her friend's name," inquired the lawyer.

"Miss Elliott."

"And her Christian name?"

"Marion."

What on earth could Blackstock have been thinking, wasting the time of the sixteen honest jurymen not to mention that of the witness and countless journalists and officials while he pursued unimportant details relating to Florence's friend! We shall see. In the meantime one thing was clear: Florence had almost certainly been schooled by Hobson to answer only the questions she was asked and not to volunteer any further information.

Blackstock persisted. Like pulling the proverbial hen's teeth, he got

Postcard of the streets of Hamilton, Ontario in the era of the Kinrade inquiry.

Florence's grudging admission that Miss Elliott, after returning to England the previous summer, had prompted a friend to invite Florence to sing at a concert in Syracuse, in Upstate New York. She named the friend, whom she'd met in Toronto and who had accompanied her to Syracuse, as Mrs. Kenneth Brown. Blackstock's picayune questions went on and on. Where had she stayed in Syracuse? Where was Mrs. Brown's husband? What was the name of a friend of Mrs. Brown's with whom she had stayed in Rochester, New York, after suffering a sprained ankle.

"Well, I don't remember," was Florence's frequent response. Marion Elliott had rejoined her in Rochester.

"Where did she come from?"

"I don't remember."

Miss Elliott had set out with her from Rochester to bring her home, said Florence, but her sprained ankle was causing pain so they stopped in Buffalo where they had stayed at someone's house.

"But you don't remember the name of the people or the address," said Blackstock with heavy irony.

"No, I can't." The day after, she started for home again.

"And did Miss Elliott come with you?"

"No, she put me on the train and wired to my father to meet me at the station."

Postcard of the streets of Richmond, Virginia in the era of the Kinrade inquiry.

It was while she was at Syracuse, she told Blackstock, that she had met Mr. Foster, the choir leader at a Richmond church who was later instrumental in getting her an invitation to become soloist at the church for $375 a year, "or something like that." By happenstance, Miss Elliott, whose grandparents originally came from Richmond, had friends there.

Blackstock: "I see, and when you decided to go down there to accept this position as soloist, Miss Elliott just thought she would jog along with you?" The lawyer was having fun now at the witness' expense.

Florence: "Yes."

And where did they meet before setting out for Richmond?

"I think I met her in Buffalo. I can't remember."

"That's a rather important matter, isn't it? Don't you think you could remember now setting out from your father's house to go off to Richmond? You had never been in Richmond before, had you?"

"No."

"Well now, can you remember where you met Miss Elliott?"

"I don't remember."

Was it in Philadelphia? She couldn't remember. Did she stop over in Philadelphia?

"Oh, I think we went straight through."

"Your father tells us that you did not go straight through, but you wrote that some delay occurred and that you had to stop over in Philadelphia." (Blackstock may be deliberately trying to fluster the witness: Tom Kinrade in fact testified Florence missed her train in Philadelphia on a subsequent trip to Virginia.)

"No, I think it was at Washington we had a few hours."

After arriving at Richmond in early March with Miss Elliott, and going to stay with Mr. Foster, the two women had enjoyed a merry round of parties and visits with friends to places of interest, with Miss Elliott, according to Florence, generally paying her friend's expenses.

Eventually Florence had moved on to Virginia Beach, and it was while she was staying at the Hotel Virginia Beach, she said, that the manager of the Orpheum vaudeville and moving picture show in nearby Portsmouth heard her sing and offered her a job in his theatre. She performed twice daily at the theatre during the week, using the name Mildred Dale, returning to Richmond, ninety minutes away on the train, to sing in the church on Sundays. At the beginning of June, she said, with her travel burden rather heavy, the church had given her a two-month leave of absence. For a month she had performed only at the Orpheum, where she received $15 a week, before returning to Hamilton for a spell.

"Did the Orpheum show consist of anything beyond singing and moving pictures?"

"There were some little plays."

"And in these plays," said Blackstock almost casually, "were there any firearms introduced?" The courtroom went tense.

"Not that I know of," the witness answered lightly, "just humourous skits and witticisms." (In Portsmouth, in addition to taking part in sketches, Florence performed as 'an illustrated songstress,' which meant she sang as appropriate lantern slides were flashed on the screen. "Her work in the illustrated songs," reported *The Virginian Pilot*, "was exceptionally attractive, as she possessed a pleasing voice of wide range which was heard to advantage in many of the musical features introduced by Manager Butler." *The Pilot* also reported that, in October, Florence had severed her connection with the Orpheum Theatre, and had gone to work at the Pastime Theatre in the Masonic Building on Court Street before returning to Canada before Christmas.)

Florence told Blackstock that she had boarded in Portsmouth with the theatre manager and his wife, Mr. and Mrs. Butler, only seeing Miss Elliott when her friend was passing through town. She had returned to Hamilton eventually, because she couldn't stand the heat of a Southern summer. Ultimately, she returned to Portsmouth after receiving several letters from Mrs. Butler urging her to come back.

"And how did your people feel about that?"

"Oh, they didn't approve of it very much. They didn't like me singing in a theatre."

"Which was the strongest against it – your father, your mother, or your sister?"

"My mother."

"Your sister was also opposed?"

"Oh yes."

"And your father took your side, did he?"

"Not quite."

Had she seen Miss Elliott since returning to Portsmouth?

"No. I think she is a little angry with me."

What had decided Florence to return home once again before Christmas?

"Oh, I got tired of it all."

"Were there any unpleasant incidents associated with it?"

"No. I didn't mix with many people."

"Were any that you met down there paying you any particular attention?"

"Oh, not particularly"

"No one went so far as to make any proposal to you?"

"Yes."

"Which one was that?"

"Mr. Baum."

"Were you pleased?"

"It wasn't agreeable to me."

"What answer did you make to him?"

"I took it more as a jest than anything."

"There was no trouble about it? He dropped the matter after your refusal?"

"No, he still persisted."

"Did that influence you at all in returning home?"

"I wanted to get away."

"Then, when you came home, you didn't think anything more about it?"

"No."

"All the time you were away, you had been engaged to a certain young man and remained so until the occurrence we are discussing?"

"Yes."

"Was there in the family at any time any discomfort or estrangement between you?"

"No."

"How did your sister, Miss Ethel, treat your being down South when you came back?"

"Oh, she didn't say much about it. She was not provoked. (Airily) I wrote and told them all at home, you see. They treated it as a joke."

"Who would you name as your father's favourite daughter?"

Not for the first time, she carefully weighed her words before answering: "He treated all his family alike."

To the jurymen, doubtless drowsy as they watched the hands of the clock pass midnight, the pattern of Florence's responses was now clear: Deny or plead forgetfulness until confronted with specifics, and then admit only the minimum. All suggestions from Blackstock of family discord were roundly rejected, as they would be by all the members of the family. "We were a most agreeable family," Florence declared.

But the jurors snapped awake as Blackstock finally broached the events of the murder day. She had stayed in bed until noon? he inquired, hinting at a pampered existence. She had one of her headaches, she said, and her mother and Ethel came in to see how she was before she got up. Her father and younger sister, Gertrude, came home and the five of them sat down to their main meal at 12:30. "We were all worked up about the night before," said Florence, referring to the tramp incidents. Dinner over, Ethel and Florence cleared up the table while her father and sister left for their schools. Her mother, she said, began getting ready to go the police station to complain about the tramps at about 1:45 *p.m.* It would take her mother half an hour to get ready, she estimated. When did she leave the house?

"I don't think she went out before three."

"Well, what on earth was she doing between 1:45 and three? Can you fix the time when she went out?"

"I have no means of doing so."

"No, you can't say when she went out. It might have been 1:45, 2, 2:15 or 3 o'clock?'

"I can't say."

(Earlier, in response to a police appeal for witnesses, Mrs. Lafayette Shafer, of Glanford, had come forward to say she had been passing the Kinrade house at a few minutes after three the day of the murder, and had heard three shots fired. She heard no commotion, and saw no one emerge from the house. If she was correct, what was happening in the Kinrade house in the hour before Florence ran into the street at 3:57 *p.m.*? Unfortunately, her report does not seem to have been followed up at the inquest.)

Florence recalled that she and Ethel went up to their rooms to get dressed before going out for a walk. "I think she was ready first. I wanted to sew a little hole in my glove, and I came downstairs for the needle. I remember she hollered to me, was I ready yet, and I said, not quite, I was sewing my glove."

The witness said she had come downstairs by the rear servant's stairway, and was in the dining room when the front doorbell rang. The inside door was locked, but the outer one was ajar. When she opened the door, a man standing there asked if she would give him something to eat. But as she went to close the door and get him something, he pushed his way in, saying, "I want all the money you have in the house."

"Then what did you do?"

"I went upstairs to get any money I could find. I had some money of my own, about ten dollars."

Passing the closed door of Ethel's room, she told her to keep her door locked. "I sort of whispered; I didn't want him to hear me."

"The door was closed and you spoke in a whisper!"

"I spoke real loud."

She got a ten-dollar bill from her bureau drawer.

"In that room of yours was a window that opens right out onto the front street?"

"Yes."

"And any time in the afternoon there are people passing on the street?"

"Yes."

"And you went over and opened that window?"

"Yes, raised it up."

"If you had stepped out of that window, you would have been on the balcony."

"Yes."

"And able to call to people in the street?"

"Yes."

Instead, she returned down the front stairs, where the stranger came to meet her. "I got awfully frightened then," she said, and ran past the man into the back parlour, where she opened the window. "He ran after me then. He pulled me back."

"Do you think you got out?"

"I don't know."

"If you said before that you got out and he pulled you back, would that be true?"

"Well, it may be. He grabbed me as I was going out of the window. He told me not to make a sound."

"Well then what?"

"I don't know just what then."

"Why, Miss Kinrade, your memory has always been very good. When is it that this haziness came? What took place after you went to that parlour window and opened it?"

"I don't remember seeing him after that."

"Did you see any person in the dining room?"

"No." She recalled seeing the kitchen door open, and dashing out into the yard to the back fence.

"You could have got over the fence if you wanted to?'

"I don't think so.'

"It is a very easy fence to get over. It has a scantling along it. Why, a child could get over it. Didn't you stand on a pile of rubbish there?"

"I don't think so."

"One cry at that moment would have brought you help in a moment. Still you didn't give it?"

"I was frightened."

"Did you attempt to get over the fence?"

"Yes."

"What was it made you change your mind?"

"I don't know. I thought he was gone and then I came back to the house."

When she re-entered the house though she encountered him in the hallway. "Instead of turning back into the yard, you kept right on?"

"I wasn't far away from him."

"Either you stopped or you went on. Now, Miss Kinrade, I am sorry to have to press you, but I am instructed you have told this story several times, and on all of these you said that, though you saw him, you kept right on. Why do you hesitate now?"

"I remember going on towards the front door."

"Did he say anything to you when you were passing him?"

"I remember I yelled and kind of shoved him away," she said, motioning with her arms.

"Did he threaten you with anything when you did that?"

"No, but he told me not to make a sound."

"Where did you go when you got out the front door?"

"Ran right across the road to Mrs. Hickey's."

"Then you didn't hear any shots fired at all?"

"Yes."

"You haven't told me anything about that so far at all. You haven't said a word up to the present about any shots?"

"I heard so many in succession, I can't remember them all. He fired at me when I ran out of the front door."

"Was that the first shot that you heard?"

"Well, I heard a bang like a house nearly going off. He told me not to make a sound and I seemed to hear something. I remember when I went up those stairs the first time to get the money, something went bang. But I didn't think of anything like that, I didn't."

"You didn't hear Ethel coming out of her room while you were in your room getting the money?"

"No."

"Where were you when you heard what you have referred to as shots in rapid succession?"

"After I had come downstairs with the money."

"Why didn't you reach over the banister when you came down and hand him the bill, or why didn't you throw it down to him?"

"He seemed to be coming to me when I gave it to him. I don't know why I didn't. I didn't want to appear afraid of him."

"As soon as he got that money there was nothing to prevent his leaving the house at once?"

"That is true."

"He didn't want to shoot you?"

"I was awfully frightened."

"Yes," said Blackstock irritably, "you told us that ever so often. But he had lots of chance to shoot you if he wanted to?"

"Yes."

"Well then, Miss Kinrade, let me ask you this: Did you tell anybody since the tragedy that the way it happened was this – that this man opened the door and fought you into the dining room; while you were scuffling with him, your sister, Ethel, came downstairs and as soon as the man saw her, he shot her right there?"

In a voice that could scarcely be heard: "No, I didn't tell anybody that."

Pressing his advantage: "Was that the way it happened? Was Ethel shot at the foot of the stairs in your sight and presence?"

"That is where I saw her lying when I came out of the backyard."

"Did you see the pool of blood?"

"I saw her lying there."

Now Blackstock tried out some of the other earlier versions Florence had given of the shooting. Did she tell someone else that when the bell rang she was sitting downstairs and called up to Ethel that she would answer it?

"I may have."

Did she tell someone else that both she and Ethel were upstairs when the bell rang?

"No."

Did she relate that, going out to the backyard, she dragged her feet one behind the other?

"I don't know how I went."

"Did you tell at first that this man was a tramp that did the shooting?"

"Not exactly a tramp."

"Would you say he was a cross between a gentleman and a tramp?"

"About that."

"How old would you take him to be?"

"Oh, nearly forty I would think."

"Was his hair short or long?"

"Not short and not really long."

It was after one thirty in the morning. Florence had been on the stand for more than two hours. Blackstock knew he couldn't keep her there much longer. If he was to break her story it must be now.

"Miss Kinrade," he pronounced with awful solemnity, "who was that man?"

"I don't know."

"Never saw that man before?"

She looked dazed; her head fell to one side. She seemed about to faint, then stammered, "Never. I would know him if I saw him. I couldn't forget how he looked." She began to cry.

At once, the Kinrade family physician, Dr. James White, was at her side, administering a glass of water. Hobson, the family lawyer, was on his feet declaring it was cruel to keep the girl in the witness box any longer, and demanding an adjournment.

Blackstock, beating a strategic retreat, said he had no desire to cause the witness suffering, and it was for Miss Kinrade to decide if she would answer just a few more questions. She would rather, she said in a weak voice, carry on and be done with it.

Blackstock resumed his hectoring tone: "Do you mean to say, Miss Kinrade, that you never saw that man before?"

"I do," she mumbled.

"You understand, do you not, the solemnity of this occasion? You realize the importance of what you are saying and the obligation that is on you to tell the truth? Realizing all that, do you say that you never saw that man before?"

"I never did."

"You are sure of that?"

"Perfectly."

"Very well then, I will not trouble you any more on that."

Florence had triumphed. As she was helped from the courtroom by the nurse on one side and her fiancé on the other, there was no doubt at all that she had secured a victory against "one of Canada's greatest criminal lawyers."

"Florence Kinrade's Story Created Good Impression," *The Hamilton Spectator* headlined on its front page next day. "There is a fair-sized suspicion that the authorities played a deep game, and that it failed," the accompanying *Spectator* report suggested. The game: to deliberately prolong the interrogation of the father, Tom Kinrade, so that it was after eleven *p.m.* before Florence took the stand.

> By then she was very tired and for over an hour-and-a-half (in fact, more than two hours) she was asked question after question in an endeavour, it was hinted this morning, to wear her down preparatory to the climax. But Miss

Kinrade was indeed more than a match for the talented lawyer examining her, and the opinion has been expressed that
the manner in which she told her story created a favourable
impression.

Certainly there were contradictions in her story: her account of her
confrontation with the 'tramp' differed from earlier stories she had told the
police, and, on some counts, seemed simply implausible. Curiously absent
from her testimony was any description of the actual murder or of her sister. Much of this could be put down to the natural confusion in her mind
following the traumatic events of that fatal afternoon.

Did the Crown lawyer still believe Florence's story of a male intruder,
perhaps connected with her time in Virginia? Or, more likely, was
Blackstock deliberately barking up the wrong tree hoping that in that tense
and obviously preplanned climax, Florence would break down completely
and make some damaging and almost unimaginable admission?

Next morning Blackstock was in Toronto, conferring at the Parliament
Buildings with the Attorney General, J.J. Foy, and his deputy about the
course the Crown's tactics should follow when the inquest resumed that
evening. As far as he knew, Blackstock told a reporter, he had no reason to
recall Florence Kinrade.

Chapter Six

A CHINK IN THE ARMOUR

George Tate Blackstock Q.C. who handled many prominent cases of the era, both as a defence lawyer and as a Crown attorney.

As George Tate Blackstock Q.C. prepared for another late night session interrogating the police and other members of the Kinrade family, one fact was becoming clear: Florence Kinrade, in her virtuoso performance on the witness stand the night before, had been remarkably economical in telling the truth.

Blackstock for one was not surprised. He told an American reporter:

> I am not disappointed about the outcome of the Florence Kinrade examination: she is the most artful woman who has ever come under my observation. I quickly realized that whatever testimony she gave must be taken for what it's worth. She was fully prepared for the trying ordeal. She was on the stand for three hours (in fact two) but I am satisfied

that she could have continued another fifteen hours if necessary.

Now the cracks were showing in her story. A dispatch from Stratford said that, in spite of Florence's claim in her testimony to having sung in concerts in Stratford and Goderich,

> … there is no one in the city that can be found who has a recollection of her being here. The 'Miss Elliott' mentioned in the evidence is not remembered, nor is her sister, Mrs. Robinson of Goderich, known here.

A few people in Goderich remembered Florence singing in a church there, but that was two or three years earlier.

Then an alert reporter tracked down a report, published in August 1907, in *The Stratford Beacon* under the heading, "Delightful Musicale." "Last evening," it read, "a very enjoyable musicale was held at the residence of Mrs. J.C. Robinson which proved a decided success." After listing those who performed, it stated,

> Miss Florence B. Kinrade of Hamilton created quite an impression by her excellent singing and charming manners. She has a wonderfully sweet, melodious voice which she uses artistically and she was given well-merited encores.

 Oddly, when a reporter called Mrs. J.C. Robinson, she said there must have been a mistake – no musicale had been held at her house.

Similarly, an August 1907 report in the Goderich Signal described a reception at Mrs. Arthur Karle's "pretty villa, Lakeview,' at which, not only Florence, but Claude Elliott, a baritone from Kingston summering at Goderich, had performed.

"It is hinted," said a report in *The Toronto World* "that both items were written by one and the same person and designed for the aggrandizement of certain ambitious young persons as a credential of the fact that somebody was in certain places at those times."

In fact *The World*, while remarking on Florence's bad memory, had discovered she was in Goderich for a week in August 1907, but had stayed alone there in room nine at the Bedford Hotel for which she paid ten dollars. "There was no Miss Elliott in evidence at the time, nor do best-informed people here recall ever seeing a likely woman of that name." The only likely Robinsons were a couple, he "a sort of a plumber," she his sister-in-law, who were "not the style of family that would likely be prominent at musicales or parlour entertainments."

In Syracuse, N.Y., a reporter was also unable to find any trace of the Mrs. Kenneth Brown named by Florence as her hostess in that city and also as her escort when she attended musical affairs in Toronto.

As for Miss Elliott, her name had come out of the blue. Said Blackstock, "We had not the slightest inkling of the existence of any Miss Elliott."

With the star turn, Florence, staying out of the limelight at the home of Nurse Walker's mother, there was less excitement as the clock came around to eight in the police courtroom that evening. Isabelle Kinrade, a portly figure accompanied by the nurse who was carrying a medicine bottle, made her way slowly to the front preparing to answer Blackstock's questions about the minutiae of domestic life at 105 Herkimer Street.

It was a familiar litany. Any estrangements or ill-feeling between family members in the four or five years they had lived in the house?

"None whatever."

"Any family dissension about Florence's engagement to Monty in October 1907?"

"None whatever."

The mother confirmed that Florence had undertaken a three-week concert tour to Goderich and other points in 1907 – "I received letters from her."

"Did you ever see the people who went with her on those trips?'

"No, I never met them."

Florence, said the mother, had been with them on trips to Atlantic City, to Niagara Falls, and to Buffalo for the Pan-American Exposition. But the trip to Richmond was the first (presumably forgetting the concert tour) that she had made on her own.

"You were opposed to her going to Richmond?"

"I was opposed to her going, and Ethel also took that view. The girls were much attached and hated to part."

Mrs. Kinrade had written Florence ordering her to come home after learning she was performing on stage. "I did not like her to be connected with a theatre."

"Everything went pleasantly after her return?"

"Oh, yes."

But, Blackstock kept nagging: hadn't there been bad feeling because

Florence, when she returned for good before Christmas, shirked her domestic duties? "Did you or Ethel ever reproach her for not taking part in the household work?"

"Not that I remember."

"On the morning of the occurrence Florence didn't rise till noon, and that was a common practice with her?"

"Yes."

"Did you and Ethel attempt to get her up before that?"

"I don't think we did."

One issue that had concerned Blackstock and the police was what time exactly Bella Kinrade had left the house to go to the police station and the Bethel Mission to complain about tramps. Why the concern? Because knowing that would help pinpoint the time of the supposed tramp incident and the time of death. Or were the police wondering if Mrs. Kinrade was actually in the house when Ethel was shot?

Dinner was finished by about 1:10 *p.m.* and her husband and Gertrude had left shortly after, she testified. She started to get ready to go out at about two *p.m.* "I may have lain down for a little while," she added.

"Now Mrs. Kinrade, may I suggest to you, if you remember anything in your life with perfect accuracy, you should remember what you did on that day."

"I don't think I did lie down."

"Sure about it?"

"Yes."

"What time did you go?"

"What time – I really didn't look at the time, but at the police office, it was four o'clock."

"So she would have left her house about three o'clock?"

"Yes."

Blackstock persisted: "What were you doing from 1:30 when your husband left until three o'clock? It would only take you a few minutes to get ready. Kit Watkins' tart comment:

> No doubt since Mr. Blackstock finds it an easy matter to put
> on his hat, overcoat and gloves, he thinks women ought to
> get ready just as quickly. Most men think so, but women
> know better, and one hour to a woman who was in no hurry
> appeared to me moderate enough—

"I was sewing."

"How long?"

"Likely half an hour." After more of what Watkins called "badgering," Mrs. Kinrade allowed, "I might have been sewing longer than half an hour."

"Am I right in saying," asked Blackstock, revealing perhaps his frustration with the Kinrade family's stonewalling, "that you would like to extend that half hour's sewing and make it longer? How much more do you want to put on – half or three-quarters of an hour? Three quarters of an hour sewing and three-quarters of an hour dressing just nicely fills up the time to three o'clock."

The barbs continued, but if he thought he could make Bella Kinrade lose her composure, he was mistaken.

Her husband had a brother, Hiram, a carpenter, with whom there had been a legal disagreement over their parents' wills. Was there anything the matter with the brother?

He was a very quiet man – "except when in liquor."

(Hiram Kinrade was certainly not in his liquor when a *Toronto Daily Star* reporter found him: he was quietly fishing through the ice in a fishing hut on Burlington Bay, kept warm by a small stove. The reporter described him as bearing a resemblance to his older brother, Thomas, though not as heavily built. There were six children in the Kinrade family: four boys, William, Thomas, George and himself, and two girls, Sarah and Caroline. William, a lawyer, and George, a blacksmith, had both died, as had Sarah. At their father's death, Hiram admitted, he and Tom Kinrade had litigated over the will, but the matter had been settled. Cordiality though was not restored. Although Hiram had worked as a carpenter with Ernest building houses in 1907, he and Bella Kinrade were not on speaking terms. "I have not spoken to her for years," he said. As for his brother, "Thomas and I always speak when we meet on the street.")

Back at the inquest, Blackstock asked Bella, why anyone would want to harm Ethel.

"She was of a very affectionate disposition, and I never heard her say anything against anybody, and I am sure no person wished to harm her."

"There was nothing which indicated that Florence had any mental trouble?"

"No, she always seemed of strong mind."

Her ordeal over, Bella looked suddenly frail and had to be helped from the stand by Nurse Walker.

And so it went. Florence's younger sister, Gertrude, swore her two older sisters never quarreled, and, no, she had never seen any firearms around the house. The brother, Ernie, 26, was asked if relations were agreeable at his birthday party the night before the murder. "You bet!" he replied. He too knew nothing of firearms at 105 Herkimer and had no idea why anyone would harm Ethel.

It was only during testimony the following afternoon from Earl, the second son, that Blackstock finally found a chink in the Kinrades' armour.

Earl, it will be remembered, had been working in a Montreal bank in the months before the murder, but was on his way home the day of the murder to take up duties at a Hamilton branch of the bank. Initially his evidence only echoed that of other family members. Relations between Florence and Ethel?

"Could not have been better."

"Was Florence's health good?"

"Except for an occasional headache."

"Was your sister, Ethel, always a strong girl?"

"She was healthy except being frightened easily."

"Apart from that, she was strong and healthy?"

"Not strong, but in good health. She didn't have the strength that Florence had."

Earl was asked if he ever carried a revolver.

Earl's answer was, "Only once."

"Were you ever in any shooting affray?"

"If you mean in a fight, no sir."

"Or in any threatening or improper way?"

He had once, he agreed, gone target shooting on Hamilton Mountain two or three years earlier using a gun he had borrowed from the bank. Another time he had fired off a borrowed revolver in an alleyway.

"Any other time?"

"Yes," he admitted. On one occasion he had been carrying a revolver in his pocket in the Waldorf Hotel in Hamilton, had been pulling the trigger, not realizing it was loaded, and it had gone off, hitting the floor.

"I am instructed that you threatened somebody at that time."

"That's not so."

He had dropped the revolver, which he had again borrowed from the bank without permission, down a grating into the cellar, recovering it a few days later and returning it to the bank. (Perhaps alerted by this evidence, the police a few days later had tardily opened the sewer outside the Kinrade house, searching for the murder weapon. It was not to be found.)

"Had you heard anything about a revolver being brought back from the South by your sister, Florence?"

"No."

"Did you hear anything about her using a revolver in the South?"

"May I ask for what purpose?'

Blackstock's dark eyebrows shot up. "For any purpose."

"Yes."

"Was that in one of her letters?"

"I heard my father say something about it." Earl explained that Florence had gone on a visit to Savannah, Georgia, where there were many "coloured people." She practiced with a revolver before going, not to injure anyone, but for protection.

The strain was showing. Earl asked if he could sit down, and landed on the chair with a thump. "If at any time you feel sick or tired," said Blackstock, "just say so and we will let you have a rest."

Was the revolver practice alluded to in the family?

"I heard them say it was foolish of the girl to go down there if there were so few civilized people there."

"And if it was necessary to have a revolver?"

"They never liked the idea."

"Did you ever learn what she did with the revolver when she left the South?"

"No." Earl added that he did not say Florence took the revolver to Savannah, only that she had practiced before going.

"Did you know with whom your sister, Florence, went to Savannah?"

"I never met the lady."

"Did you hear her name?"

"Miss Elliott."

"Did you understand that when Florence first went south to Virginia, she was going with Miss Elliott?"

"Yes, sir."

"But you never saw Miss Elliott?"

"No."

"No member of the family ever saw Miss Elliott?"

"They talked as if they knew her."

"Miss Elliott was never at your father's place?"

"Not so far as I know."

"But she seems to have been a great traveller," observed Blackstock wryly.

"Yes."

The Crown lawyer wanted to make it quite clear the Kinrades had been given every chance to uncover any hidden facts. "As far as you know," he asked Earl, "the family has told everything that can throw light on it?"

"I certainly believe that."

"You are not aware of any information being held back by any member of the family?"

"No, sir, I am not."

"You are not able to throw any light upon the location of the revolver used on the day of the murder?"

"No."

"Or what became of the cartridges?"

"No."

"That will do."

Earl's evidence plainly contradicted his father's blanket statement that his children knew nothing of guns, and for the first time revealed that Florence herself had handled and perhaps possessed a revolver. And that information, he had revealed, came from his father.

Blackstock's intentions were plain: he was laying the groundwork for a murder charge against Florence following the inquest, and he wanted no more surprises like the 'Miss Elliott' episode. With remarkable – perhaps reckless – frankness, he told a reporter,

> We are plugging up the holes to prevent new evidence being sprung at the trial. We don't want any will-o'-the-wisp being brought up. We don't want to be confronted with any theory of insanity or fits or anything else that might tend to cover up the truth. We are giving them the chance to tell everything at this inquiry and when an attempt is made at the trial to introduce anything new, we will be able to say, 'We gave you every chance at the inquest, but you said nothing about it.'

Was Blackstock disappointed by the family's evidence? "No," he told the reporter,

> … we got all from the family we expected. But we were probably not prepared for such incessant assertions of the lovely

relations of this angelic family. The absolute state of felicity that seems to have existed has not a parallel!

Meanwhile, patiently, doggedly, he was filling in the small details. Mrs. Hickey, from across the street, sewing in her front upstairs room that day, had seen no one come out of 105 Herkimer, nor heard any shots. When Florence, wearing her hat and coat, had come running to her house, she had foam on her lips and her voice sounded thick, said Mrs. Hickey helpfully.

Was she quite sure Florence was wearing a hat?

"Oh yes, I took it off."

A next-door neighbour, Mrs. Kitson, testified that she was in the back sitting room that afternoon, but had heard no shots.

Dr. McNichol testified that when he arrived at the murder scene both the inner and outer front doors were open. He found Ethel on her back, her feet at the foot of the back stairs, dressed in her hat, veil and coat. The only sign of blood – until the body was moved – was in her hair. The clothing was burned to the skin, suggesting the gun had been held to her chest when three shots were discharged at her heart. "She may have been dead fifteen minutes to an hour-and-a-half," he estimated.

"Did you feel her hands?"

"Yes, and I thought they were fairly cool."

"Was there any smoke in the house when you arrived, doctor?" asked a perceptive juror.

"No, but I think I smelled powder." Detective Bleakley had noticed the smell of smoke, and also that several windows had been thrown up, some so hard it was difficult to close them.

Inspector of Detectives McMahon recalled a "perfectly cool" Bella Kinrade coming to the station to complain about tramps. He advised her not to sign Bethel Mission meal tickets indiscriminately, and to phone the police if she had further problems. Curiously, she made no mention of the incident the night before when a man had rung insistently on their door, but she spoke of the gouge in the windowsill beside the front door. Within minutes of Mrs. Kinrade leaving, he testified, there was a phone call reporting the murder.

McMahon had later noticed the mark on the windowsill.

"Did it look anything like a bullet mark?"

"No."

Detective Bleakley testified there was a chair near Ethel's feet. If she had been sitting in the chair when she was shot in the head, agreed Bleakley, she would likely have fallen forward, her head landing where the pool of blood was eventually found.

Blackstock: "Then the position of the body must have been changed?"

"It must have been."

Bleakley repeated his assertion that, on arriving at the house, Tom Kinrade's first words had been, "I've just expected something like this would happen."

The officer had searched the house, finding no sign of an intruder or a weapon. The only two bullets discovered were one in the pool of blood, the other near Ethel's feet with a piece of bone or ivory.

Bleakley was present for the meeting between Florence and her father, and asked to interview the daughter. Florence was giving him a description of the tramp-intruder when her father came into the room and said, "I do not wish my daughter to be interviewed in this manner."

Before the inquest resumed the following afternoon, Friday, March 13, the jurors spent an hour inspecting the murder scene, guided by Detectives Bleakley and Coulter. They showed particular interest in the back parlour window and Coulter indicated where he had observed the marks of a woman's shoe heels in the snow outside, as if she had stood with her toes in the snow-free area near the wall. At the back fence, Coulter showed them a garbage box opening directly into the laneway through which someone could, at a pinch, have crawled to escape.

And then, late that Friday afternoon, with the jurors looking forward to a weekend's respite, Blackstock sprang his surprise: "Florence Kinrade," called the court constable.

Chapter Seven

I LET OUT AN AWFUL YELL

Quebec lawyer and newspaperman Hon. T. Chase-Casgrain who criticized the inquest
as being contrary to the best British legal traditions.

THIS TIME there was no grand entrance, no swooning approach to the
witness box supported by her nurse and fiancé. Once her name was
called, Florence Kinrade, still dressed all in black, walked in unsupported
and, apparently, in the pink. "Her step was firm and she seemed stronger
and more composed than at any time since the shooting occurred. She had
remarkable control of her features, and her voice was more distinct."

She needed her strength because in the four hours to come she would
be subjected to one of the most rigorous cross-examinations imaginable.
A leading Quebec lawyer and political figure, the Hon. T. Chase-Casgrain
would describe the episode as "very shocking and very scandalous" and
contrary to the best British legal traditions. Blackstock, with generous
walrus moustaches and a pugnacious, terrier aspect, would use the classic

'sweat box' techniques familiar to police interrogators around the world: going over and over the same ground, by turns bullying and cajoling, hoping to trip her up over inconsistencies, and, after lulling her with innocuous queries, firing off damaging leading questions to catch her off guard. It would end with a scene not even he would have imagined.

"Have you slept well?" was Blackstock's barbed opener.

"Off and on," replied Florence, knowing it wouldn't do to admit to completely untroubled slumbers. And while she was in Toronto with her parents prior to the inquest, had she gone out every day?

"Nearly every day."

"Shopping?"

"Occasionally." She had also, she allowed, played the piano to pass the time while her fiancé, Monty Wright, sang.

The lawyer couldn't wait to confront her over her brother, Earl's statement that, despite her earlier denials that she had ever handled a gun, she had practiced with one while down South. Had she visited Savannah?

"We took a trip down there. I don't remember if it was Savannah or Atlanta."

"Was it Savannah or Atlanta?"

"I think it was Savannah."

She had gone there for two or three days with her friend, Marion Elliott, and Colonel Warburton, a friend from England who Miss Elliott had since married. Warburton, a man of about fifty, had arrived in New York from England shortly before, she said, and he had known Marion Elliott from childhood.

"During your stay in Savannah, what did you do with yourselves?"

"Mr. Warburton was on business and we didn't do much. Just went out in the air for a walk."

"What was Mr. Warburton's business?"

"I hardly know. I never heard."

"Did you have occasion at any time to familiarize yourself with firearms?"

"No, I remember when we were going there, Mr. Warburton told us he would have to be armed on account of the coloured people there."

"Did you practice with a revolver at all?"

"He did not say we had to."

"No, but did you practice?"

"No."

(It was becoming a familiar trait: asked a direct question, Florence would answer a different question, requiring Blackstock to pose the original question once again. Her manner too seemed designed to keep Blackstock at a distance: she kept her eyes on the ceiling most of the time, only occasionally glancing at her interrogator.)

"What did Miss Elliott do in Richmond while you were engaged as a soloist at church?" He asked on a new tack.

"Just amusing herself."

"There was no reason for her to go (to Richmond) except to accompany you?"

"She had friends. Richmond was her grandparents' birth place."

"Where was Miss Elliott when you left the South to come home in July 1908?"

"I believe I left her there. They were going down to San Francisco. They got married before I left."

"They got married before you left?"

"No, they got married in Norfolk after I came home. She sent me a postcard telling me of the marriage."

"You have never seen her since?"

"No."

"That card was your last communication with her?"

Florence asked for time to think, then finally said she thought it was.

Like a dog with a bone, Blackstock kept coming back to the mysterious Miss Elliott who, Florence claimed, had paid her expenses in Savannah and elsewhere, and who no one except Florence had apparently seen. The case had received wide publicity throughout North America: if she could corroborate so much of Florence's evidence, why on earth had she not come forward! Blackstock still had no idea what bearing Miss Elliott might have on the murder of Ethel Kinrade. All he knew was that it was a particularly puzzling piece of the mystery and might explain much.

And then it was back to the 1908 tour of southwestern Ontario when again Florence claimed she had been accompanied by Miss Elliott, staying often, she said, with friends of her patron. They had stayed in Galt, Guelph, Stratford, Kincardine and other towns, said Florence, and she had performed at house parties and Miss Elliott had again paid the expenses. They were accompanied at one point by Miss Elliott's brother, Claude, down on a visit from Montreal with his wife. Blackstock was especially interested in Florence's week-long stay in Goderich with 'Mrs. Robinson,' who was proving so elusive when journalists there tried to find her.

"Mrs. Robinson was supposed to be Miss Elliott's sister?" he inquired skeptically.

"Yes, the Robinsons had a summer house near Goderich."

There was a small child in the house; Mrs. Robinson was stout, Mr. Robinson had a small moustache and was very pale, and the house was on the lakeshore. Blackstock extracted these small crumbs of information almost playfully, but to other queries about the location of the house and the domestic details, Florence claimed ignorance.

The geography lesson switched to Virginia: "Is Portsmouth on the sea?"

"No," she answered correctly.

"Is there any military or naval station there?"

Again the right answer: "The navy yard is there."

Had she met any of the naval officers who attended her performances at the Orpheum?

"No, except the captain of one warship. On two or three occasions I was invited to dine with the captain. Sometimes Mr. and Mrs. Butler (the theatre manager and his wife) were there."

Mr. and Mrs. Butler were bona fide people who had been interviewed by reporters in Portsmouth. Perhaps Florence felt on surer ground in offering their names. If so, with his next question Blackstock again tried to rattle her: "Then did you ever fire off a revolver at any time?"

"I remember seeing one down there."

"Down where?"

"Down in Portsmouth, when we were having some kind of an affray in town between some coloured men and a policeman. He (the policeman) was in the theatre showing us the revolver that the deed had been done with."

"And did you shoot it off at all?"

"Oh, no!"

"Was it shot off in your presence at all?"

"I don't remember that it was."

One of the boys in the theatre had a revolver too, she offered. "He liked to take it out and show it to me 'cause I always told him to put it away."

Postcard of Confederate Monument in Portsmouth, Virginia in the era of the Kinrade inquiry.

"Did you ever take it in your hand?"

"No, he would ask me to take it because he wanted to tease me. He knew I wouldn't." (The reporters are too discreet to tell if this exchange provoked laughter from the onlookers.)

Suddenly, from no knowledge of guns at all, there seemed to be guns everywhere. She was sure that Mr. Butler kept a revolver at the theatre, "most all the men carried them."

"When you came from the South, did you bring a revolver with you?"

"No, I didn't have any."

"Did your people write to you when in the South telling you not to use a revolver?"

"I don't remember. They wrote so much. When I wrote home I told them so much that it is likely they did write me."

"Why likely?"

"Because they might have been frightened about me down there."

"Then it is probable that a revolver was mentioned in the correspondence?"

"Yes, probable."

Blackstock was tiptoeing now, sensing a disclosure: "Did you write to your family and say that, before you went to Savannah, you were practicing with a revolver?"

"Well, I don't know that I did. I don't think I told them of the Savannah trip. I wrote to tell them I thought I might go."

The lawyer contained his impatience: "Did you tell them about practicing with a revolver?"

"Why, no, I did not write anything like that."

"And you don't know how such a report got abroad?"

"No, unless I told them Col. Warburton was armed."

It was 6:10 *p.m.* Florence had been on the stand for nearly ninety minutes. The jury foreman suggested an adjournment. "I would like to get through with this witness," insisted Blackstock. He would keep her feet to the fire – and the jurymen waiting for their suppers – for more than two more hours.

The questions came relentlessly. No detail was too small. The colour of Jimmy Baum's hair? Dark. Her escort at a Toronto reception? Mrs. Kenneth Brown. The monthly rents she collected for her father? One hundred and six dollars, of which she got five.

Inevitably, Blackstock moved on to the day of Ethel's murder. Where was she when the doorbell rang?

"In the dining room, mending my gloves."

"And Ethel, where was she?"

"In her bedroom."

"Had you your hat on?"

"Yes."

"And your furs?"

She gave a wan smile: "I only have a muff."

"And what furs had Ethel?"

"She had a mink set – muff and boa."

"Your muff was what?"

"Mink."

By now it was a familiar story to the jurors, who must have had difficulty listening for fresh nuances as their stomachs grumbled.

After the man had prevented her escaping from the open bay window in the back parlour, why hadn't she made a run for the front door, Blackstock wanted to know.

"I don't know."

"Now I ask you to be serious about this. Please give me your attention. When you walked from the front window to the hall, where was the man?"

"I don't think I walked."

"This is something new. Did you run?"

"I must have fainted or something."

Blackstock looked up with renewed interest: "Now, Miss Kinrade, of all the times you have told of this incident, this is the first time you have told any person you fainted."

"I was very frightened."

"Since the incident, have you been talking this over with members of your family?"

"Not a word."

"Now we are getting something entirely new about this fainting. When did this idea about you fainting at the window first occur to you? Remember, this is the first trip for that remark. Did it come to you just now?"

"Yes, it came to me just now." Florence's explanations had rarely sounded weaker. Returning from the back yard and finding the man in the dining room, "I saw something in his hand."

"Did it look like a revolver?"

"Something like one."

"Haven't you said a good many times that you pushed the revolver away from you?" Besides, said Blackstock, by her account, the man was ten feet away from her when she encountered him.

"And the gunshots? You heard the first sound when you were upstairs and Ethel was not then downstairs. Then the next bang sounds you heard were after the man seized you at the bay window?"

"Yes." She didn't know where the sounds were coming from, but it sounded as if the house was being blown up.

"When you had all this time to go into your room and open the window, why did you not open Ethel's door and speak to her?"

She hesitated. "Now, Miss Kinrade, you are a woman of intelligence, why didn't you open her door?"

"I never thought of it."

And then, she thought of a reason: "I didn't want to alarm her until I got the man out of the house."

"But you called through the door and alarmed her."

"Yes, I wanted her to know there was danger."

"Very well, now, Miss Kinrade, in all this story you have never mentioned any shooting except the shots fired at you (as she fled out of the front door). How do you account for that?"

"I heard this bang, bang, bang."

"When was that?"

"After he dragged me away from the window."

"Then the first sounds you heard were when you were in your bed-room getting the money, and you thought it was connected with the gas?"

"Yes."

"And Ethel was in her room at that time?"

"Yes."

"So she could not have been shot then?"

"No."

"And the bang, bang, bang you heard were after the man dragged you away from the window?"

"Yes."

"And where did the shots come from?"

"I couldn't just say."

"Now, Miss Kinrade, don't trifle with me. If those sounds were the shots which killed Ethel, they were fired in the dining room, were they not?"

"Yes."

"Which way did the sounds bang, bang, bang come from?"

"I just seemed to hear them in the distance."

"If you were in the back parlour near the window at the time, and if those shots were fired at Ethel in the dining room, they were fired within a few feet of you?"

"Yes."

"Did it seem so far?"

She faltered and mumbled: "I remember... I don't."

"I ask you again, hearing those shots, why did you not jump out of the wide-open window?"

"I don't remember thinking of it."

It had been a devastating exchange, exposing many of the weaknesses of Florence's story. There were more, many more inconsistencies.

She claimed, for the first time, that the tramp had entered through the unlocked outer door and was standing behind the glass of the locked inner door when she answered the bell. Then why, with the family fear-ful of tramps, had she opened the door to a man bold enough to barge through the outer door?

"I have nothing," she faltered, "except that when I got to the door I did not know what the man was; he might be no one particular – anything, you know." Her answer was delivered in a whisper, and two jurymen got to their feet to protest they could not hear.

"Then what about those times, Miss Kinrade," Blackstock resumed after she had repeated her earlier answer, "when you said this man fired at you when you went out of the back door? Have you said that?"

"I don't remember."

"Then Dr. McNichol tells us that you told him you ran to the front door where the man seized you and dragged you back to the dining room, and while you were struggling with him, Ethel ran downstairs and he turned the revolver on her and shot her. Did you tell Dr. McNichol that?"

"I couldn't tell you whether I did or not."

"If you did tell Dr. McNichol that, was it true?"

"No."

"If you did tell him that, you told him something that was not accurate?"

"Yes."

Did she remember telling Mrs. Hickey that the man shot her sister six times?

"Yes, I may have."

"How did you come to know that it was six times that Ethel was shot?"

"It might have been seven or eight times, I don't know the exact number."

"But that is what we are talking about. Did you tell Mrs. Hickey Ethel was shot six times?"

"I may have."

"Then why did you mention six?"

"I just thought it sounded like six times."

With Blackstock fixing his dark eyes on the witness with intimidating intensity, the hearing moved towards its startling climax: "Now I'll ask you, Miss Kinrade, a question that is most important. And that a strong woman like you ought to remember. I am asking you, when you came out of your house, knowing your sister lay in that house dead, and that the man was in there, did you give the alarm?"

"I let out one awful yell."

"Such a yell that everybody must have heard?"

"Yes."

"Did you ever say that before?"

"I would have if asked."

"I am asking you now, have you ever up to this moment told anybody that you gave that yell and gave that alarm?"

"When I have told the story before…"

"Please bear in mind, I am asking you: have you ever told any person up to this moment that when you got out into the street, when you were free, that you yelled and gave the alarm?"

"Nobody has asked me."

"You've told me that twice. Kindly answer my question."

Hesitating, "I may have told Mrs. Hickey."

"Can you account for no person having heard such an alarm?"

"No."

"And if you didn't give the alarm, would it be very surprising?"

"Yes."

"Miss Kinrade, do you know anything about the revolver with which the deed was done?"

"No, I don't. I cannot say clearly whether I saw it."

"Do you know what became of the cartridge shells after your sister was shot?"

"No," with a shake of her head.

"What do you think became of the revolver?"

"I don't know." Her voice now hoarse and almost inaudible: "I would not know what he did with it. I would not know."

Loud, compelling: "Do you know?"

"No."

"Eh?"

"No."

"You do know, of course, the solemnity of these questions?'

In a faint voice: "Yes, I do."

"You know it would be an awful sin to vary a hair's breadth from the truth?"

"Yes."

"Do you now tell us in this solemn moment, and under these solemn circumstances, that you know nothing about who killed your sister?"

She answered firmly: "I do not know."

Then Blackstock finally put into words what no one in the hours of testimony had dared to say: "Then that man did it, or else – " he let his words hang in the air, "or else the only other persons in the house were you and your sister, Ethel. And if no man was there – only you two girls were left."

Not waiting or expecting a reply, he dismissed her: "That will do, Miss Kinrade."

Even Blackstock could not have expected what followed. Florence's head fell back and she seemed to faint. The court constable called for Nurse Walker, who hurried forward with Florence's fiancé, Monty, and together they struggled to extract her from the narrow witness box. Suddenly she emitted a shriek. "Oh, that man! I see that man! He will shoot me!" she screamed.

"Hush," urged Monty.

"I see that man," she kept on. "He'll shoot me."

They carried her apparently unconscious form into the witness room, closely followed by a mild-looking man with a white, droopy moustache who had sat watching Florence and the other witnesses attentively throughout the inquest. Dr. C.K. Clarke was Canada's most eminent psychiatrist of the age; we shall hear more of him.

With the inquest adjourned for a week, the courtroom emptied. *The Globe* reported that in the ante-room where Florence now lay screaming on a table, her father raised his hands above his head and cried, "Were there ever such brutes of men!"

"Be quiet father," said his son, Ernest, taking his arm, "Don't get excited."

"Get a doctor," someone cried as Nurse Walker bathed her charge's temples with water.

Dr. Bruce Smith (the provincial inspector of asylums who was attending the sessions with Dr. Clarke) was found and, after looking at the patient, he declared, "Come, come, there's nothing the matter with you. You're all right." Florence quieted right down, and a few minutes later was able to leave with her fiancé and the nurse in a closed carriage.

The reporters, the police and the lawyers all considered it now just a matter of hours or days before a charge of murder was laid. And there were no prizes for guessing against whom. Asked the following Monday morning if he thought an arrest would be made, Detective Inspector John Miller replied, "Don't you think there should be one made after last Friday night's exhibition!"

Crown Attorney Washington seemed to be of similar mind: "From the questions the jurors have been asking, and from various remarks, I think they have some person or persons in mind. It would not surprise me at all if a verdict was returned against some definite individual." He smiled wryly: "But it won't be any tramp."

It would take a remarkable effort now to reverse the tide running so strongly against Florence.

Chapter Eight

THE PET OF THE TOWN

Vintage postcard from Virginia Beach, Virginia, circa 1910.

S OME TEN DAYS AFTER Florence Kinrade's dramatic exit from the
Hamilton inquest, a tall man of military bearing stepped down from the
train in Richmond, Virginia, the old capital of the Confederacy. Detective
John J. Pender, assistant superintendent at the Pinkerton detective agency
in New York, had been assigned by the Ontario government to find out
once and for all what Florence had been up to during the months she had
spent in Virginia the previous year.

George T. Blackstock and the agents of the Crown had listened with
increasing frustration as Florence related details of her various travels with
the mysterious Marion Elliott and Marion's friend – now husband – Col.
Warburton. Newspaper reports from the South contradicted Florence's
stories, yet these were not evidence enough to challenge her veracity in the
witness box.

At the resumed inquest session on March 19, 1909 Blackstock had
put into evidence the autopsy report that established beyond a doubt that
Florence's account of the shooting could not be true. Dr. J.W. Edgar, one of
the two doctors who examined Ethel's body at the city hospital morgue the

night she was murdered, testified that the young woman, who was five feet six inches tall and weighed 110 pounds, had been shot seven times, four times in the scalp and face, and three times in the left breast. It was a shot to the breast that had penetrated her heart, killing her, and from the burned clothing and flesh, he calculated the gun had been held one foot or less from the body.

Blood continued to flow from the head indicating, said Dr. Edgar, that she was still alive for, he estimated, fifteen minutes before the final fatal shots were administered to the heart. This was damning evidence indeed, and did not tally at all with Florence's story of a tramp or intruder. But if she, or someone she knew, had killed Ethel, there was still nothing to indicate a motive. By having the inquest adjourned to April 22 – more than a month away – Blackstock now hoped that the Pinkerton man would provide him with irrefutable evidence about Florence's activities in the South with which he could confront her when she next testified.

After registering at a Richmond hotel, Detective Pender made his way across the James River to adjacent Manchester where, Florence claimed, she had been hired as a paid soloist with the Presbyterian church choir. The church was hard to miss: the Manchester Presbyterian Church, the only Presbyterian church in town, was a large edifice, and Pender was able to talk to the pastor, the Rev. J.J. Fix, who told him Florence Kinrade had certainly not sung in his church. And he was equally blank about the Mr. Foster who Florence had claimed was the choirmaster who had hired her. In fact, Pender discovered, there was no one named Foster serving as choirmaster in any church in Richmond or Manchester. He interviewed many people prominent in local musical circles, yet none had heard of Florence Kinrade. Which makes all the more intriguing reports published in Richmond newspapers and reprinted in Canada giving fulsome accounts of Florence's local performances.

Some of the reports were remarkably detailed. The Warren, Virginia, correspondent of *The Richmond Times-Dispatch* described Florence's impressive performance at an anniversary concert at the Warren First Presbyterian Church where, "her hearers were delighted with her clear, sweet voice." Wrote the correspondent,

> Undoubtedly the climax was reached when the choir's final number, Buck's *Deo Gratius* was given, with Miss Kinrade's high soprano voice soaring above the entire assemblage until a final B flat was reached and maintained without the

slightest effort, but with a distinctness and power that truly stamped her as a singer of merit.

Another report in the social columns of a Norfolk newspaper described a reception Mr. and Mrs. J. Wells had given Florence at their home on Fairfax Ave. and which was also attended by 'Fred W. Warburton and Marion Elliott' and the elite of Norfolk and Portsmouth. Yet Mr. Wells told Pender he did not know any Florence Kinrade, and no such reception had taken place. The local elite, said Wells, would hardly attend a reception in his modest home, and, Pender discovered, the report was a fabrication sent in by someone unknown to the newspaper.

Florence had told the truth about one thing: Detective Pender found that, after arriving in Richmond about April 10th, she had arranged to pick up her mail from the Manchester post office. She had crossed the James River by trolley from Richmond daily for that purpose. After about three weeks, she left for Virginia Beach, some ninety-five miles away, ordering her mail to be forwarded there.

Her story back home was that she had gone to stay at Mr. Foster's cottage in Virginia Beach, but again Pender could find no trace of a cottage owned by anyone named Foster.

Local newspaper reporters had also been following Florence's trail in Virginia, and *The Virginian-Pilot* reported that Florence had arrived at the Hotel Virginia Beach, "in a condition of great distress."

"She seemed to have some great trouble," Mrs. Forman who, with her husband, owned the hotel, told a reporter, "but we could never find out what it was. She would never say anything about herself or her relatives or what she had been doing before she came here. We felt sorry for her, but she was a mystery to us."

The woman related that Florence had arrived one evening on the streetcar from Norfolk, and had been given an ocean-view room. But when a member of the hotel staff checked on her, she found her walking up and down her room, wringing her hands and crying. "The woman told me," said the hotel owner, "and I went up to see what trouble she had, but she would not say anything about it."

Florence had arrived before the summer season began, the hotel was empty, and so, said the landlady,

> … as we were alone, we had her come and have her meals
> with us. We were with her a good deal. We understood from

her that she had been at Richmond about two days, that she had come south with two other relatives, one of them a brother-in-law or sister-in-law, we thought she said.

Her relatives, she told them, had gone further south, but would call for her on their return. She was waiting for them, but they never came.

For days after her arrival, she cried a good deal and stayed in her room. "When she came down to her meals, she could not restrain herself. I remember once we tried to talk to her, we asked her something about what kind of fish they got for the table at home, and she burst out crying," said the kindly landlady.

And then another small mystery: Stephen P. Butler, manager of the Orpheum Theatre in nearby Portsmouth, on the lookout for singing talent, heard of a 'Miss Kensington' staying at Virginia Beach. 'Miss Kensington' (a name which, while familiar as that of a fashionable district of London, is almost unknown as a surname) was not there when he and his wife arrived, but Miss Kinrade, whose name he had also heard, was. Florence later told Mrs. Butler that she had a cousin on the stage, name, Miss Kensington, but never mentioned a Miss Elliott.

Mrs. Butler recalled that when she and her husband called on Florence in Virginia Beach, "she sang so well that Mr. Butler said he must just have her. I told her that she could come and live with us at the Hotel Monroe at Portsmouth, and she did so."

Florence had only one stipulation: that her real name must be concealed. She explained that she did not want people in Hamilton to know she was singing on the stage, so the name 'Mildred Dale' was selected for her, and even at the Orpheum Theatre she was known to her friends as 'Miss Dale.'

"Miss Kinrade," added Mrs. Butler, "conducted herself as a perfect lady; she was quite unassuming, and sometimes I was really surprised that she was so quiet. Never a night was she out. After the theatre closed, she would go with me to the hotel, and seldom had a caller."

Florence had come south with, Mrs. Butler thought, an aunt, and had sung in a church choir in Manchester. "When she left, they gave her a handsome bracelet; she had it here and she showed it to me."

Florence, she said, had written to tell her mother and sister she was on the stage, but her father did not know for the longest time, and, not knowing she was earning her own money, continued to send her money to support herself. "I know this because I used to see it when she got it."

"She was the pet of the town," according to Special Officer Broden, of the Portsmouth police. It was Broden's job to visit the Orpheum regularly to check that fire precautions and exits were in order:

> I was often up behind the stage, and I became acquainted with Miss Kinrade. Everybody in town liked her and talked about her. My whole family used to like to hear her sing because she had such a sweet voice. After she went home (to Hamilton) on a visit, and the announcement was thrown on the curtain with a lantern that she was coming back, the whole audience applauded and just went wild.

A Mr. Kirby, manager of the Colonial Theatre, gives us a snapshot of the offstage Florence:

> I remember being over there with Mr. and Mrs. Butler in their parlour, and Miss Kinrade was there too. We had some sandwiches and beer during the evening. She took a sandwich, but would not drink anything, and she would sit for an hour and not join in any conversation of her own accord.

As Detective Pender would put it in his testimony, "She lived like a good, respectable girl, so far as I could learn." But of Miss Elliott or Col. Warburton, the detective would say, "I found no trace of them at all."

Pender may not have been the only investigator looking into Florence's activities in the South. On April 19, 1909, *The Richmond News Leader* reported that a man identifying himself as 'W.M. Clare, Washington, D.C.' had registered at the Lexington Hotel in that city.

'Clare' immediately received two telegrams, delivered to his room, and the suspicion must be that the manager or desk clerk read them, intuited the true identity of the guest, and tipped off a journalist. The name was suspiciously close to that of Clare Montrose Wright, Florence's fiancé, who may have eased his conscience by simply reversing his initials when he registered.

"Were you ever a resident of Toronto?" inquired the reporter when he called on the visitor who he described as about 23 years old, six foot in height, and cordial in manner.

"I have not lived in Toronto," was the evasive reply.

"Are you a native of Washington, or are you from some of the States?"

"I don't think that is material. I came here from Washington."

"Would you object to stating the nature of your business?"

"That is not a matter that interests the public," said Clare.

Had he heard anything of the Kinrade murder case?

"Oh, yes. I have read something of it in the papers. Has the case been finished yet?"

"Have you any acquaintance with a lady by the name of Miss Kinrade?"

"No," he replied, "I do not recall that I have any such acquaintances."

How long would he be in the city? A day or two, he responded. "I may leave tomorrow."

Was the stranger Monty Wright? Had he been dispatched by Florence's father to provide the family with its own version of events in the South? A May 4th report in *The Hamilton Spectator* would suggest that Wright, who was absent from the city about the time the stranger appeared in Richmond, had gone in search of clues to the identity of the mysterious Marion Elliott.

If so, the expedition was quickly aborted: early the next morning, 'Mr. Clare' left town, adding just one more question to the mounting mysteries surrounding the Kinrade murder.

A few days later, a Hamilton reporter tried to catch Monty off-guard by asking him, "Did you find out anything down in Virginia?"

"You don't know that I was down there," he replied coyly. "You don't know whether I was there, or in Dundas, or Brantford, or Hamilton!" A young minister would never lie, but it certainly did not sound like an out-right denial.

Chapter Nine

ESCAPING THE VELVET PRISON

Photo of a typical Edwardian 'velvet prison', parlour, circa 1909.

S O WHAT WAS IT ALL ABOUT? What was the explanation for Florence Kinrade's mysterious travels? Why did she keep inventing characters that, so far as anyone could determine, simply did not exist?

Some explanations for Florence's strange behaviour flow directly from the role of women in the nineteenth and early part of the twentieth century. The parental home was for young women of that time not only a refuge and a support but a velvet prison. "Among middle-class families it was quite accepted that a girl not go out to work, and there was no economic justification for doing so," wrote McMaster University sociologist Jayne Synge after interviewing forty-nine Hamilton women born between 1880 and 1905. Where a girl did want to work outside the home, "the only suitable jobs open to her, office work, teaching or nursing, all required some investment in training, thus placing the daughter more directly under the control of her parents."

Often too, there were family rows over girls working outside the home. One of Synge's subjects wanted to train as a surgical nurse, but was prevented by her parents from leaving the city to take the necessary training.

"In the early twentieth century," added Synge, "marriage involved a far greater transition than it does today. For most women, this would have been the first occasion on which they left the parental home."

Indeed, there was a fear among these women of being entombed in the home. "In those days," one of the women, interviewed in 1976, told Synge, "there were a lot of girls stayed home. I mean, in the (social) class I was in (she was the daughter of a small businessman). If there was more than one (daughter in the family), one always stayed home. That was the one thing I was afraid of."

"At the same time," wrote Synge, "upper middle-class girls were encouraged to choose their mates from a limited social circle, to choose at a late stage, and to go out in groups rather than twosomes."

For the young Hamilton women of Florence and Ethel's generation then, the matrimonial dance was everything. And, says Synge, the women who had the hardest time finding mates were those of comfortably-off families who were not part of the social set, plugged into the round of midnight lake cruises, dance parties, and sports clubs and the like. If they were also forbidden to work, "their social worlds could be very narrow indeed." Her description neatly encapsulates Florence and Ethel's comfortable but constricted existence.

It would not be true to say young women never travelled. Wrote Synge,

> The daughters of the middle class often spent periods away from home. In upper-middle-class circles, the number of eligible young men was limited. Some had in any case gone off to college; leaving home (for the girls) was important in enabling young women to widen their social circles.

But otherwise travel was nearly always to relations, who could keep an eye on the girl, or involved a chaperone. E. Pauline Johnson, the famous poet and performer of the period (and a member of the Hamilton Dramatic Society), "resisted maternal opposition to a stage career and self-consciously seized opportunities to occupy the spotlight." Yet, in a sketch she wrote for the American magazine, *Rudder*, she acknowledged the single woman's need for a chaperone by humorously claiming that her show business partner, Owen Smiley, was her cousin – and so safe!

In his questioning at the inquest, George Blackstock returned again and again to the issue of whether Florence had been allowed to travel alone

– as if that was in itself evidence of wantonness. In a typical exchange, after Mrs. Kinrade said she could not remember if Miss Elliott was to accompany and pay for Florence on her first trip to Richmond, Blackstock blustered: "I should think you would remember an important trip like that, as to who paid the expenses!"

"I can't remember."

When the mother could not remember other details, the lawyer declared, "Do you mean to suggest to us that you allowed your daughter to go there not knowing the church or the salary she would receive!"

"It was left in her father's hands," the witness replied weakly. "I did not like parting with her and letting her go away."

It is difficult to see Florence Kinrade adjusting to this restrictive model. From all we know of her, Florence was not only artistically gifted, but a spirited and self-centred woman who, it is clear, yearned to perform on a larger stage – literally and metaphorically. On the facing page across from the preface of this book, there is an original family photograph of the young Florence, taken at the Andrews studio in Hamilton, showing a handsome young woman with the trace of a wistful smile on her face. On the back she has written: "18 yrs old – how could anyone fall for me..???" It speaks of a young woman always concerned about how the world saw her, determined to be the centre of attention.

She was a survivor and a woman of independent spirit, and the one thing you can't possibly imagine her being is the wife of a clergyman in a small town in Ontario. You can though imagine her reading Jane Austen's *Persuasion* in her teens, and smiling in wry agreement as the heroine reflects on the female role: "It is, perhaps, our fate rather than our merit. We live at home, quiet, confined, and our feelings prey upon us." The heroine's name, coincidentally: Anne Elliot.

So the fate of most young middle-class women waiting for Sir Galahad to rescue them from spinsterhood, was, in Hamilton in 1909, not so different from that of Jane Austen's young women in eighteenth century vicarages and country houses. We can see just how stultifying that existence could be in the domestic details George Blackstock extracted regarding the lives of the two sisters following Florence's return from Virginia.

Florence commonly stayed in bed until noon – probably because there was nothing to get up for. The two girls had a midday dinner with their parents, did a little sewing, then put on their fur muffs and boas and went for a walk. Apart from light work around the house, the only real connection the two young women had with the real world of work was in collecting the weekly rents for their father. It would have taken them, unaccompanied, down some of the city's poorer streets, exposed them, we can assume, to difficult or even drunken tenants, and tested their hardiness in summer heat and winter cold.

Other than that, there was church on Sunday, choir practice during the week, and the occasional family birthday party, such as the one they attended at Ernest's house the night before the murder. Their mother had a visiting day every second Thursday – but hardly anyone ever came. That left the church as the only place where the girls were likely to meet suitors, and here Florence soon trumped her older sister.

Initially, Montrose Wright, the earnest, young theological student they had met at choir practice, would accompany both sisters on outings. It is not hard to imagine that Florence, always thinking how she could exert her charms, would make a play for the boyish, idealistic minister to be. There would be a natural competitiveness with her older sister, and what could better trounce Ethel than an engagement ring! After that, Ethel stayed home and, we can guess, quietly stewed.

But ministerial candidates were not allowed to marry prior to ordination, and when they became engaged, Montrose still had a couple of years to go at Victoria University. Gradually it must have dawned on Florence that, when she married Monty, she would face a lifetime of manse teas, church bazaars, Sunday school teaching, and presenting a cheerful front to church folk who would, in turn, be watching her for any signs of deviant behaviour.

If Florence decided at this point that she had to escape at all costs, she was not the first woman to do so. In December 1926, the grande dame of mystery herself, Agatha Christie, in the midst of turmoil with her husband, simply disappeared. Rewards were offered, huge headlines announced developments, and thousands scoured the countryside in search of her. She was found eleven days later staying at a hotel and spa in Yorkshire where she had registered as 'Mrs. Neele' – the name of the woman with whom her husband was having an affair.

In 1909, at the time of the Hamilton drama, the New Zealand writer, Katherine Mansfield, newly arrived in England, was going through a series of episodes where she changed her identity and even married on the spur of the moment, "just to know what it felt like" for a book she was writing.

Kit Watkins 'Kit of the Mail' who has already appeared in this narrative, forged a new identity for herself when she came to Canada from Ireland at the age of twenty-eight. She gave herself a new name, shaved years off her age and told a tall story of having been left a penniless widow forced to work in London as a pound-a-week governess.

Florence had no need to disappear or disguise herself. It was enough for her to somehow find a way to be away from her family. It must have occurred to her early on that her singing talent provided the perfect cover and from that realization grew the great scheme of deception.

At the concerts in which she performed she would have met interesting and influential people and, itching for greater freedom, the thought must have occurred to her that if she invented an out-of-town patron, she could spend nights or weeks away from home, no questions asked. And false reports in local newspapers of concerts in which she had appeared would provide a perfect backup for her stories. She must have discovered that when reports of concerts at homes were sent in to local newspapers, no one ever checked on their accuracy. If she was careful to pick either non-existent households or, as in the case of 'Mr. and Mrs. J. Wells' in Portsmouth, choose ordinary folk who would not be looking for their names in the society news, there was almost no risk at all of discovery. The clippings, especially those mailed home later from Virginia, must have been immensely gratifying to her family in Hamilton.

Mrs. Kenneth Brown, of Syracuse, was an early invention that allowed Florence to stay overnight in Toronto, ostensibly attending a musical evening at a grand home on Spadina Avenue with Mrs. Brown. But 'Mrs. Brown' could not be everywhere. She had a home in Syracuse and could be checked up on. Florence needed someone altogether more fluid – someone who could not be pinned down, someone always on the move – someone like Marion Elliott. She was from England – an ocean away – and had no fixed address in Canada or the United States, she had social contacts and even relatives everywhere, she had the money to travel and even to pay for many of Florence's expenses. In short, she was Florence's most brilliant invention, and when Florence tried her out on a dry run, staying a week at a hotel in Goderich in 1907 and, the following year, three weeks in southwest Ontario, she worked like a charm.

What Florence did that first week is a mystery. She knew no one in Goderich so far as we know. Outwardly, nothing could seem more boring – getting up, walking the streets of a small town, dining, going to bed. But, sitting in her room, polishing the concert reports she would send off to newspapers in Stratford and Goderich, dreaming of the new places and experiences now open to her, free to come and go with no one to answer to, she must have simply revelled in the experience.

But what was the reason for it all? Was Florence simply looking for escape, adventure and perhaps romance? What was the explanation for her state of upset when she arrived at Virginia Beach? Logically, an unwanted pregnancy and the need for an abortion must be considered. And then dismissed – because the Pinkerton man, Detective John Pender, doubtless on the lookout for such an eventuality, found nothing. Florence was a romantic and an adventuress and she may have been upset over an affair. But we have to give her this: for a young Canadian women from a sheltered background, travelling alone to a post-bellum South, where violence was still a presence on the streets, this was immensely daring.

Freedom was one thing, but when her ambitions came to focus on a career in vaudeville, she entered another dimension entirely. For a young middle-class woman in Hamilton in the early twentieth century, such an ambition would simply be considered beyond the pale. Class was everything: Florence Bridgewood, born in Hamilton in 1886, went on (as Florence Lawrence) to become The Biograph Girl – the first 'movie star,' and by 1909 was making dozens of silent movies every year. But she began her career at the age of three performing in her parents' tent show as 'Baby Flo, the wonder whistler.'

Caroline Crerar, another Hamilton girl, was less lucky. In 1897 at the age of fifteen, she gave a brilliant performance in the (amateur) Garrick Club production of *Baby Clive* and scored another triumph in *Not Such a Fool as He Looks* which won a Dominion drama award in Ottawa in 1906. But when Caroline received an offer to go professional, her father, a lawyer who was also president for many years of the Garrick Club, simply refused permission, and she remained a mainstay of the Hamilton amateur dramatic scene.

Earlier, Georgina Treherne, the talented and beautiful daughter of a Welsh landed gentleman, thought she had found a way to overcome the objections of her family to a stage career. When she married the impecunious Henry Weldon in 1860, although it was a love match, she made it a condition that she would be allowed to "go on the stage and make a fortune." But once married, Weldon reneged on the deal and Georgina, like Caroline Crear, in Hamilton, had to settle for performing in amateur theatrics and society events.

And if the dramatic stage was dubious as a career choice, vaudeville was unthinkable. Even though, as John E. DiMeglio would write, "As the 20th century began, vaudeville was the unrivalled king of entertainment." It is difficult now to appreciate just how popular an entertainment medium it was – Hollywood, Broadway, and television all rolled into one, as it were. By 1914, the weekly capacity of Toronto's four major vaudeville theatres was nearly 150,000. It meant that potentially close to a third of the city's population of 470,000 could attend vaudeville weekly – and full houses were common.

The great stars of the day were not simply shadows up on the screen, they were flesh and blood performers at the local theatre where, for tickets ranging from twenty-five cents to sixty cents, you could get an intimation of greatness. So crowds thronged to hear stars like Vesta Victoria singing *Waiting at the Church* or Eva Tanguay (The "*I Don't Care Girl*") singing *A Bird in a Gilded Cage*. As our drama unfolded in Hamilton, the whole of Canada and America was whistling and tapping – and playing on a million front-parlour pianos – vaudeville hits of the day like *I Wonder Who's Kissing Her Now*, and *Yip-I-Addy-I-Ay!* and *Shine on Harvest Moon*. It wasn't just music: the crowds saw every kind of novelty act, from ice skating, to sword swallowing. One week it would be the escape artist Houdini, the next comedian W.C. Fields. The rewards were immense: Vesta Tilley, an English performer, was paid $2,500 a week when she came to North America, while Lillian Russell, who appeared in Toronto sixteen times, received a phenomenal $3,100 a week. Even famous actors from the legitimate stage like Ethel Barrymore and Mrs. Patrick Campbell were tempted by its rewards, and regularly appeared in the vaudeville houses between plays.

One thing the owners of the major vaudeville circuits, including the Shea Brothers, the Buffalo pair who owned three of Toronto's largest theatres, were absolutely clear about: In contrast to vaudeville's bawdy cousin, burlesque, there would be no smut in their theatres. At matinées, two-thirds of the audience consisted of women, in the evening half, and children were commonly allowed in unaccompanied. So any performers who broke the rule would quickly find themselves without employment: vaudeville was strictly family entertainment.

Yet vaudeville performers got little respect. "The overall view of vaudeville," writes DiMeglio, whose father and grandfather were vaudeville stars, "was that, having emerged from the lowest classes, though destined to entertain a basically middle-class America, they were considered social undesirables. A staunch middle-class citizen would probably oppose his child's wishes to become an entertainer."

For instance, the comedian Jack Benny's parents (his father was a haberdasher in Waukegan, Illinois) felt disgraced when their son became a vaudevillian. Lillian Russell, a beauty who was regarded as the belle of the 'Gay Nineties,' describes in her memoirs how she had to go behind her mother's back to get a tryout at Tony Pastor's famous Broadway theatre. For more than a month, while her social activist mother was out lecturing as a suffragette, Lillian would slip out of an evening in her costume, and be walking on to the Broadway stage fifteen minutes later. Luckily, when her mother saw the rapturous reception her daughter received, and, more importantly, what she was being paid, she had no further objection.

Society's attitude toward vaudeville artistes was pungently described by the impresario, B.F. Keith. He wrote,

> There is a quite ignorant hostility among those women who rule the social destinies of the world to anybody associated in their minds with music halls. They imagine a vaudeville lady as appearing, dressed in little, in a hall filled with tobacco, casting immodest winks at not wholly ideal men.

Indeed, vaudeville's origins were, in some regards, less than respectable. In *A Prescription for Murder: The Victorian Serial Killings of Dr. Thomas Neill Cream*, Angus McLaren describes how the prostitutes Cream preyed upon touted openly for business in music halls, as vaudeville theatres were called in Britain. The music halls had originated in public houses and by the late nineteenth century were the target of the National Vigilance Association which, with the blessing of Prime Minister W.E. Gladstone, "attacked the moral excesses of music halls and theatres on one hand and established rescue homes for 'fallen' women on the other." The Cream murder trial, opined the *British Medical Journal*, was of interest because of what it revealed of "the manner of life led by the degraded women who haunt the street, the gin palace and the music hall." Even in far-away Hamilton, Ontario, some of this mud would have stuck.

Apart from snobbish attitudes, there was indeed a difference in social background between the vaudeville stars of the day and aspiring artistes like Florence Kinrade. "We all sprang from the same source, the same origin," said Sophie Tucker at a dinner at the New York Public Library in 1954. "We were all swept to the shores of this country on the same tidal wave of immigration, in the same flight from prejudice and persecution. Our life stories are pretty much the same." Vaudeville's stars, as Tucker pointed out, tended to emerge from the immigrant hordes of New York's slums, and certainly not from respectable neighborhoods in small Canadian cities.

Florence's first exposure to vaudeville must have come on family outings to the theatre. Tom Kinrade, in his inquest testimony, mentioned a family excursion to see *The Merry Widow*, and it is inconceivable that a well-to-do family of that era would not also have attended one of the several Hamilton vaudeville theatres. There might too have been excursions to Toronto, by steamer in summer, by train in winter, to attend one of Sheas' grand vaudeville palaces. The most popular stars of vaudeville were overwhelmingly women singers and comediennes, and it would only be natural for a girl whose singing talents were so admired to see herself as one of those glamorous figures on the stage.

But how could that be achieved? There is no mention of Florence revealing her ambition to her parents. Perhaps she realized that in just about any middle-class family such an ambition would be laughed off. She may have made secret inquiries in Toronto or Buffalo with the Shea theatres about a career on the stage and quickly learned three hard facts: that New York was the vaudeville fountainhead where careers were launched, that most performers worked their way up, usually starting in their teens, and that, besides, Canadians seemed to be at a disadvantage, ranking well behind American and, more particularly, experienced British music hall performers. And even if she found a way to start a career close to home, there was no way of keeping it secret from her parents.

It must have seemed a hopeless project. Her mind must have turned around and around the conundrum. New York would have been the natural place to make a start, yet mention of that Sodom on the Hudson would certainly have alarmed her parents.

It may well have been that on one of those mysterious trips under the fictitious Miss Elliott's wing that Florence met someone – certainly not a choirmaster – from Richmond which put into her head the idea of starting a vaudeville career in Virginia. Perhaps upon her arrival in Richmond she did use church contacts to sing with choirs, but she decamped for Virginia Beach after only three weeks in a state of emotional turmoil. Rather than over a failed romance, it could have been that she had been rebuffed after approaching theatres in Richmond. Her tears at the Atlantic Hotel may have been due partly to homesickness and partly despair because her dream of going on the stage seemed to be coming to nothing.

It was only when she sent a letter in the name of 'Miss Kensington' to Stephen Butler, the manager of the Orpheum Theatre in Portsmouth, that her fortunes finally began to look up. Even then, secrecy was paramount. She signed the contract as 'Mildred Dale' (a pseudonym, we shall learn, that she had already used, and which may have been inspired by Violet Dale, a well-known vaudeville performer). Again, according to Detective Pender, she registered at the Hotel Monroe in Portsmouth under a false name, presumably 'Mildred Dale.'

Florence and her parents, in their testimony at the inquest, give the impression that her stage venture, as well as her involvement with the actor Jimmy Baum, were entirely casual and just innocent amusements to pass the time. That is hard to believe. However sincere or otherwise her love for Jimmy Baum, her debut on the stage of the Orpheum Theatre must have been a great revelatory moment for her. In the past she had been admired for performing popular classical and religious material in church and at concerts. Now, almost magically, she found she could win the applause, affection and approval of theatre audiences for material that was a great deal more fun to perform. She would not easily give up that thrill. George Blackstock could only have guessed at some of this. But with the information gathered by Detective Pender, he no doubt looked forward to confronting Florence once more when the inquest resumed on April 22. This time, he hoped, he would find the connection between Florence Kinrade's Virginia adventure and the murder of her sister.

Chapter Ten

KING VS KINRADE

Defence lawyer George Lynch-Staunton Q.C., retained by the
Kinrade family to appear for them at the coroners inquiry.

⚮

T HE DRAMATIC POSSIBILITIES were not lost on Constable Robert Lentz.
From the very beginning, when he had been called from his bed the
night of Ethel Kinrade's murder to assemble a coroner's jury, the constable
had been at the centre of the action. As the officer in charge of maintaining
order in the coroner's courtroom, it was his voice booming, "*Oyez! Oyez!*"
that announced the opening and closing of the interminable sessions; it
was he, acting as a sort of master-of-ceremonies, who called the witnesses.
And he, as much as any of the journalists present, had a first-hand view of
the legal tussles, the sometimes harsh interrogations, the contradictions,
and the hysteria – an experience that for the rest of his life would make him
the object of interest and curiosity in a city that would never stop talking
about the Kinrade affair.

On April 22, 1909 though, Constable Lentz sensed his greatest moment
had arrived. As the hour hand on the courtroom clock approached eight

111

p.m., Coroner Dr. Anderson, the Crown Attorney S.F. Washington, and Mr. George Blackstock also representing the Crown, were huddled in the witness room. Phone calls were made; in the courtroom, more crowded than ever, with newsmen at one point spilling beyond the railing protecting the officials, there was a constant buzz of excited speculation. Finally, at a half past eight and without a word of explanation, the three officials filed into the jam-packed courtroom, Constable Lentz called, "Order!" and Blackstock, with no great enthusiasm, questioned several unimportant witnesses, including Mrs. Ernest Kinrade, Florence's sister-in-law, who was able to add little.

It was getting late. There was an air of anticipation. Finally Blackstock turned to the constable. "Call Isabelle Kinrade three times," he ordered.

"Isabelle Kinrade," boomed Lentz. Then, after an appropriate interval and when no one appeared, "Isabelle Kinrade." Then: "Isabelle Kinrade." The witness room door remained empty.

"Call Florence Kinrade," directed Blackstock.

Lentz's loud voice echoed back from the bare, dingy walls: "Florence Kinrade." Not a sound in the room. "Florence Kinrade." No response. "Florence Kinrade."

"Mrs. Kinrade and Florence Kinrade," Blackstock told the coroner, "were summoned to be here tonight, and our information was that they would be here, but they have not appeared." It would be necessary to ask for an adjournment until, he added with a hint of menace, "the Crown can take such steps as are necessary to enforce their attendance."

Battle had been engaged. In Thomas Kinrade's view, enough was enough. Following the previous hearing, when he had rent his hair and cried, "Were there ever men so brutal!" Tom Kinrade had evidently decided to put a stop to what he saw as the persecution of his daughter. Now, among the lawyers crowding the front seats of the courtroom to witness the legal spectacle, one immensely tall, thin man with a goatee beard sat almost without a word. George Lynch-Staunton Q.C., one of the country's most distinguished lawyers, had been hired by Kinrade to represent the family's interests. Staunton had already issued a warning to newspapers that he would hold them legally responsible for slanderous statements they were making about Florence Kinrade. And, on March 20, he made a scathing attack on the whole coroner system, an institution with seven hundred years of legal history behind it.

Staunton was damning. He told a reporter:

> It's simply awful, this system of coroner's inquests. There sits a man, the coroner, who knows nothing about the rules of evidence, nothing about the protection that should be thrown around witnesses, and the Crown lawyers are permitted to drag out information that should never be told and has no bearing on the question before the jury. They are permitted to ask any questions they like, make all kinds of insinuations, and work things generally so that every half-baked citizen all over the country can hear or read them, formulate foolish theories and pass along their impure suspicions.

The lawyer was in full flow:

> You may talk as you like about the United States' sweat box system, but I tell you that their system of investigating crime is a thousand times more preferable, more decent and more just than the exhibition we have had of the Canadian system in connection with this case.

Was there any necessity, he asked, "for putting witnesses upon a lamppost and shouting questions at them for all the world to hear the answers! You can depend on it," Staunton declared, "the case is not closed as far as we are concerned – no, not yet!" Now, having played his first card, he was content to be silent. Staunton, in comparison with whom, a reporter would write, "an oyster is garrulous," had no word for the journalists as he left the courtroom.

The following evening, with the courtroom in an even higher state of excitement, Constable Lentz had the opportunity for a repeat performance, and once again there was no response when, on this occasion, he just called Florence Kinrade's name.

In response to Blackstock's questions, Detective Inspector John Miller testified that he had that morning served Florence with a subpoena to attend the inquest. "Upon hearing the statement of Detective Miller," Blackstock told the coroner, "I request the issue of a bench warrant for the arrest of Florence Kinrade in order to compel her attendance at the inquest."

The until-now-silent Lynch-Staunton leaped to his feet objecting:

View of Osgoode Hall, home to the highest courts in Ontario.

"Miss Kinrade is acting under the advice of counsel in the action she has taken. Besides being physically unfit, she has been advised that you have exhausted your authority, and proposes to test this before the proper forum." He demanded an indefinite adjournment.

Blackstock had again been taken by surprise in this remarkable proceeding. "This is the first intimation that the Crown has received that the delinquent who has disobeyed the subpoena was acting under the instructions of her counsel!" he bristled. "She did not comply with the subpoena, therefore there has been entire disrespect to your authority and the authority of this court," he told the coroner. "Consequently I cannot consent to the request of my learned friend for an indefinite adjournment."

The legal niceties may have been observed, but tempers were flaring. Lynch-Staunton muttered something about the coroner being hectored into issuing the bench warrant.

"Mr. Staunton," said the coroner with strained dignity, "you should not insinuate that the coroner can be hectored into doing anything contrary to his duty. When a witness refuses to recognize my authority, I must issue a bench warrant."

"You have no such authority," snapped Staunton.

"I have authority under the law, and we will not discuss the point."

The view of Toronto streets from Osgoode Hall, over the 'cattle gates' in about 1920.

And Coroner Dr. James Anderson, who must at this point have wished he was back in his office dealing with simple bunions or sore throats instead of refereeing a legal imbroglio between two very angry lawyers, ordered the court cleared and the session ended.

An unidentified Crown officer (likely Mr. Washington) told reporters that Friday night that there was no question of executing the warrant on Florence immediately, as that would necessitate her being in custody over the weekend. "We don't want to antagonize the public," he explained. In any case, he said, the Crown knew where Miss Kinrade was and there was no danger of her fleeing. For all that, two private detectives from the Thiel Agency were posted to watch the Kinrade lodgings at the Abberley apartments, on Sherbourne Street, in Toronto with, according to one of the detectives, instructions to follow the Kinrades if they emerged, and to intercept them if they attempted to leave the country.

By next morning, Thomas C. Robinette Q.C., another famous name in Canadian legal history, briefed by Lynch-Staunton, was calling on Mr. Justice James V. Teetzel in chambers at Osgoode Hall, in Toronto, seeking a motion to prevent Florence Kinrade's arrest. His grounds: Dr. Anderson, being in Wentworth County, had no jurisdiction to issue a warrant against a witness in Toronto, which is in York County, and where Florence was now staying with her parents. And besides, Robinette told reporters after lodging his application (on which Judge Teetzel reserved judgment), "Florence Kinrade has already given her evidence, having been on the stand for seven hours under cross-examination. She has told all she knows."

The clash between the Kinrades and the officers of the Crown had turned rancorous, and the public waited eagerly for new developments. It was exactly the moment for some light relief – which arrived in the jaunty figure of Jimmy Baum, Florence's actor-boyfriend, from Virginia.

A very reluctant Jimmy had taken more than a week to travel from Portsmouth, Virginia, to Buffalo, New York, where he was met by two detectives, a Pinkerton man, John J. Panday, and Ontario Detective Inspector Joe Rogers. He was inclined to go no further – until an attorney he consulted told him it was his bounden duty to testify at the Kinrade inquest. And that, if he didn't, the Canadian authorities were likely to send a commission south to interrogate him.

"All right, I'll go," said Jimmy, and boarded a train for Toronto where, the next morning, Detectives Pender and Rogers picked him up at the Iroquois Hotel and gave him the Cook's tour of the city. There was a ride on the streetcar, an inspiring view of the University of Toronto's Gothic towers, a tour of the Queen's Park Parliament Buildings including, oddly, an introduction and a lengthy talk with Dr. Bruce Smith, Provincial Inspector of Asylums.

Next morning, with Detectives Pender and Rogers sticking to him like glue, and with strict instructions not to talk about the Kinrade case, Jimmy, discovered by the press at the Royal Hotel in Hamilton, was "willing to talk to anybody about almost anything under the sun."

"You Canadians are great for walking!" he announced. "Yesterday, in Toronto, they walked me around about five miles." Dr. Smith? "A rattling good fellow," he allowed. The Toronto police? "Say," he said, "I stopped one of those Toronto policemen and got him to show me how to draw that club out of that leather case. I'd like to see them up against our people in the South, our Negroes and rough fellows," he chuckled. "I tell you what, they would be busted to pieces in a minute!" (The unthinking racism of the era is frequently in evidence and never challenged.)

"He is a blithe, light-hearted chap, about twenty-nine years of age, of medium height and build," observed a *Toronto Star* reporter. "In his hazel eyes there is a continual merry twinkle, and the general expression of his healthy-looking face suggests that it's mighty hard for him to be serious about anything."

"Going to tell them something startling at the inquest?" a reporter asked.

"Oh yes," he replied, adjusting his polka-dot bow tie, "I'm going to tell them what a pretty country Canada is."

He was interested to see Bennett's Theatre, which, in view of his notoriety, had offered him an engagement for the week, an offer he had turned down.

"That was an easy $250 you missed, Jimmy," said Pender.

A morning stroll with his keepers was suggested. "Better try the mountain," someone urged.

"The mountain!' he said, stopping as he went to light a cigarette. "The mountain – Miss Kinrade used to tell me their backyard ran up to the mountain."

A reproving wink from one of the detectives warned him to change the subject. Then, overcoat flapping, hat at a cocky angle, and using a large handkerchief to conceal his face whenever a newspaper photographer appeared, the actor allowed his two guardians to guide him to Herkimer Street where he had his first sight of the house where the drama had begun.

"Aren't we having lots of fun!" he joshed Detective Rogers after successfully evading three more cameramen. The detective did not reply.

It must have seemed questionable whether Jimmy Baum or anyone else would ever testify in Coroner Dr. Anderson's courtroom again after George Lynch-Staunton broadened his attack in the Divisional Court at Osgoode Hall the following Wednesday (April 28).

Staunton, in a ninety-minute address to the three justices argued:

That no coroner has the power to issue a warrant for the apprehension of any witness.

That no coroner has the power to issue a warrant outside his own jurisdiction.

That the law gives coroners no power to arrest for contempt of court.

That the inquest, being an investigation at which the liberty of witnesses is in jeopardy, no witness can be asked incriminating questions.

That Florence, having told all she knew about the death of her sister, could not be called again because such a procedure is a vexatious abuse of the process of the court.

And that neither George Blackstock nor anyone but the Crown

Attorney had the authority to cross-examine witnesses at the inquest.

In the case that was now called 'King vs. Kinrade,' Staunton was chal-lenging the powers of an office first mentioned in England's *Articles of Eyre* in 1194, and which may have existed earlier. The modern day function of the coroner – who is appointed in Canada, but generally elected in the U.S. – in investigating sudden or suspicious deaths goes to the very heart of the legal system, and his or her powers are rarely challenged.

But suddenly, under Staunton's withering attack, the institution seemed on shaky ground. The essence of the Kinrade lawyer's argument was that coroners are little more than civil servants, gathering facts, and having none of the powers of arrest accorded a court of law. The heated tone of the hearing can be detected as one of the three judges, Chancellor Boyd, read aloud the warrant issued by Coroner Dr. Anderson.

"...Florinne, or whatever her name is—" he said, squinting at the paper. Staunton interrupted:

> If there ever was authority for a coroner to issue a warrant, it has been destroyed by the law as laid down in England. The coroner's warrant says that the reason he wants the girl to attend is for contempt of court, and not to give evidence. Every warrant must show the cause on its face, and the coroner knew what he was doing. He didn't issue a proper warrant.

"It doesn't matter," snapped Mr. Justice Magee.

"It does matter!" shot back Staunton, showing little respect for the judges. "He issued a wrong warrant, and has no authority for the warrant he did issue."

The lawyers could argue all day over the finer points of the law, but Staunton was eager to get on to what he called the "vexatious" behaviour of Coroner Dr. Anderson and George Tate Blackstock. The justices had before them an affidavit sworn by Thomas Hobson, the Kinrade family lawyer, who had attended all the inquest sessions, giving his account of events. He had, he said, been surprised when on March 12th, Florence had been recalled after already having testified for four hours on March 10th.

Both examinations, said the lawyer, "were so severe that the witness fainted at the completion, and on the second occasion the examining coun-sel, by his questions, in my judgment practically charged said Florence Kinrade with the murder of her sister."

Hobson drew a dismaying picture of the inquest procedure:

> The coroner did not exercise any control over counsel whatever, allowing him to examine the witness without any restriction, and to keep her on the witness stand for a time which was beyond all physical endurance, and, in my opinion, it was torture.

On both occasions, argued Hobson, the coroner should have adjourned the inquest to allow Florence, who was suffering from physical and nervous weakness, meals at the proper time.

The lawyer pointed out that the overheated courtroom was packed with journalists from all over Canada and the U.S., necessitating the witness climbing behind the coroner's chair to reach the witness box. "It represented a theatrical spectacle more than a judicial inquiry," he observed.

Now Staunton was ready to fill in more brushstrokes: "They dragged her all over her past life; they led her away down to the South and made her tell about her experiences there. They led her far afield from the subject of the inquest."

Chancellor Boyd: "That's what they call the sweatbox, isn't it?"

Staunton: "It's what one of the newspapers spoke of as the third degree in public. It was a scandal, an absolute abuse of criminal law. They examined that woman there and charged her with murder – in distinct words charged her with murder."

If, he said, "she goes before a real court and is charged, she cannot be made to testify by any power under the sun."

Staunton, in the view of many, was right. Florence had been abominably treated, was indeed asked questions which could incriminate her, and was bullied. Reading the evidence, it is easy, in fact, to wonder who was in charge of the inquest – the coroner or George Blackstock. The Crown lawyer boldly took it upon himself to say when sessions would be adjourned, and personally refused requests from jurymen to take breaks for refreshment. He acted the tyrant and, though he may have been exasperated by Florence's evidence, went far beyond what was permissible in accusing her of murder.

Yet Blackstock had his defenders. Although some newspapers had faulted him for using the third degree, *The Hamilton Herald* in an editorial argued that his methods were entirely justified. "A foul and mysterious murder has been committed," it reminded its readers. The attorney-general deemed the investigation important enough that, not content with putting provincial detectives to work on the case, he had appointed one of the province's most eminent lawyers to represent the Crown at the inquest and question witnesses. "Such a thing has not been done in Ontario for many years at least, and it is doubtful if it was ever done before."

The inquest, pointed out the newspaper, had been postponed for weeks out of consideration for the chief witnesses, "who are reported to be in too nervous a condition to give evidence." The Crown though must explore the various theories, straightening out discrepancies revealed in the testimony. *The Hamilton Herald* editorial continued to say:

> It is a painful process – doubtless painful to the inquis- itor as well as the person whom he is examining. Unfortunately, the chief witness – a young woman of attractive appearance and interesting personality – gives testimony which is in essential points so confused and contradictory that the Crown representative finds it nec- essary to go over the ground again and again with the hope of getting from her a clear and connected account of what she had witnessed. That is what he is there for: that is his duty.

Blackstock, wrote the editorialist, "… is charged with having virtu- ally accused Miss Kinrade of the crime. This is not true." What he did was to suggest to the young lady an inference which might be drawn from a portion of testimony – a suggestion which was doubtless offered in a kindly spirit.

What has been described as a "gruelling" examination was indeed a persistent course of interrogation, but through it all the demeanor and tone of the examiner were the reverse of hectoring – were "courteous and even deferential."

Surprisingly, the jurymen too, in spite of having been denied their supper at one point by Blackstock, were also on his side. When the inquest had, of necessity, to be adjourned while the Osgoode Hall hearing was taking place, the jurymen told journalists they wanted it put on the record that, in their view, Blackstock had conducted the interrogation with great care, and they saw no reason for Staunton's protest.

Interest in the Kinrade affair had abated not one iota. In Hamilton, when word came that the justices had made their decision, hundreds crowded around newspaper office windows to read bulletins and to snap up special editions of the papers. The news was that Staunton had won his point – sort of. The justices gave it as their opinion that Coroner Dr. Anderson's warrant could not be served outside Wentworth County. (Staunton had indeed found a loophole in the law, and two years later the Ontario government changed the law so that coroners would have the same power to summon witnesses as the Supreme Court.) More to the point, the justices wagged a warning finger at George Blackstock, opining that, if Florence Kinrade returned to the witness box, they would assume she would not be unduly harassed, would not be forced to go over ground already covered, and that the questioning would not be intended to lay the foundation for "collateral purposes." In other words, for laying a murder charge. At the same time, the justices refused to issue an order preventing the arrest of Florence Kinrade on the coroner's warrant.

It was legal stalemate. J.R. Cartwright, the Deputy Attorney General, quickly announced his intention of securing a Crown warrant to force Florence to appear at the inquest. Staunton, bowing to the inevitable, but having scored points too, wrote to the attorney general's department, agreeing that Florence and her mother would testify, but insisting that the justices' restrictions on evidence be observed. In addition, he requested that the press and public be excluded from the inquest from now on.

Again it was the remarkably able jury, proving itself just as diligent in its pursuit of the truth as Blackstock, that intervened. "I object to any star chamber methods in any public affair," declared the jury foreman, R.B. Spira.

> If we have any say in the matter, I am convinced that the entire jury will be in favour of admitting the press. The information will leak out anyway, and it might as well come out in proper form than to have it whispered around.

Within hours of the justices' decision being announced, Detective

Inspector Miller finally called on the Kinrades' Sherbourne Street lodgings in Toronto with Crown warrants ordering Florence and both her parents to appear at the inquest the following Monday.

Blackstock would have his final chance – let's not be too delicate – to skewer Florence on the inconsistencies in her many stories.

Chapter Eleven

PRETTY INCONSEQUENT BUTTERFLY

Ottawa Journal of March 11, 1909 featured stories about
evidence given by Florence Kinrade in the coroner inquest and her fainting spells.

THE CONTRAST between mother and daughter that afternoon of May 3, 1909 as they testified at the long-drawn-out inquest into the death of Ethel Kinrade, could not have been more striking.

Florence entered once more on the arm of her fiancé, Monty Wright, with all the cockiness of a champion. "She walked in a sprightly manner and seemed greatly improved in health and nerves," reported *The Hamilton Spectator.*

The throng around the snowy door of number three police station certainly expected blood sport and was, wrote a *Toronto Daily Star* reporter, "like the crowd at a theatre entrance on matinée day." Seats in windows overlooking the police station were going to ladies for between a quarter and a dollar, and "even the windows of the Bethel Mission (where Bella Kinrade had gone to complain about tramps) each had their fashionably dressed occupants."

After arriving earlier veiled in black, a self-confident Florence now took her place in the witness box and turned to face her tormentor, the Crown's lawyer, George Tate Blackstock.

Yet, only minutes before, her mother, Bella, had been carried out by Constable Lentz and Detective Bleakley, each holding one side of her chair, after she fainted giving testimony. "Bella—" Kit Watkins observed "appeared to have aged twenty years in the past six weeks."

Blackstock's questioning of the mother had broken little fresh ground. Of the invitation to Florence to sing at a church in Richmond, she only knew what Florence had told her, reading from a letter from the church. Florence had also read her a letter she had received from Marion Elliott about the trip south, although, said Mrs. Kinrade, she had never met Miss Elliott herself. When she was due to visit Herkimer Street, said Bella, the Englishwoman had not turned up. Had she or her husband given Florence money to go to Virginia?

"I didn't. I believe she'd always got money from her father when she wanted it."

Mrs. Kinrade claimed to have known little at the time about Florence's journey, the church she was going to, or the salary she would receive. "I was ill at the time. I didn't take much interest in it," she explained. All she knew was, "I didn't want her to go, and I took no interest."

(You can almost hear Bella Kinrade telling Florence and her father, "Well, do what you want! I wash my hands of it.")

Blackstock's questions never stopped; it was all getting too much for her. "Oh. Oh, you're hurting my head," she said, pressing her hand to her forehead. "You're hurting my head."

"I am very sorry, Mrs. Kinrade," he apologized. Would she prefer to postpone the examination?

"No, Mr. Blackstock," she replied. "It is my child that's gone. My memory is gone."

"When did you first hear that she was acting in a theatre?"

"I—" She got no further. Her head fell back and she fainted away.

"Pretty, inconsequent butterfly," Kit Watkins called Florence as she took the stand. And like a luckless butterfly, collector Blackstock would mostly swat empty air with his net trying vainly to trap her: the famous lawyer would never face a tougher witness.

It took her less than a minute to revert to her old standby: "I can't remember."

The name of the church where she sang? "Manchester Presbyterian Church," she answered. Name of the clergyman?

"I can't remember."

"Choirmaster?"

"Mr. Foster."

George Lynch-Staunton, trying to head off any damage, reminded Blackstock that the Division Court decision had warned against going over the same evidence over and over, and pointed out that Florence had the right to refuse to answer any question that might incriminate her.

He needn't have worried: Florence was as hard to pin down as ever, especially on the subject of the moveable church.

"Then, Miss Kinrade—" resumed Blackstock, "when you went to the South, did you sing at the church at Manchester?"

"I can't say that the church was at Manchester."

Yes, she agreed, she'd sung in a church for a salary.

"Was that church in Manchester?"

"I couldn't just say where it was."

"Can't you recall it?"

"I understood it to be there."

"How long did you sing in that church?"

"I couldn't say just how long it was."

It might have been three or four weeks, she finally agreed.

"Was that church a white church or a coloured church?"

"White people, certainly."

She had only received her salary – about $30 – after she left, and it was sent on to her in Portsmouth, she said.

"Then, Miss Kinrade, why is it you say you don't know whether the church is in Manchester or not?"

"I am just telling you what I think. I can't say some thing positively."

She had gone to Richmond about Easter. Did you commence singing at once at the church?

"I believe it was the next Sunday after I got there."

"And you sang each Sunday for the weeks you were there?"

"Not consecutively."

"Well how many Sundays did you act as soloist?"

"I can't remember just how many."

"You were the soloist, were you?"

"I understood so."

"Did you live in Richmond or Manchester while you were singing at the Manchester church?"

"I couldn't state positively."

"What was the name of the street you lived on?"

"I don't remember."

"Did you receive your mail at Richmond post office while you were singing at the church?"

"I think not."

"Did you not leave a direction in writing with the postmistress at Manchester when you left to forward your mail matter to Virginia Beach?"

"I may have."

"Do you still persevere in saying you can't remember receiving mail matter at Manchester post office?"

(Tartly) "I didn't say I hadn't."

(Exasperated) "Oh yes you did, but say what you please."

"I don't know whether I did or not."

"Well now, Miss Kinrade, I am instructed that, for a period of between three and five weeks you called at Manchester post office and received mail there, and that when you left, you left a written direction to forward your mail matter to Virginia Beach. Is that statement true?"

(Grudging) "It may be."

"I am instructed that you came in a (street) car across the bridge that spans the James River and got out at the post office and got your mail and got on the car and returned to Richmond in the same manner. Is that true?"

"It may be."

"I am instructed that you did that week after week for several weeks. Is that statement true?"

"I don't remember."

"Now," he said, fixing her with that fierce gaze, "I am instructed that you never sang at any church while you were in the South, and I ask you now if you can name the church."

"I can't name it any more than I could before."

"Did you, when you turned up in Portsmouth in the month of May, show the people a bracelet bearing the inscription that it had been presented to you by the choir at the church at which you sang for three or four weeks."

"Yes." (A collective drawing in of breath in public gallery: Florence had finally answered a question.)

"Did you procure it yourself and give directions to have the inscription put upon it?"

"No, I did not."

"The inscription said it had been presented by the choir."

"That's what it said."

"That wasn't true, was it?"

"I understood it was."

"Now I am instructed no such bracelet was given to you by the choir. Do you still say it was?"

"It was presented by the choir leader and I believed it was on behalf of the choir."

"Who was present."

"I don't remember."

"Not a single person?"

"I remember Mrs. Warburton (Marion Elliott that was)." She thought the presentation had taken place in the choirmaster's house in Richmond.

"That was not the Mr. Foster you met at Mrs. Kenneth Brown's house in Syracuse—" he raised a humourous eyebrow, "was it?"

"I think not."

He was making a fool of her now: "Another Mr. Foster entirely?"

"Yes."

Staunton at this point asked a very natural question: what did Blackstock's line of questioning have to do with the murder of Ethel Kinrade? It was, Blackstock said that evening, to establish Florence's credibility.

(If her statements about her stay in Virginia could not be trusted, what credibility attached to her description of events the day of the murder?)

As Staunton continued his protests, Blackstock made an admission: he would have preferred, he said, if the inquiry had been conducted in private, "but the coroner has already given his reasons for holding this open to the public. And they are good reasons," he added.

"I cannot alter it," Coroner Anderson chimed in. "The jury are entirely with me in this matter."

Dr. Anderson might have added that the spectators, leaning on walls and radiators, standing in aisles, filling every square foot of the courtroom, were equally on his side: they were being treated to a remarkably unrestricted public exploration of one of one of Canada's greatest murder mysteries.

Now Blackstock prepared to spring the Marion Elliott trap. Florence had said Miss Elliott accompanied her part of the way from Hamilton to Richmond: "Any person else accompany you?" he asked mildly.

"No."

"And you cannot tell us where you met Miss Elliott on that trip?"

"I think it was Washington or Philadelphia. I cannot recollect."

Blackstock showed Florence a letter. "Is it from Miss Elliott?" he inquired.

"Yes."

The lawyer handed the letter to Crown Attorney Washington to read, and the courtroom grew very still.

> Philadelphia, Saturday, October, 1908
>
> My Dear Florence,
>
> I am sorry things have turned out so contrary to our plans, but of course under the circumstances it was entirely out of our hands. The remains were brought to Philadelphia for burial (Miss Elliott's aunt had apparently died), and as I am one of the chief mourners, I had to come with them, and I gladly did so, even though it is a disappointment for you.
>
> However, our plans are not completely frustrated because you must come on the 5 p.m. train and Mrs. Goldsmith – you remember the lady you met in Buffalo – will meet you there, and together you can travel to Philadelphia.
>
> I think it will be advisable for you to take a sleeper: I believe Mrs. Goldsmith prefers that kind of travelling

for long distances. She knows you, and so there will be no difficulty whatever if you take the 1:05 p.m. (from Hamilton), and then all will be right at the depot here in the morning when your train is due. Then we will complete our journey in time as Mrs. Foster wishes us to remain with her over Sunday.

I was extremely sorry and disappointed not to have met your parents and sister, but I was hardly prepared for the return trip to Buffalo and of necessity came here. I hope to have the pleasure and opportunity of welcoming them in Virginia some time in the near future. Kindly tell them to rest assured that everything will be done for your comfort and that you will be well looked after.

Now I hope you will follow up these few directions, dear. I will meet you here on Wednesday morning, and, with Mrs. Goldsmith, I know you will have a pleasant journey. Just bring a suitcase because I will have all I can do looking after the luggage. Kind regards to your parents, and tell them that perhaps at some future time I will be pleased to spend a few days with them as I pleasantly anticipate with you.

Goodbye until I see you soon,
Ever your friend, Elizabeth Elliott

The letter certainly has the ring of authenticity, but it contains several puzzling features. Blackstock picked up immediately on the error of the signature, but he missed the fact that the letter is dated October 1908 when, Florence had earlier testified, she had never again seen Miss Elliott following her return to Hamilton from Portsmouth in July of that year. The letter also seems to be referring to her fist trip to the South – to Richmond – adding to the confusion.

"This is the letter of instruction you received from her before you set out for Richmond?"

"Yes."

"Then the writer was the person you referred to as Marion Elliott?"

"Yes."

"And who signs herself Elizabeth Elliott?"

"It was Miss Elliott's other name," she insisted.

"Before you got to Richmond you met this Mrs. Goldsmith?"

"Yes."

"Although you told me before that no other person accompanied you. Where did you meet Mrs. Goldsmith in Buffalo?"

"At the depot."

"Had you known her before this?"

"She was a friend of Miss Elliott."

"Had you met her in Buffalo before?"

"I don't remember where I met her."

"When Miss Elliott mentioned the name, you could not recall the woman?"

"No."

"But although you had forgotten Mrs. Goldsmith, she was able to pick you out in the crowded station in Buffalo?"

"Yes."

"Why then, Miss Kinrade, when I asked you before why did you not tell me you were accompanied by Mrs. Goldsmith?"

"I guess I forgot."

"And you now ask us to believe you forgot that on this trip to Richmond you forgot Mrs. Goldsmith after having travelled all night with her in a train to Philadelphia?"

"Yes."

"Did any person else accompany you on that trip?"

"Some of her friends."

"How many?"

"There were two."

"Were they men or women?"

"Why, two ladies."

"How did you get this letter from Miss Elliott? Did it come from the post office or was it handed to you?"

"I do not remember."

"See, Miss Kinrade—" he said, showing her the envelope, "it has no postmark and the stamp appears never to have been used."

"No, it doesn't appear to have been used."

She had reached Richmond in the evening with Miss Elliott, they had driven in a cab to a private house which she thought might have been the Fosters'.

She had eventually moved on to Portsmouth, "for no particular reason." On the way, she agreed, she had stopped for a day in Norfolk, when she had simply gone about the shops, before continuing to the seaside resort. She had chosen to go there because, she said after being pressed by Blackstock, "Mrs. Foster was there, and I wanted to see the place." She had only returned to Canada in July, she testified

"Now, Miss Kinrade, I am going to give you the opportunity of making a statement," said Blackstock, always his preliminary to confronting her with inconvenient facts: "Did you come back to Toronto, Canada, between the time you left Richmond and the time you turned up in Virginia Beach?"

A definite: "No."

"Were you in Toronto in April of last year?"

A small: "I think I was."

"How long did you stay then?"

"About a day."

"Where did you stay?"

"I did not stay anywhere."

"Are you clear about that?"

"Well I remember having dinner at the Queen's Hotel."

"Alone or with anybody?"

"With Mr. Wright."

"But you did not stop in Toronto that night?"

"No, I came home late that night."

"Well now, Miss Kinrade, I am instructed that you stayed in the Queen's Hotel at Toronto from the sixth to the eighth of April. Do you say now that is true?"

If Blackstock thought his revelations would crack her composure, he was mistaken. "I believe that I did," she declared, as if grateful to him for jogging her memory. "I remember now." (This surprising revelation – that Florence, without informing her family, had travelled all the way back to Toronto and stayed two nights at the Queen's Hotel before returning to Virginia – was never explained or even explored. Was she missing Montrose? Unlikely. Was she considering ending her engagement? Was there already another matrimonial correspondent in the picture?)

"When you went to Virginia Beach, you went to a hotel there kept by Mr. and Mrs. Forman?"

"I don't remember their names."

"What! Are you serious? You lived with them several weeks, taking your meals with them, and you wish us to understand you don't know their names?"

She hesitated: "I remember now."

She had arrived, he said, about April 11th and stayed until May 15th. "It was not that long," she insisted.

Had she gone anywhere else between leaving Richmond and arriving at Virginia Beach? Florence knew better now than to be caught out again by Blackstock's research.

"I think I was at Fortress Monroe."

"Who went to Fortress Monroe with you?"

"Miss Elliott."

When she first arrived in Virginia Beach, said Blackstock, she had parked her suitcase in a pavilion by the sea, gone into the hotel and bargained for a room. Because it was off-season, the Formans offered her a bargain rate of $7 a week, and she would live as a member of the family, taking her meals with them. She shortly returned with a boy carrying her suitcase.

"Now, Miss Kinrade, were you in any trouble at that time?"

"No."

"I am told that you arrived at three o'clock in the afternoon and that you were in a great degree of distress for the next ten days. Would that be true?"

"No."

"Is it a fact that a considerable amount of mail matter was waiting for you at Virginia Beach at the post office?"

"It may be true."

"At any rate, you found a number of letters for you?"

"Yes."

"While there, did you have any callers?"

"Mrs. Warburton (Miss Elliott)."

"Did the people at the hotel see her?"

"I couldn't say."

"Did she ever stay at the hotel?"

"I am not positive."

"Now, Miss Kinrade, did you tell Mr. and Mrs. Forman on your arrival that you came south with your brother-in-law and his wife, that he was connected with a railway, that he and his wife had gone further south, and that they would come back for you?"

"They are mixed (up) there. I told them that I came with my aunt."

"Who was your aunt?"

"Miss Elliott. I called her aunt."

"Did you tell them there was any man or woman you came south from Canada with?

"Well, I may have put it that way – that they had gone some place to return again."

"And they tell me that you stayed there with them for five weeks expecting them to return."

"They never saw them," was her curious answer.

"Where did you meet them?" asked Blackstock, going along with Florence's trance-like thinking.

"On the boardwalk, I think."

"Did you meet this man and woman at Virginia Beach?"

"I do not remember just where."

"I am instructed," said Blackstock, off on a new tack, "that no such persons were in Virginia Beach as Mr. and Mrs. Foster."

"I remember meeting them on the boardwalk."

"Was this Foster the choirmaster named Foster?"

The jurymen were not going to miss their supper this time. They had had enough of Blackstock's marathon interrogations, and before Florence could reply, a jury member proposed that, as it was 6:20 *p.m.*, an adjournment should be called.

After supper, Blackstock persuaded Florence to tangle herself further in the Foster business. When Florence told him she had secured the position in the church through Miss Elliott, he asked how she had arranged it.

"She had me sing for somebody connected with the choir."

"Where?"

"At Toronto. At the Queen's Hotel."

"This is the first time, Miss Kinrade, we have heard of Miss Elliott being at the Queen's Hotel. And she got you to sing for somebody from Richmond?"

"No."

"Where from then?"

"I don't know."

"Who was it?"

"A man named Foster."

"Another Foster!"

"Yes."

"And this was the first time you met this Foster?"

"Yes."

"He was choirmaster Foster?"

"No."

"Have we heard of all the Fosters you've met now?"

"Yes."

"We've got them all – the Queen's Hotel Foster, and the choirmaster Foster?"

"Yes."

"I must remind you that you said before that you met this Foster at Mrs. Kenneth Brown's at Syracuse. Which is right: the story you now tell or the other one?"

"I met him at the Queen's first."

"You didn't tell us that before."

"I didn't think it was necessary."

It is clear that Florence Kinrade was making it all up as she went along. She had lied to her parents, lied to her friends in Virginia, lied, as we shall see, to her lover, Jimmy Baum, and lied repeatedly during her testimony before the coroner. She had invented a whole alternative existence based on a web of untruths. Blackstock would point out to her that, woven into her account, were no fewer than six people who did not appear to exist, starting with the ever-present Marion Elliott. Perhaps, though, her lies can be better understood in an era when middle-class women were forced to conceal their true motives and inclinations.

Prof. Mary S. Hartman, a Rutgers University historian, says in her study of thirteen middle-class Victorian murderesses that,

> All the women here lied… Their lies, which were ultimately used to cover illicit sexual behaviour or criminal acts, originally served less shocking but still forbidden ends: a secret tryst, an opportunity to read forbidden literature, an escape from unwanted marital sex. For most women, of course, the new opportunities for dissimulation were restricted to goals within the domestic sphere, which could be achieved through lying.

Prof. Hartman goes on:

> For some of the accused women the lies themselves
> became a kind of game, carried on partly for itself as
> escapist fantasy and partly as a means to allow them to
> integrate socially expected behaviour with their own
> contradictory feelings and urges. This may account for
> their creation of elaborate and intricate tales which
> became a kind of secret code, identified as such only by
> other women.

In other words, she says, other women could recognize themselves in these "romantic fabrications."

She could have been writing about that great inventor, Florence Kinrade.

Chapter Twelve

LOVE LETTERS TO JIMMY

An example of 'matrimonial ads' that were ubiquitous in
newspapers around the turn of the twentieth century.

IT HAD TO BE the greatest puzzle George Tate Blackstock faced in a distinguished career. The Crown had dispatched Detective John Pender of Pinkerton's to Virginia to find out the truth once and for all about Florence Kinrade's sojourn in the South. Yet every fact uncovered seemed only to add to the mystery. At every turn in the maze, Blackstock seemed just as far away as ever from the goal of somehow connecting events in Virginia with the murder of Ethel Kinrade.

Now, in the second half of Florence's final-marathon six-hours of testimony, he had his last chance. And, as he broached the subject of her short-lived theatrical career and her romance with actor-singer Jimmy Baum, he knew he had information she would have difficulty in explaining.

First there was the odd business of Miss Violet Kensington, another of those phantom figures who only Florence seemed to have met. Her responses to questions about Violet were classic Florence evasions.

How had Florence come to leave Virginia Beach, Blackstock inquired. She replied that Mr. Butler, manager of the Orpheum Theatre, in Portsmouth, had asked her to perform at his theatre.

"You saw an advertisement of the Orpheum Theatre in a paper, did you not?"

"That wasn't the way."

"Didn't you see that advertisement, and didn't you reply under the name of Violet Kensington?"

"I wrote for Miss Kensington. She asked me to write."

"Then what you swear is that there was a girl at Virginia Beach named Violet Kensington and you answered for her?"

"Yes, I think – though her name was Edna Kensington."

"Did a young man come down from the Orpheum to your hotel and inquire for Miss Kensington?"

"Yes."

"And Mrs. Forman (the hotel proprietor) told him she was looking for you, and you said Miss Kensington was your cousin."

"No."

"Will you swear you didn't?"

"No."

"Did Mrs. Forman tell you she told the man there was no one there named Kensington, but that there was a young Canadian singer named Florence Kinrade?"

"Yes."

"Did she ask you to see him, and you refused?"

"Yes."

"Anyway, Mr. and Mrs. Butler came down to see you."

"And you engaged with them to go to this dime museum?" said Blackstock, revealing the prejudices of his class.

"It isn't a dime museum!" Florence replied indignantly. "It's a theatre."

"Well don't let's squabble. A 10-cent theatre then."

And then, a different tack: "Did you ever hear the name Violet Kensington before you went south and met Miss Kensington?"

"No, I can't recollect what names I've heard."

"Did you ever answer any matrimonial advertisement?"

Florence's composure was never put to a greater test. But she met Blackstock's broadside with a merry laugh, and she continued smiling as the lawyer conferred with his colleague, S.F. Washington.

(In fact, today's dating websites would not have surprised people of Florence's era in the least. Throughout most of the nineteeth century, newspapers featured matrimonial ads, and soon there were newspapers devoted entirely to this form of advertising. Then, more than today, men and women lived within their own spheres – men in the world of out-side work, women within the home. Matrimonial ads were one of the few ways of breaching those walls. At their most extreme, the ads could expose women to the dangers of swindlers or even murderers. Or, as in the case of the two Hamilton sisters, they could be the source of a little innocent fun at the expense of would-be suitors. But that batch of mail waiting for Florence in Portsmouth and her emotional upset at the time suggests one of those ad responses could have led to a serious liaison.)

"I asked if you ever answered a matrimonial advertisement," persisted the lawyer.

"Not exactly that. It was just a little fun."

"This advertisement was inserted by whom?"

"Some gentleman, I forget the name."

She agreed that the man lived in Ithaca, New York, and she had been responding to an advertisement in an American paper.

"Is this letter in your handwriting?"

"Yes."

George Lynch-Staunton was on his feet immediately: "Surely, Mr. Coroner, there is a limit to this sort of thing. He's trying to make a fool of this girl. He ought to be ashamed of himself!" The coroner refused to intervene, and Washington read the letter:

Dear Harold,

I enclose my photo as you requested. I got it taken in Philadelphia while visiting there a few weeks ago. They say it is not a good one of me, but I think it will give you some idea of my style. This is my new opera hat that I am taken in. Is it not fine?

I do not sing, "Won't you come and spoon with me?" (Harold, hearing she was a singer, had evidently asked play-fully if she knew this favourite of his.) What is it like? Did you hear it in 'Lovers and Lunatics' at the theatre? I know you would surely go there often. I do now.

I always was (susceptible) to Yankees on account of their fickleness, but I am sure you are not that kind…Have you an auto? I know some men in Cornell (University, near Ithaca) – Mr. Notfair, Mr. Halfspace and Mr. May. Have you any nice girls over there?

Now, Harold, be sure and send me your photo in return. How old are you?

Sincerely yours, Violet.

Blackstock showed her a letter, which she agreed she had received in reply from Harold. "It is addressed, "Miss Violet Kensington, 105 Herkimer Street, Hamilton?"

"Yes."

Florence admitted that the letter, dated March 14, 1907, showed she had been using the name Violet Kensington a year before she went to Virginia Beach.

"And you wrote several letters to this young man in Ithaca using that name?"

"I wrote two."

"And your sister wrote also?"

"Yes."

Certainly Blackstock had caught Florence out in another lie, but overall, the letter weighed in her favour. For the first time jurors got a glimpse of Florence as a giddy, fun-loving young woman no doubt giggling as she and Ethel concocted mischievous letters and those comical names for rubes who put matrimonial advertisements in the newspaper. The letters though might also have given her an early notion of the potential power of literary invention.

Then another minor mystery: According to Mrs. Butler, five mornings out of seven while she was staying with them she went to Norfolk (a ferry ride away). "Is that correct?" asked Blackstock.

"Yes."

"She says she never found out what you went for. She says she wanted to go with you, and that you refused her permission, and she gave up the idea. Is that correct?"

"No."

"What were you doing in Norfolk?"

"I went shopping and for the trip."

"Was there anybody you went to see?"

"No."

Shortly after she arrived in Portsmouth, Mr. Butler introduced her to Jimmy Baum who gave her some instruction in stage technique and wrote a sketch in which they acted together.

"And in this sketch one of the things you did was to chase him with a knife?"

"Yes."

"And once you changed the knife for a revolver without his knowing it, and fired it off?"

"I tried to but it wouldn't go off."

"Did you ever fire the revolver off?"

"I don't remember."

"While at Portsmouth, did you tell Mr. Baum you had been married?"

"I may have. I don't remember."

"Did you tell him your husband was much older than yourself and that you'd been compelled to marry him?"

"No."

"Did you give him to understand your sister, Ethel, had been instrumental in forcing you to marry the man?"

Outraged: "Why, no!"

"And that your husband was following you to get you to go back to him?"

"No, I didn't say so."

"Did you from time to time while in this theatre receive notes and letters and tell Baum and Butler you were in mortal dread of the writers?"

"No."

"Do you remember showing Baum a letter you received from a man who said if you didn't leave the theatre at once and go home, he'd shoot you on the stage and drag you off?"

"No, I think you're mixed some. I only got letters from Mr. Wright."

"Do you remember a box of flowers being sent to the theatre about the middle of July, after you had left (to return to Hamilton)?"

"Yes."

"The box arrived after you'd left, and Mrs. Butler brought it home?"

"Yes."

"Did you tell her that, had you received that box on the stage, you would have collapsed?"

"No, I never said so!"

"Well Mrs. Butler instructs me that you told her so. Did you tell Baum that, had you seen it while you were on the stage, you'd have had to be carried off?"

"I don't remember."

"Did you tell him your husband sent it."

"I don't remember."

"Will you swear you didn't?"

"Yes."

When the Crown lawyer returned to the matter of the flowers later though, Florence told him she thought they came from Marion Elliott's brother, Claude, who she had encountered in Goderich on the Ontario tour the year before.

She also, under Blackstock's prodding, recalled a box of sweets she'd received from an admirer at the theatre. She may, she agreed, have said she feared they were poisoned, "but I intended it as a joke." And she had certainly not peeped through the stage curtain to see who had sent them.

"I am instructed that you did," said Blackstock dryly. "Did you tell Baum on one occasion that you were going to Norfolk to meet your husband and that you were afraid to go, and he said, 'Let me go with you.'"

"I may have said it in a joke."

Blackstock was wearying of her evasions. "I ask you again, did he not offer to accompany you to Norfolk to protect you?"

"I don't remember."

"Will you swear he didn't?"

"I don't remember."

"And that's as far as you'll go?"

"Yes."

"Now did you not tell Mr. and Mrs. Butler about the middle of July you'd have to leave as this man was persecuting you?"

"That wasn't it."

"Did Butler induce you to stay five days longer by telling you that if a man could get you to give up your position that way, he must have a wonderful power over you?"

"Well, no, it wasn't that way."

"Well, Miss Kinrade, I'll let you give your version."

Miss Elliott, Florence explained, disapproved of her performing at the Orpheum, as did Col. Warburton, and from that time on, her friend had not paid her expenses. Now Miss Elliott was anxious for her to quit the stage.

Archly: "Did you tell them it was Miss Elliott who threatened you?"

"No!"

"Did you tell them it was a man?"

"I may have."

"And was there a man?"

"Mr. Warburton spoke to me."

"Who was the woman, the stout blonde, that Mr. Baum saw you with on the streets of Norfolk?"

"I don't know."

"Was it Miss Elliott?"

"No, she hasn't blonde hair."

"Did Warburton live in Richmond?"

"I couldn't say where he lived."

"Where did you first meet him?"

"In Richmond."

"What was his business?"

"I don't know."

"You understood he lived in Richmond?"

"No, I understood he lived in England."

She had left Portsmouth towards the end of July, calling at Virginia Beach before coming back to Canada, and then had returned to the theatre in Portsmouth in October, she confirmed.

"And when you left in December, your mother gave us to understand it was because Baum was pestering you with his attentions, although he knew you were engaged to Mr. Wright?"

"Yes."

"If we stopped there, we'd know all about matters between you and Baum?"

"It was all a joke, anyway."

Baum, standing at the courtroom door, flushed red as people turned to see how he was taking Florence's casual dismissal of their relationship.

"You didn't mean anything in your relationship with Baum?"

"It wasn't serious."

"When you left Portsmouth, Baum saw you off?"

"Yes."

"And went across on the ferry with you?"

"Yes."

"Had you promised to marry Mr. Baum?"

"No."

"Did you ever promise him you would?"

"No. I may have in a joke."

"Then it would be entirely erroneous to represent that you left Portsmouth in December engaged to Mr. Baum, and informing him you would go and tell Mr. Wright of that engagement?"

"I was never engaged to him."

"And you never intended he should so understand? And there was no promise that you'd go home and tell Mr. Wright so?"

"No, I never did. I might have told him a lot of things as a joke."

Detective Pender now rose to read a letter which, Florence agreed, she had written to Ethel from Virginia Beach on April 22 – about the time the Formans said she was constantly upset. Full of girlish chatter – and the prevailing racial prejudice of the time – it read in part:

> My Dear Caroline (Ethel's second name),
>
> Heaven help any poor soul that has to live for a year long down here among the cotton, tobacco and coons. It's fierce. I saw some little shacks with big, fat mammies with 52 kids. In Norfolk it's worse than Richmond.
>
> Virginia Beach is okay, not as nice as Atlantic City (which she had visited some time before with her family), but the hotels are dandy. It's sad to sit alone in a bedroom and hear an ocean rolling in—

It was a nuisance not having a permanent address, she complained to Ethel in the letter, but the following Saturday she was returning to Manchester for good, and expected to receive lots of letters from home. She had come down for Easter with the Fosters, she explained. She described the church as a fashionable one with "a steeple so high you can't get it on a postcard."

The parson "is an old, bald-headed soak that reads his sermons. He has an assistant who needs his moustache off and some firecrackers behind him before he will interest me!"

Her commentary crackles on: "There was a Kentucky lady in the congregation who never saw a Canadian before. She looks at me with her mouth open. I'll shut it some time!"

She's seen a persimmon tree with yellow fruit, just like in the love song of that name, and a possum. On Sunday afternoon Aunt Marion took her to Fortress Monroe where there were hundreds of soldiers in gold and grey uniforms marching up and down with their guns. "I said to Marion, 'Say, if they ever knew there are two Canadians here, we'll get shot!' And she laughed like a son of a gun."

Giving details of the church choir to Ethel, she continues,

> The alto is a big fat woman with a pretty good voice. Our tenor is rather young, of the white-haired variety as most tenors are, and sings the best of the bunch. The baritone is a nice, fat man with a real basso.

Through an advertisement, wrote Florence, she had been picked to sing in an upcoming concert, which she was looking forward to. She also mentions that 'Marion' is resting in the same room while she's writing the letter.

But, resumed Blackstock, the Formans claimed Marion Elliott was never there.

"I say she was there."

"I want to know the name of the church you describe in that letter."

"I understood it was the Manchester Presbyterian Church."

"Very well then. Now the clergyman, choir leader and leading members of this church affirm that they never heard of you, that you never sang in that church and that your statement is a tissue of falsehoods. What do you say to that?"

"All I know is that I understood that was the church."

Had she written a false account of a reception given for her at the home of Mrs. Jake Wells and attended by Miss Elliott and Col. Warburton and sent it to the *Norfolk Ledger-Dispatch*, which published it on May 14?

"I didn't write it," she said cagily.

Had she sent home a clipping of the article?

"I may have."

"Now Mrs. Wells tells me there was no such reception."

"It may have been Mrs. Jones' place."

Sometimes it all got too confusing even for Florence. On June 14th, according to another letter read aloud by Detective Pender, she had told her father that she was to be given a reception by Mrs. Jake Wells, a friend of Marion's, for which she intended to buy a new dress. The 'reception' of course, had already taken place a month earlier. She had also told her 'Dearest Daddy' in a letter notable for its coy, little girl tone, that she had a long chat with the choir leader, Mr. Foster, who said everyone was most satisfied with her singing.

"You were deceiving your father by writing untruths to him," accused Blackstock.

"I can't say that."

"You know they were all false."

"I did not want him to know I was singing in a theatre, but they were not altogether falsehoods."

Now, just like a prospector in the Yukon gold rush of 1896 that still tickled the imagination of Canadians, Blackstock revealed his own small vein of gold: a little bundle of letters that Florence agreed she had written to Jimmy Baum since returning finally from the South just before Christmas. Here at last might be some clue to what was happening inside the Kinrade family circle in the weeks leading up to the murder. But Blackstock, uncharacteristically, was prepared to spare Florence's feelings.

"So far as I am concerned," he told her, "I am willing to read these letters. Do you desire to have them read?"

"No."

In that case, he said, he would offer her a deal. If she would confirm certain facts contained in the letters, then it would not be necessary to read them to the court. She nodded her assent.

"Now is it a fact that you came back from the South engaged to Mr. Baum, and that you told him you would inform Mr. Wright on your return of this engagement?"

Florence could not resist dissembling: "I may have led him to believe that, but it was for fun." And perhaps at that point Blackstock should have dropped the gloves and insisted on all the letters being read.

Instead, he inquired, "Did you upon your arrival home write him a letter stating the position to him in that way?"

She did not answer, and the lawyer repeated the question.

"Yes."

"Did you write telling him you would tell Mr. Wright?"

"Yes, I was keeping up the joke."

"Did you receive a letter from Baum shortly before Christmas telling you that he was going to send you a present for Christmas, and you, between Christmas and New Year's, wrote back to him telling him that if he had sent you a present, it must have been intercepted at home by your family, as you did not receive it?"

"Yes, I did."

"This letter is in your mother's handwriting?"

"Yes."

The note, dated January 13, 1909 and read aloud by Crown Attorney Washington said:

> Dear Sir, As my daughter, Florence, is engaged to a man, I do not think it right that she should accept presents from another gentleman. I therefore return the present you sent her. Yours truly, Isabella Kinrade.

Blackstock resumed: "Now, in your second letter, in which you told him that you thought your people had intercepted your letter and brooch, you directed him to write to you under the name Mildred Dale at the Hamilton post office so you could get his letters without them knowing it."

"Yes."

"And you and Baum continued to write in that way – he to write on Sunday night, and you to get it on Tuesday?"

"He suggested that."

"No, Miss Kinrade, you suggested that."

"Well, it was partly my suggestion."

"Then the family discovered that."

"Yes."

"And there was a family row?"

Florence could see the danger. "Ethel didn't say anything."

"Did Ethel intercept a letter?"

"No."

"Was Ethel opposed to what you had done?"

"She never said so."

In one of the letters, said Blackstock, finally clearing up the matter of the fur coat, she tells Baum her father has given her a fur coat for Christmas. No, she admitted, he had not. In another she tells him the family has seen one of his letters arrive, but she has brushed off the contents as "just chit-chat." If they knew what it really contained, there would be trouble, she writes.

In another letter, she tells Jimmy she is a member of a proud and wealthy family, and if they found out she was in love with an actor, there would be trouble ("I tried every way to break it off," she explained to Blackstock). In yet another, she tells him she is being urged constantly by her family to marry Montrose Wright, but doesn't intend to ("I may have kept it up for a little while," commented Florence).

"And in one of those letters," said Blackstock, "you said you thought you would go crazy with your troubles. What did that refer to, Miss Kinrade?"

She was silent.

"What did that refer to, Miss Kinrade? Was that a joke?"

"I was very much undecided. They came out of the question of marrying either Mr. Baum or Mr. Wright."

"And the arrangement between you and Mr. Baum was that if you married him you should go upon the stage?"

"He wanted me to."

She continued the correspondence, she agreed, until her family had forced her to break it off.

On January 29th there is a postcard informing Jimmy that the family has moved to Niagara Falls, and is now living at 34 Clifton Avenue, and that he should write her care of the Niagara Falls post office.

"So this continued until February 10th when you wrote this letter," he said, handing her the note. "Look it over and possibly you won't object to having it read."

She nodded: "I would like to have it read."

This letter, dated two weeks before the murder, was written at the King Edward Hotel, in Toronto:

> Dear Jim,
>
> Of course by now you have come to the conclusion that I have forgotten all about you. Well not quite so bad as that. I was really sorry to hear of your illness, and hope you have completely recovered. I should have written before, I know, but thinking of the news that this letter will convey would not hasten your recovery, to say the least.
>
> I have put it off, but after reading your last letter, I feel the time has come. You ask me to tell you the truth. I will. I will speak frankly. I have learned to love the gentleman to whom I am engaged with all my heart. In fact, I am utterly devoted

to him. In all sincerity I say that I cannot marry anyone else in the world. I do not wish to go into details, but I know now that my heart is entirely in his keeping. We must let bygones be bygones.

I am spending a delightful week in Toronto. When we leave here we go to Niagara Falls. You know we have moved there. Our correspondence must end. I hope you will forgive and forget, which will not be hard for me to do.

Yours sincerely, Mildred Dale

It is a poignant letter, with its share of irony. By signing it, 'Mildred Dale,' is Florence saying farewell to that brief and glamorous life she had enjoyed in vaudeville? And why the sudden turnaround? We can imagine that the Kinrades, shocked at their daughter's apparent intention of marrying an actor and going on the stage, had sought for some way to distract her. And what better than a week in Toronto, staying at the sumptuous King Edward Hotel, a high temple of Edwardian elegance, opened only four years earlier, and with Montrose Wright close at hand studying at Victoria University! A lover present generally has the advantage over a lover absent.

We can easily excuse the one tiny repeated fib at the end of the letter about the family moving to Niagara Falls: her intention likely was to ensure that a lovelorn Jimmy did not turn up at her door in Hamilton.

The letter though is almost too final, too sudden, and so lacking in regret, especially in its final unkind words, it has the mark of being composed for other eyes as well as Jimmy Baum's. No doubt she showed it to Monty and also, perhaps, to her parents and Ethel as proof that the folly was at an end. But was it?

Blackstock continued for an hour more taking her through the many contradictions in her evidence. He pointed out that there were six people with whom she had been on terms of intimacy – Miss Elliott, Col. Warburton, Mrs. Kenneth Brown, Mrs. Goldsmith, and Mr. and Mrs. Foster, and about none of them was she able to give personal details, such as their addresses.

"I cannot explain it," said Florence. But, during this long session of intense questioning, she was not once flustered by Blackstock's interrogation nor at a want for an answer.

Finally, as the courtroom clock indicated 10:30 *p.m.*, Blackstock gave her a last chance to straighten things out: "Now Miss Kinrade, is there any kind of explanation you wish to make regarding any matters on which you have been examined?"

"There is nothing."

"You've already told us that you understand the desirability of our knowing what reliability we can place on your statements?"

"Yes."

"And you are not, I suppose, surprised that it has become necessary to ask you about your occupations in the South?"

"I am a little surprised."

"Do they appear to yourself to be somewhat mysterious?"

Staunton jumped up to protest that the question was improper, but Coroner Anderson, after a long and weary day, did not even seem to be hearing the lawyers' arguments.

"No, I don't think so," Florence replied when the bickering ended. A few moments later, Blackstock told her, "I'll not detain you any longer then."

The main headline on the front page of the *Toronto Globe* the next day expressed the public feeling exactly: "Florence Kinrade Suffers Greatly from a Very Defective Memory."

Chapter Thirteen

Tain't That L'il Girl

It would be natural for a girl whose singing talents were admired to see herself
as a glamorous figure on the vaudeville stage.

J IMMY BAUM ENTERED THE WITNESS BOX the following evening in the undignified role of discarded lover. But by the time he had given his testimony the soft-spoken Southerner had become, to quote Kit Watkins, "the only heroic figure in the story."

The little vaudeville performer had watched in obvious discomfort the evening before as Florence had airily dismissed their engagement as "a joke." It was never a joke to him. Initially, he told Blackstock, she was his student as he taught her what he knew about stagecraft. Between May 15th and the end of July, when she returned to Canada, he was with her, "nearly every day and night in the week and an hour or two every Sunday." For the jurors and the inquest crowd it was easy to see how his Southern charm and manners would win his way with Florence. "Ah done tole her so!" he exclaimed at one point.

He in turn was drawn to the vivacious and gifted performer from Canada and had readily accepted her many deceptions at face value. When she told him she had come south with her brother and sister-in-law and was waiting for them to return from their travels further south, he saw no reason to doubt it.

When, about June, she told him she had been forced to marry a man twice her age and had come to the South to escape him, she had his entire sympathy. He believed her completely when she said that, although she was divorced from the man, he had come in pursuit of her, and "she hated, despised and feared him."

When she became alarmed at receiving a letter and later flowers at the theatre, he teased her. He accepted it as gospel when she showed him the engraved bracelet which, she said, had been presented to her by the choir at Manchester Presbyterian Church. She also told him her uncle was a judge in Toronto and that her father was a professor (both untrue).

Nearly every day she took the seven-minute ferry ride across to Norfolk, but never told him why. Then,

> … she came to me the week before she left and told me that she had to go home. Somebody had threatened to shoot her and drag her across the footlights if she did not leave the stage.

She even showed him the letter and said she was going to see the person in Norfolk. He offered to go with her to protect her, but she turned him down. Once he had seen her in Norfolk with a woman with light brown hair, but Florence never told him who it was.

Another time she told him she had been sent a box of chocolates. "I saw them on the shelf at the theatre. I said I would have one, and she said, 'No, they might be poisoned.' I said I would eat one and take a chance."

Jimmy was transparently honest, telling the truth even if it did not help Florence's cause. About the gun incident:

> I wrote a little sketch in which she was a crazy girl and chased me with a butcher knife. There were two other boys in the act, and they put up a joke. Instead of using the knife, they gave her a pistol. That was the first time that the weapon was used.

"Was it fired at him?"

"It exploded and she dropped it."

"Was that practice continued, or did you get back to the knife?"

"It made such a big hit, I decided to keep it in."

"How long was it kept up?"

"Just one night more. I saw the way she shot the gun off, and I made her stop. I was burned with the powder."

And then, a rare moment of levity: "What was her demeanor as to spirits?" inquired the lawyer.

"What do you mean, liquor?"

"No, I don't mean that! There is no suggestion of that. I mean whether she was happy or unhappy."

"At times she appeared happy, and at other times very unhappy. Often in the dressing room I saw her crying."

"Would you think her fear to be genuine?"

"I certainly would."

"Noticeable?"

"Yes, by everybody in the theatre."

Had Florence ever told him what Ethel's view was of her engagement to Montrose Wright?

"She told me Ethel had said that even though she'd gotten rid of the older man she'd been forced to marry, she would not get rid of this one: she would have to marry Mr. Wright."

Then, interestingly, to a question from Blackstock about whether Florence appeared to have money, Baum replied, "Always seemed to have plenty of money."

"Did he ever see how much she had?"

"Yes, on one occasion I saw that she had forty or fifty dollars."

On her return to Virginia in October, had an attachment sprung up between them, asked Blackstock. Jimmy hesitated a moment, as if he wished to say something, then, gruffly: "Supposed to be one, yes."

"And it is in respect of that the letters referred to last night were written to you?"

"Yes."

It was only fair to say, declared Blackstock, that it was Baum's wish that the letters not be read except with Florence's permission.

"That was my desire," confirmed Jimmy.

Had she made any statement to him about her engagement to Montrose Wright?

"She made a whole bunch of them!" he said to general laughter.

"I mean as to her feelings for Mr. Wright?"

"She told me that, when she got home, she would tell this chap that she didn't care for him."

What was the arrangement when Florence returned to Hamilton in December? "Were you engaged or not?"

"I thought I was."

Jimmy had accompanied Florence on the ferry to Norfolk where she would catch the train home. He had bought her chocolates and magazines for the trip, and they talked of their plans – to be married in Philadelphia in the spring, and then go on the stage together.

Shortly after, he sent her a little pearl and diamond brooch for Christmas, and she sent him a stick tie pin. Perhaps it was no surprise when Isabelle Kinrade wrote her curt letter and returned the brooch – it only confirmed Florence's stories of being pressured by her family to marry Montrose Wright. Writing to her secretly, using the name Mildred Dale, made it a romantic conspiracy.

Jimmy Baum was given little chance to express his disappointment and hurt. Yes, he had told a reporter at the inquest the night before, he thought her change of heart was entirely due to pressure from her family.

But he had also that evening spoken kindly of Monty Wright, and had shaken hands with him.

Now George Blackstock allowed him to at least set one wrong right:

> Now, Mr. Baum, it is only fair to you to give you a chance to speak in view of the statement made last night by Mrs. Kinrade that you had pestered Miss Kinrade during her stay in the South, and she was obliged to return home in consequence.

"There is no truth in that statement," replied Baum, and tactfully said no more on the subject.

Baum, said Blackstock, had been quoted in a newspaper as saying, no one could say anything bad about Florence Kinrade. "You said that?"

"Did I make a statement like that?" said Jimmy, his voice rising. "I certainly did, and I make it again!"

"You, as I understand," began Blackstock, fumbling to express emotional words not normally in his vocabulary, "have still a very strong regard for her… I mean that you have not any feeling against her."

"No, sir, certainly not!"

"That will do, Mr. Baum," he said, indicating his testimony was at an end.

Jimmy asked to make one final statement. Struggling to control his emotions, he aimed his words at the jury:

> I should like to tell the coroner and the jurymen that if they think that this girl committed this crime, they're wrong. If they catch the party who chased this girl from Portsmouth, they will get the one who killed her sister. Tain't this li'l girl.

This he said in his soft Southern drawl.

If courtroom protocol had not forbidden it, Jimmy Baum would have received a sympathetic ovation as he stepped down. Wrote Kit Watkins, revealingly:

> If at times during the inquiry, you felt your faith in human nature at breaking point, you had it firmly reestablished the moment Jimmy Baum began to talk in that musical voice of his…. He is small of stature and slight and weak of chin… but he carries a mighty big heart in that small body of his.
>
> There is nothing in man more fascinating to women than his chivalry, his courage, his defence of her – even when she is in the wrong.

When he had told the jury, "Tain't this l'il gal," suggested Watkins, "James Baum did more for the girl who jilted him than he may ever know."

Throughout the inquest, there had been repeated hints from the Crown that new, sensational evidence would be presented – even on this, what turned out to be the last day. But now, with the frustrated jurymen feeling as much in the dark as ever, the inquest seemed to be hurrying towards a close, and it was only at the request of the jury foreman that the promised testimony of Pinkerton detective John Pender was heard. The detective told the now familiar story of the Manchester church where no one had heard of Florence Kinrade, the reception for her that was reported in the newspaper but which had never taken place, her mysterious travels, her arrival at Virginia Beach in a state of emotional distress, and the phantom Miss Elliott and sundry other ghostly characters who no one had ever set eye upon.

Withal, he said, she had deported herself, so far as he could discover, "like a good, respectable girl."

As his final witness left the stand, George Tate Blackstock had to admit defeat. He had failed to point the jury decisively towards a perpetrator, and was not even able to give a plausible explanation for the murder of Ethel Kinrade. It was all bound up in a confusion of hints and lies and whispers that he had not been able to untangle. Now it was time for him to explain his actions and then, ultimately, to be graceful.

Speaking without notes, he said:

> I have frequently been asked what the theory of the Crown was as to this matter. The answer is that the Crown has no theory, and ought not to have. That is an expression that may be very legitimately used if criminal prosecution was a fact against anybody, but, as has been said here frequently, no person is on trial. The evidence brought forward might result in some person or person being charged, but, for the moment, no one has been prosecuted.

The duty of the Crown, he said, was to bring forward any evidence that might throw light on the crime. "In consequence of that feeling, we have brought before you some evidence that we ourselves thought had no bearing whatever on these proceedings." For instance, he said, they had heard witnesses who claimed to have seen various strange characters within several blocks of the Kinrade house on the day of the crime. Although he attached little importance to it, he felt the jury should hear such evidence.

And now Blackstock came to his essential quandary: "The murder took place, and a young woman who was undoubtedly there at the time came forward saying, 'I know the circumstances under which that murder was committed, and will tell you what they were.'"

> The moment that you accept the story of the woman, I agree that every other question asked is a cruel impertinence. The moment you say... you have implicit faith in the account given by the young woman as to what took place, then it must be obvious to everybody that to continue to ask her any questions except those designed for the purpose of identifying the criminal who committed this crime is an absolutely cruel and improper proceeding.

But two other responses were possible on hearing Florence's story, said Blackstock.

That her story "has incoherent marks of improbability about it, as to which I say nothing at all."

Where the person hearing the story says, "I have passed the stage of doubt, and I am now in the frame of mind where I absolutely decline to believe that story at all."

When such doubts arise, continued Blackstock, "it becomes extremely important to know who is the person who asks you to believe this statement."

It had been the Crown's duty to answer that question as fully as possible, but for him,

> … a more odious, distasteful and unpleasant duty was never cast upon me. It is one from which, as my friend, Mr. (Crown attorney) Washington and others know, I endeavoured to escape.

He admitted:

> It may indeed be that mistakes, errors of judgment have been made. If so, the blame is entirely mine (but) it is important for the proper administration of justice that the truth should be made known.

He reminded his listeners that it is the purpose of an inquest also to exonerate those facing unjustified suspicion.

> Take the case of Mrs. Kinrade. She was in the house at a time so close to the commission of this offence as to suggest she may have some knowledge of or complicity in it. I need scarcely say that a more awful suggestion could be made in connection with a mother.

Answering his critics, both legal and journalistic, who had faulted him for his 'sweat box' methods, Blackstock employed the elaborate rhetoric of the time:

> One would have thought the voice of criticism would have been silenced in the presence of the awful fact that in one of the principle thoroughfares of this city, well nigh three months ago, was committed this foul and bloody deed. And at this moment, no explanation of that offence has taken

place. Surely we have not arrived at a pass where, in our anxiety about those who are alive, we forget the voice hushed in death!

It had been a remarkable inquest. As Coroner Anderson said in his brief address to the jury:

> It is unparalleled in the history of Canada, not only for the interest it (the inquest) has aroused throughout the whole country, but by reason of the legal points raised (over the power of a coroner's warrant), which I am glad to say have been settled once and for all.

The courtroom was cleared, leaving the jurymen to come to their verdict. Journalists outside the doors heard voices raised, discovering later that the only issue over which the jurors had been divided was whether to specifically cite the unreliability of certain evidence – presumably the Kinrades. One juror, J.F. Stenabaugh, suggested to his fellow jurors that the verdict should say,

> … that Ethel Kinrade came to her death through bullet wounds in the head and chest, and there is no reliable evidence to show that there was any person else in the house outside members of the family.

His proposal was rejected.

At twenty minutes before midnight, the coroner was called back in. Shortly after, he read the verdict to the small group of newsmen who were all that remained of the earlier large crowd. The verdict:

> We, the jurors assembled to investigate the death of Ethel Kinrade, find that the deceased met her death by shot wounds inflicted by some person or persons unknown to this jury.
>
> Owing to the fact of the unreliability of some of the evidence adduced, the Crown is especially requested to continue its investigation. We also desire to express our hearty appreciation of the able, courteous and kindly manner in which the inquest has been conducted by Coroner Anderson and the counsel for the Crown.

The verdict would cause debate, but there was no argument at all about the verdict on these remarkably able jurymen, who had been plucked at random from their homes and businesses by Constable Lentz on the night of February 25th, the day of the murder, assembled at the City Hospital to view the body, and then had seen their lives disrupted by attending no fewer than fifteen hearings, some of them running into the early hours of the morning.

Their ordeal was at an end: "*Oyez, Oyez*," intoned Constable Lentz, and it was over. The inquest had heard fifty-four hours of testimony from thirty-two witnesses over sixty-eight days. Representatives from fifteen newspapers covering the inquest had filed an estimated 800,000 words.

At the Royal Hotel half an hour later, Jimmy Baum asked a *Toronto Daily Star* reporter, "What did they do?"

"They returned an open verdict," he was told.

"What does that mean?," he inquired. When it was explained to him, he exclaimed, "Well, I am powerful glad of it. God bless them. I'm glad I came up here now," he said.

Yes, he admitted, he had almost broken down at the end of his testimony. "I intended to say some more, but my voice choked up, and I couldn't go on."

He was less pleased about Florence's letters to him turning up at the inquest, feeling no doubt that she would believe he had handed them over to Detective Pender. "I don't know how they ever got hold of those letters," he said. "I certainly did not give them up, and I have an idea who is the responsible party. The letters were in a trunk, and I would not have given them up for the world." Baum only became aware the detectives had them on his arrival in Buffalo from Virginia, and then refused to travel further until he was given an assurance that they would not be read in court unless Florence gave her permission.

Earlier in the day, out for a stroll, he had met Florence and her father, also out walking near the Kinrade home. Florence introduced him to her father, and they chatted for a few minutes. "He certainly is a fine gentleman," commented the actor.

Next morning, any hard feelings about the letters forgotten, Jimmy Baum left on the 10 *a.m.* train with his new friend, Detective Pender. Pender was bound for his office in New York; Jimmy would continue to Portsmouth. But, he told the people of Hamilton before leaving, he had signed on with a vaudeville circuit, and expected to be back in town performing within the next year.

About the time Jimmy's train was leaving, Florence and her fiancé were enjoying a walk in the Dundas Valley where the birds had returned and the trees were just coming into leaf. For Monty, these were bittersweet days. Recognizing the favourable impression Jimmy Baum had made in Hamilton and after witnessing the man's charm first-hand, he no doubt realized Jimmy was an altogether more appropriate partner for Florence. Add to that the glamorous possibilities of a life together in vaudeville that he offered, and Monty was very much a second choice. All the young minister could offer was the one thing Florence most needed at that point – the stamp of respectability. And on that count, controversy still swirled around Florence's head.

The inquest had wound up so abruptly that it was fair to ask whether the Attorney General intended right away laying charges against her. At Queen's Park, the provincial detectives as well as the alienists (psychiatrists) Dr. Bruce Smith and Dr. C. K. Clarke who had attended the inquest, filed their reports with Deputy Attorney General Cartwright. The Attorney General, J.J. Foy, conferred long into the night with Ontario Premier, Sir James Whitney.

The provincial government faced a difficult decision: the Ethel Kinrade murder had attracted huge national and international interest, and the public demanded a resolution. The Whitney government had done its best to provide it, appointing George Blackstock as the Crown interrogator, spending some nine thousand dollars on the inquest alone, and plenty more besides on travel and investigation. Yet, after three months of unsparing effort, they had no motive and no weapon. All they had was a suspect – a suspect who it would be difficult, if impossible to convict.

In the witness box Florence Kinrade had been nothing short of formidable. She had withstood everything that Blackstock could throw at her. Her answers may have been contradictory, confusing, and sometimes downright lies, but she was admitting nothing. In a trial she would have the option of refusing to testify, and if she did go into the box, under the rules governing such legal proceedings, she would be far better protected by her lawyer than had been the case in the inquest. In addition, she was a talented and attractive young woman who any jury would be loath to convict of murder in an era when the death penalty was the normal punishment for that crime. Public sympathy too might swing strongly in Florence's favour, leaving the Attorney General and his officials looking like bullies out to persecute a vulnerable and perhaps unbalanced young woman.

These, undoubtedly, were the thoughts going through the mind of Premier Whitney. According to Hector Charlesworth, city editor of the *Toronto Mail and Empire*, officials in the attorney general's department, responding to public demands that they take some action, had at one point decided to arrest Florence and charge her with murder. Whitney though called in the officials and asked whether there was any possibility of securing a conviction. "They had to admit," wrote Charlesworth, "that conviction was extremely doubtful," but pointed out the popular clamour for 'action.' Whitney scoffed at this, and asked again if they thought any judge would permit such a case to go to a jury, "in which direct evidence was so lacking." They had to admit that the absence of a gun was an almost certain obstacle to a successful prosecution. "Sir James," wrote Charlesworth, "was firm in his declaration that nobody would be arrested merely to satisfy public opinion… that was the end of the Kinrade case."

A week later though, the Whitney cabinet appeared still not to have made a decision. Emerging from a cabinet meeting, Premier Whitney said he and his colleagues had not even reached consideration of the Kinrade case before adjourning.

By then though Tom Kinrade had again stolen a march on the investigators. On the Monday morning, five days after the inquest concluded, Florence, her mother, and Montrose Wright arrived in Montreal on the morning train from Toronto, all three of them dressed in black. The following evening, in a gusty wind and pouring rain, and travelling under the names, Norman Latchford, Miss Latchford, and Mrs. Latchford, they left Montreal for Sherbrooke, Quebec, on their way to Boston. U.S. immigration officials seeking advice from their superiors on whether to admit them, held their train up an hour at Newport, Vermont. Reassured that the three were only entering the U.S. for a short visit, they were cleared and sent on their way, with only the usual pack of Canadian reporters in pursuit.

Although he did not travel with them, the guiding hand of Tom Kinrade can be seen behind the trio's peripatetic journeying. From the moment of the murder, Kinrade's instinct had been unerring in trying to protect Florence from the police interrogators, Blackstock, the Crown's lawyer, and the press. He must have seen plainly that the best solution now was to get Florence well away from Hamilton, to deter the detectives as well as the newsmen who followed her every movement. In this, his best ally was her fiancé, whose divine calling, you might say, cast a cloak of piety over his errant daughter.

Kinrade's plan seemed to be working when, on May 13th, following another cabinet meeting, the Attorney General, J.J. Foy issued this statement:

> The Crown investigation of the Kinrade murder will continue. The case has not been dropped – it will never be dropped until it has been solved. The mills of justice may seem for a time to grind slowly, but, in the view of the department, the slow course is the sure course.

The final piece of what had surely been Tom Kinrade's hopes and plans fell into place when, in June 1909, he sent the following announcement to the Hamilton newspapers:

> The marriage of Miss Florence Belle Kinrade, daughter of T.L. Kinrade, principal of Cannon Street School, Hamilton, to Mr. Clare Montrose Wright, BA, of Victoria University, Toronto, took place yesterday (Monday, June 28) in New York City. The ceremony, which was very private, only the nearest relatives being present, was held in the Madison Avenue Methodist Church, and was performed by the Rev. Dr. Wallace McMullen. The bride, who was handsomely gowned in white, was given away by her father. Mr. and Mrs. Wright left the city on their honeymoon soon after. It is understood they may spend some time in England and principal European cities.

Monty's devotion to Florence had been sorely tested. He had been forced to fight for her against a rival, Jimmy Baum. He had, apparently, been sent to Richmond by Tom Kinrade to look into the Marion Elliott business. He must, in any case, have known that much of Florence's story of what she had been up to in Virginia was false. Yet, he had stood beside her throughout, his tender concern obvious to everyone. Now though he was being asked to make the largest sacrifice. As *The Hamilton Times* put it, "Locally, it is believed the marriage will bring about two things – the end of the Kinrade case, and the close of Mr. Montrose Wright's career as a Methodist probationer."

Students or probationers were simply not allowed to marry in the Methodist church. Even if he had been marrying a saint, he would be dooming his chances of a career in the ministry. By marrying Florence, a now-notorious woman who had not only performed in vaudeville, but who was also suspected by many of having murdered her sister, his career hopes were doubly dashed.

It is hard not to believe that, in the weeks before the wedding, Tom Kinrade did not offer to smooth the way ahead for the couple by paying, not only for their travels, but to launch Montrose in a new career, and to set them up in a new life far from Hamilton. Because, by October 12th, the same year, we find Montrose and Florence living in Calgary, Alberta where Monty was now studying law (he was admitted to the Alberta bar December 3, 1912). Tom Kinrade, meanwhile, had resigned his post as school principal, and on September 9, 1909, the Hamilton School Board passed a resolution of appreciation for his thirty-six years of service.

The wedding day, Monday, June 28, 1909 was also a date with fate for Frank Roughmond, the Black tramp who on October 1, 1908, the previous year, had been found drunk and asleep in a farm cellar near Stratford, Ontario beside the body of Mrs. William Peah, whom he had raped and murdered. The reports in the newspapers of that crime may have registered in the mind of Florence Kinrade, who would travel later that month from Hamilton to Portsmouth, Virginia, to resume her brief vaudeville career. It could have been a memory of that murder by a tramp that influenced her to tell her highly implausible story of a tramp murdering her sister, Ethel, on February 25th.

While Florence prepared for her wedding that June morning, Roughmond had a different appointment. Saved from a lynching by local farmers at the time of the crime, he had been put on trial, found guilty of murder and sentenced to death. Roughmond declined to eat breakfast that morning, and told Hangman John Robert Radclive, for whom he was the twelfth execution of the year (bringing his career total to 450), "I guess I will take my breakfast in Heaven this morning." He was hanged at five o'clock sharp.

— Part Three —

FINDING FLORENCE

Chapter Fourteen

HOLLYWOOD TERMINUS

In the early 1920s Florence, now Florence Wright, toured across Canada and US with Mildred Perkins' Pantages Grand Opera Company. Florence is seated at the piano.

S O WHAT HAPPENED TO FLORENCE after she and her husband, Monty, left behind the relentless glare of the legal spotlight and moved to Calgary, where he became a lawyer? Peace at last? A quiet perhaps boring life as the respectable wife of a professional man? Hardly.

If I was to write a book about the case, it was essential to find out how the story ended and to discover whether any further light could be thrown on the crime. The one thing I knew was that she had, against all odds, finally achieved her ambition of becoming a vaudeville performer. According to a small item in *The Hamilton Spectator* of September 3, 1921, "Mrs. Montrose Wright, formerly Florence Kinrade, has scored a great success as one of the leading singers in the Madame Dorée Grand

Opera Company. After touring all the centres of the United States, the company finished its season by taking part in the opening of the new million-dollar Pantages Theatre in Los Angeles in April." Mrs. Wright's performance on that occasion had been so well received, she was engaged as a leading star of the Pantages Grand Opera Company. "After rehearsals in New York," went on the article, "the company has been out since June and everywhere Mrs. Wright's popularity has been pronounced....Mrs. Wright is undoubtedly the star of the... company," continued *The Spectator*, saying she had been particularly outstanding in a thrilling duet from *Il Trovatore*.

The 'Grand Opera' tag should not be taken too seriously. This was not the Metropolitan Opera; rather both companies put on abbreviated versions of popular operas on the vaudeville circuits.

But how had Florence, who would now be about thirty-seven, once again escaped the restraints of a tedious middle-class existence to seek the glamour of a stage career? The explanation came in a 1922 interview she conducted in Toronto where she was appearing with the Pantages Grand Opera Company at the local Pantages Theatre. She had returned to her singing career following the death of her husband four years earlier, she told the reporter, who described her as having, "dark hair and eyes and a clever, piquant face." Montrose, a victim of the 1918 world flu epidemic, had died in New York following a business trip to Trinidad.

She was living in Philadelphia as a widow, she explained, when she decided to take up her musical studies again in New York. There, Madame Dorée had heard her sing, and had sent her immediately to Binghamton, N.Y. to fill a place in her opera company. When Mildred Perkins founded the Pantages opera group, it was Alexander Pantages, a colourful one-time sailor and gold prospector turned impresario, who remembered Florence's performance at the opening of his Los Angeles theatre and suggested Miss Perkins recruit Florence Wright. At the end of the current tour, Florence revealed, she was going to Europe with Miss Perkins intending to study music in Paris.

And then Florence, as far as the Canadian newspapers were concerned, ceased to exist. Apart from periodic retrospective pieces on the crime, there is no further mention of her. Had she continued to perform? When and where had she died because, of course, by 1987 it was 102 years since her birth?

Detail from previous photo of Florence Wright performing with the
Mildred Perkins' Pantages Grand Opera Company, circa 1920.

Seeking Details in Hamilton, from Ken Kinrade

Seeking answers, I went first to Florence's nephew, Ken Kinrade, on his
return from Florida. He met me at the door of his tenth-floor apartment in a seniors building on King Street, Hamilton, Ontario wearing fawn pants and a short-sleeved shirt. Slim, near six feet, with steely
short hair, he needed no encouragement to tell the story of his early
troubled years.

He was born, Theodore Lachlain Kinrade in 1913, four years after
the murder, but he hated the name, Theo, and only used it for legal purposes. He was the baby in a family of six. His mother's younger sister,
Norah came to live with them and his father, Ernie, who built many
of Tom Kinrade's houses, started taking her out for rides in his buggy
with the big white horse. Norah became pregnant, and that was when
his mother, Margaret, walked out. Ernie and Norah had three children
together.

"I knew there was something wrong, back in the past," he said in that choppy, oddly aggressive tone. He was always hearing about the murder. "People said, they (the Kinrades) lost one daughter (Ethel), and they didn't want to lose another." One time, he said, a fireman told him "the gat (gun) went over the side" of the boat on which the family travelled to Toronto (hardly likely because, it being winter, they travelled that February by train). He recalled:

> When I was about ten, and we were living over Stewart's candy store, my grandfather and grandmother came to pay a visit. They lived in Jacksonville, Florida. My grandfather (Thomas Kinrade) was a big, tall man, six foot three, but my grandmother, (Isabelle Kinrade) she was a little, dumpy sort of a woman. And he put a snowball down the back of her neck. She lets a whoop out of her – because they're not used to snow down in Florida.

> He (Thomas) had a kind of handlebar grey moustache, and he built all the houses down on Kinrade Avenue and a good number of the ones on Chestnut Street. They used to call that part of Hamilton, 'Monkeytown.' The girls (Ethel and Florence), when they came back from collecting the rents, would take off their high boots which were all covered in mud, and put on their shoes to go back to Herkimer Street.

He remembered talk in the family about the two sisters "Florence had lots of jewelry, but Ethel was a plain Jane."

Ken, seventy-four when I talked to him, had lived over the candy store with his brother, Tom, his half-brother, Jim, and his father Ernie Kinrade, who was a travelling salesman for the Dominion Belt Co., at that time.

> My father would say to Tom, 'I'm goin' away for a couple of days, here!' and throw him a quarter. 'Git yourself a loaf of punk (day-old bread) and some beans.' At that time you could get a huge can of pork and beans and pay four or five cents for it an' dump the beans in the big iron pot and add water to it. And we'd tear the bread up and when that was gone, fend for yourself.

His face became animated as he played the roles of his father and himself as a small boy: "He'd come home, get dressed in a hurry, an, 'I'm goin'. Set up in that chair!' I'd get up in the chair in a hurry. 'Now, listen to me,' and he'd be just glarin' into me, 'if anyone comes and asks where I am, what are you going to say?'"

In a small voice Ken says, "I don't know."

"Father says, 'That's fine,' and then, quick as a bunny, he has me by the throat and up against the wall. 'If you tell anybody any of my business, I'll kill you!' Then he throws me back in the chair."

Once, as Ken and Jim walked with their father past a boys' charity home surrounded by a high fence, Ernie said, "I can't keep you guys any longer. I'm going to have to put you in that home."

"I said," recalled Ken, "that fence isn't high enough to hold me. The first night I'll bust out and take him with me." Soon after, Ken left school at fourteen, Ernie "more or less kicked me out of the house. Kids I hung around with, they'd bring me out a sandwich. Later I did a little bit of boxing. You could get a fight any time you wanted. Go down the North End, they'd accommodate you."

He said: "No matter where I went, if I applied for a job and they heard my name, they'd say, 'Oh, Kinrade – you any relation to the murder case?' That was thrown up at me all the time." Eventually, Ken went to work at the Westinghouse factory, where he stayed for thirty-nine years.

One time, in later years when his father was ill, he took him some paperbacks and detective magazines. "He just happened to grab one that said, 'Who Killed Ethel Kinrade?' on the front. 'Anything to sell their ten-cent novels!' he said, and he took the magazine and threw it across the room."

Ken recalled, "My father loved to gamble." Tom Kinrade had given Ernie seven houses when he and Bella left Hamilton and moved south – "'Look after them, and watch the roofs.' And he gambled them all away. He liked the horses, and he went down to Florida following the horses."

Ernie, who sometimes worked as a painter and decorator, had no time for his sister, Gertrude, who remained single, but the one person in the family he got along with was Florence. At one point he visited her in California, reporting that she had a nice place but that he'd had to sleep in the chauffeur's quarters. "When I was first married, that's when (my father) told me, 'You know, I've got an arrangement with my sister (Florence). If I die first, she gets my money, and vice versa.' He was telling me right out, nothing was coming to me."

When his father, living in a room, was dying of cancer, Ken would drop in every day. "Is there anything I can get you?" he asked Ernie one day as he was leaving.

"Yeah, a bottle of root beer," Ernie said, but Ken, not hearing right, said, "Did you say ginger beer?"

"What did I tell ya," he said, imitating the snarl he's never forgotten. "I want root beer."

"Okay, I'll get you a big bottle. I'll see you tomorrow then, Dad," said Ken.

"Wait," said his father, then Ken said, "And he went like this, as if he'd seen something. 'All right,' he says, 'so long.' And that was the last I saw of him."

The next day a friend of his father's called to say he'd found Ernie dead.

Ken sent Florence a telegram – "I don't know where I got the address – in California." She sent him a letter saying not to worry, she would pay the funeral expenses. But she didn't. "She whipped up here," said Ken, did not attend the funeral, but cleared out Ernie's bank account. "I went to my lawyer, and he says he'll try and freeze that money, but it was too late. She grabbed the money and beat it back to California. She didn't see me or anything. Shows how callous that woman was." He never once saw his aunt, even though she came to Hamilton to perform at local theatres on numerous occasions.

Throughout his growing years though, the murder was always in the background. "Stay the hell away from the graveyard," Ernie would always tell him, and Ken only saw the family grave, where Ethel is buried, years later when he was taken there by a *Spectator* reporter for a photograph (a copy of which he kept embossed in plastic).

"My mother drank quite a bit, and she'd say, 'Kinrade, I hate that name.' She'd say, 'I got a secret, and I'm taking it to the grave.' Her secret went to the grave with her, but one time she told me she found a spent bullet."

Seeking Details in LA

July 12, 1987. The plane carrying me from San Francisco dips towards LAX airport, and I have that familiar feeling of apprehension. It is a feeling that always dogged me in the past as a foreign correspondent: arriving in some unfamiliar city whether Kampala or Budapest or Tel Aviv, I would look out of the window at the city lights, the huts or spreading suburbs, and wonder, how can I make sense of this, who can I talk to, where do I begin?

My early attempts to pick up the trail of Florence's life have been particularly discouraging. Early last month I called Ken Kinrade again. He had been going through all his documents and old letters, looking for an address for Florence, but without success.

"It was a city in California. Could have been Pasadena," he said. "That's where (her younger sister) Gertrude lived." I called the public library in Pasadena, and a librarian kindly looked up a city street directory for 1960. No luck. "We have Los Angeles phone books up to 1941," she offered. She was away a while checking. When she came back to the phone, she had four Florence Wrights, the last of them listed as an actor, living at 411 Northcroft Avenue. "That's the address!" said Ken, when I asked him. But it was a very thin straw.

In the following days, I checked with various theatrical and movie archives in Los Angeles as well as the California State Library in Sacramento and, using my newspaper contacts, the *Los Angeles Times* library, all without getting even a nibble. I wrote to the LA Hall of Records, enclosing a seven-dollar fee, and inquiring if Florence Wright, born in Hamilton, Ontario in 1884, had died subsequent to 1960, and again received a negative reply. I had an upcoming conference to attend in San Francisco; it provided a chance to flip down to Los Angeles to conduct on-the-ground research. But as the date approached and I lacked even a single solid clue to Florence's fate I wondered if it was even worth the effort. So as my twenty-five-dollar discount flight landed at Los Angeles, I had no great hopes.

Next morning, leaving my room at a Motel 6 discount motel beside the highway in Torrance, I drove to the Hall of Records, a huge, Soviet mausoleum-style building on North Broadway. In its echoing, marble halls, I found a kindly assistant named Billie, who showed me how to search the microfilm records and use the machines. Within ten minutes, as the microfilm for Los Angeles County rattled through the machine, my eye caught the word 'Canada' under place of birth. A few moments later I knew when and where Florence died.

The record showed that Florence Wright, a naturalized American citizen born in Canada November 7, 1884, died August 20, 1977, aged ninety-two, in the Royal Palms Convalescent Hospital in Los Angeles. Her maiden name, it noted, was unknown. Causes of death included the usual heart and circulatory problems associated with advanced age. A check with the Los Angeles county courthouse showed that she had died insolvent. The funeral director was listed as Pierce Brothers, in Hollywood.

If it had been seemly to let out a whoop in those somber surroundings, I would have. Instead, I thanked Billie (the Registrar-Recorder later
returned my seven dollars, covering the first ineffective search), bounced
out of the building, jumped in my rental car, and wheeled around headed
for Pierce Brothers on Santa Monica Boulevard. Then, with the wail of a
police siren, I came sharply back to earth. One of those LA cops, complete
with tan and wrap-around sunglasses, climbed off his Harley and explained
that U-turns were against the law in that part of town. Pleading ignorance
got me nowhere: he slapped me with a fifty-dollar ticket.

But as I got out of the car at Pierce Brothers, glancing up at the smog-
shrouded Hollywood sign in the hills above, nothing could dampen my
spirits. Inside, in the grey hush, an administrator with a bushy moustache
explained that, sorry, he could not possibly release private details of one
of their clients. But after some pleading, he went away, and a young man
appeared quite miraculously with a ledger containing details of that 1977
funeral. The public administrator had handled the ceremony. Burial had
cost $705 which, the young man explained, must have meant Florence
had some modest funds or she would have been cremated at the public
expense. Florence was buried in an orchid-coloured dress. No relatives had
been present – there was a daughter, Joan, 'whereabouts unknown,' but the
funeral home had not been able to contact her.

Florence was buried, quite conveniently, right across the street in the
Hollywood Memorial Park Cemetery, founded in 1899, and part of which
had been severed to create the Paramount Studios. Catching what shade I
could from the rows of stately royal palms, I discovered 'Innocents Corner'
– where children are buried, the stones topsy-turvy from subsidence. And
there, incongruously, was the flat stone engraved 'At Rest, Florence Wright,'
and her dates. Her grave was shaded by a large crimson bougainvillea.

And then the irony struck me: Fame was the spur that had driven
Florence – perhaps even to commit that awful crime. She had overcome
serious obstacles to re-start a career in vaudeville after Monty's death
and at an age when few would have even contemplated it. She succeeded,
although perhaps never as she had hoped. Her impecunious end suggested
that it had all come to nothing. Yet, in death, she may have achieved what
eluded her in life – to see her name alongside the great names of show
business. Because, as I wandered around, I found the graves of Cecil B. de
Mille, Tyrone Power, Marion Davies, Nelson Eddy, Paul Muni and Harry
Cohn. This modest 60-acre plot is the last resting place of names that once

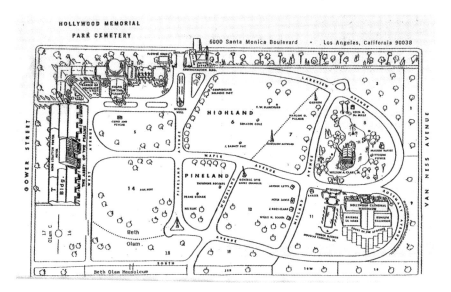

Final resting place at the Hollywood Memorial Park Cemetery. Graves of Eleanor Powell, Jayne Mansfield, Cecil B. DeMille and many other stars are also located here.

shone in lights – Edward G. Robinson, Rudolph Valentino, Peter Lorre, Douglas Fairbanks Sr., Adolphe Menjou, Eleanor Powell and Peter Finch. She could not have wished for a better outcome.

For the humbler reality of Florence's Los Angeles years, it was back to the libraries and directories. In the collections at the stunning hilltop Huntington Library I found no mention of Florence's musical career. But the street and phone directories at the Spanish Colonial Pasadena public library yielded the information that from the 1930s on, Florence led a nomadic life, changing her address nearly every year. In 1941, for instance, Mrs. Florence Wright is listed as a saleswoman living at 1532 Wilshire Boulevard. But by 1965 she seems to have settled down, living in 'The Edgemont', an apartment building at 5406 Lexington Ave., where she is still to be found six years later.

As a long shot, I called by The Edgemont, a turreted, four-story building with small prison-like rear windows overlooking the Hollywood Freeway. Inside, the paint was dirty, door handles rattled, and the carpet was threadbare. I knocked at several doors to be answered by elderly women wearing housecoats over their sleeping apparel and who, regarded me suspiciously from behind security chains, while television soap operas blared behind them. None of them could recall Florence Wright living there.

The Edgemont apparently is the last step before the nursing home for some of its elderly tenants, and so it was for Florence. The Royal Palms Convalescent Hospital, where she died, is not far distant on Rowena Avenue. It has since, I discovered, become the Skyline Convalescent Hospital, and a very helpful bookkeeper named Sandra looked up the records for me. Florence had been moved to the Royal Palms from The Edgemont June 1, 1977, only a couple of months before she died. Ten years later no one, of course, remembered her.

Flying home to Toronto next day, I was feeling disappointed. After a promising break, the trail had once again turned cold. I knew now that Florence had a daughter; if anyone could throw light at all on Florence's career and subsequent life, it must be 'Joan.' But how on earth would I find someone simply named Joan, who might have been right under my nose in Los Angeles, who might be dead, or who might be living just about anywhere in this wide world? Impossible!

꧁꧂

Chapter Fifteen

KINRADE FAMILY MENTAL HEALTH DIAGNOSIS

Known as the 'father of Canadian psychiatry', Dr. Charles Kirk Clarke was an
early promoter of the later-discredited 'selective breeding' eugenics movement.

FOR MORE THAN A CENTURY, the number 'nine-ninety-nine' carried
a special stigma for the people of Toronto. Nine-ninety-nine Queen
Street West was the address of the Provincial Lunatic Asylum (later called
The Ontario Hospital), a classical revival edifice designed by the great John
G. Howard and opened in 1850. With its dome and Greek portico, it was
one of the finest buildings in the city, but by the time it was wantonly torn
down by the Ontario Government in the 1970s, nine-ninety-nine had
become indelibly connected in the public mind with insanity.

Today, its number changed to 1001, the more acceptably named
Queen Street Mental Health Centre occupies a set of mediocre modern
buildings. In these reduced surroundings I occasionally had lunch during
the 1980s at the centre's cafeteria with Cyril Greenland, a University of

Toronto criminologist, and Dr. Jack Griffin, a founder of the Canadian Mental Health Association, usually to talk about their project to create a Canadian mental health archive. Sometimes we talked about the Florence Kinrade case.

One day, when I was telling them about my recent trip to Los Angeles to find out what had happened to Florence, a student of Cyril's who had joined us said the name 'Kinrade' rang a bell with him. He thought he might have seen something about the case in the archives at the Clarke Institute of Psychiatry in downtown Toronto. The facility was named after Dr. C.K. Clarke, the brilliant but highly controversial clinician who was regarded by his colleagues as 'the father of Canadian psychiatry,' and who died in 1924.

A Slim Grey Folder

Immediately after lunch I telephoned to make sure the archive was open, mentioned the subject of my search, and said I would be by later. When I arrived, the archivist handed me a slim, grey folder. As I took it to a table, sat down and opened it, I could not have anticipated the surprise it contained.

Dr. Charles Kirk Clarke, who in his time held just about every eminent position available in the Canadian mental health field, worked constantly during the asylum phase of his career (up to 1911) to improve conditions for patients.

According to the file, Dr. Clarke possessed an authentic fondness for the mentally ill, abhorred the stigma they traditionally bore, and worked strenuously to make their conditions more humane.

In the second phase of his career though, concerned initially about the disproportionate numbers of immigrants in the asylum population, he became preoccupied with the admission to Canada of mentally defective immigrants. While his concern resulted in useful immigration changes, he was an early convert to the 'selective breeding' eugenics movement, forever discredited by Adolph Hitler's social engineering experiments. A brilliant and affable all-rounder who played the violin and cello as a non-professional member of the Toronto Symphony Orchestra, Clarke's correspondence reveals him as snobbish and "venomously anti-Semitic, bigoted against vulnerable immigrant and ethnic minorities, and a promoter of eugenics."

What I knew though was that, at the time of the Kinrade murder,

The Ontario Provincial Lunatic Asylum at 999 Queen Street West in Toronto where Dr. C.K. Clarke worked to improve conditions for the mentally ill.

Clarke was superintendent of the Queen Street hospital, had the respect of his peers, was at the peak of his fame – and that the newspapers of the time mentioned his attendance, along with Dr. Bruce Smith, provincial inspector of asylums, at every session of the Kinrade inquest.

In the folder, I found a sheaf of notepaper-sized sheets covered with a flowing and mostly legible handwriting. As I began reading the slightly faded script, I realized they were Clarke's notes on the Kinrade case. It was more than I could ever have hoped for – the privately expressed opinions of a master interviewer, quite used to separating fact from fiction, and who had been privileged to listen to the main actors in the Ethel Kinrade drama and pose his own questions.

In his first undated note, Clarke mentions that the inquest has been postponed because neither Florence nor her mother are in a fit mental state to testify. He writes that

> The tramp theory has been largely abandoned by the detectives, as nothing has happened to make it even probable that a tramp was mixed up in it. In view of the mysteriousness connected with (the murder), and the character of the shooting, which was done apparently in the most frenzied way, the Attorney General has asked Dr. Bruce Smith and myself to examine Flossie Kinrade and the members of the

family with the idea of finding if an explanation can be found within the household.

The previous day, he writes, the Kinrade family had refused to cooperate,

> ... but today we were permitted to examine the daughter in the presence of the nurse, Miss (Loula) Walker (a registered nurse hired by the Kinrades and who accompanied Florence throughout), for two hours. Of course, no reference was made to the tragedy and the conversation ran along general lines.

Clarke, like many psychiatrists of his time, attached, as we shall see, great importance to the physical aspect of patients in assessing their mental fitness or deficiency. He notes that

> Miss Flossie Kinrade is a tall, handsome girl of 23 – fairly well-nourished and of light and vivacious manner. She says she has always enjoyed good health, has never had menstrual irregularities, although she has frequent vaso-motor (vascular) disturbances, clammy hands, etc. Has many headaches, which are common in the family, has many fainting attacks, which are also frequent with her mother. Pulse is small and feeble, somewhat hurried, as was to be expected during the excitement of the interview. Hands rather abnormal in shape, fingers not symmetrical, nails short. Ears ill-formed. Patient somewhat manneristic, with peculiar mouth puckering-up. Would not look one in the face; in fact, during the whole examination did not once face us, but kept her eyes directed towards the nurse.
>
> Gave an animated and light account of her life, dwelling particularly on her experiences in Virginia last year, where she was a professional singer in church and on the concert stage.

Clark further opines:

> If she is suffering from the shock occasioned by the tragedy, gave no indication of it during our interview which might be described as a 'merry one' as she seemed to enjoy any little jokes that were made and was willing to indulge in repartee. She said she had no enemies in particular, was not the

subject of persecution, any jealousies that existed were not more than might be expected in everyday life. Was much disturbed when I proposed examining her patellar reflexes (the familiar 'knee-jerk' reflex test doctors administer) and hurriedly left the room with her nurse. They returned in about five minutes, the nurse explaining that Miss K. had misunderstood and was frightened. Patellar reflexes quite normal.

Next he gave her a mathematical test, counting back in sixes from one hundred,

> ... which she ran through in 57 seconds but was strangely inaccurate, going astray after the second subtraction and persistently adding new mistakes. As I propose making a further psychological study of her associative powers, I prepared her for it by submitting a sheet of our stock words.... Much to my surprise, she proved to be exceedingly slow in her reactions nearly all the way through.

> In fact, Florence took a painful five seconds to respond to many quite simple words, for instance, flower ('a perfume, pretty little thing with perfume'). And for the word 'chair', which could have a connection with the crime, she took a thoughtful eight seconds. Observing that Florence took fourteen seconds to respond to 'line' and sixteen to respond to 'egg', it would be easy to conclude she was either slow-witted or was carefully avoiding any perceived trap. We know from her testimony though that she was not deficient in intelligence.

"After our interview with Miss Flossie," Clarke picks up the tale,

> ... we conversed for some time with Nurse Walker, who has been with her since the time of the tragedy. She appeared to be frank and admitted freely that her patient has been in varying states of incoherence and 'something more than hysteria' at different periods while under her care. Says the girl sleeps soundly, and the patient admits this. Would not think that hysteria would account for her condition at times – cannot 'just describe it', but certainly she has been absolutely incoherent at times. Thinks Miss Flossie has been trying to

pull herself together and feels that when the inquest is held she will tell a more coherent story than she has yet done. Admits there is a period of time not accounted for, explains this on the supposition that Miss Flossie fainted. Miss F. is a creature of impulses and startled them all on the day of the funeral by suddenly rushing downstairs into the room where the funeral service was being conducted, shouting out dramatically, 'Ethel, lock your door!' and then fainting.

Does not put too much belief in the story that Flossie was engaged to an actor in Virginia and a divinity student here – was simply having a good time with the actor, who was also having a good time and regarded the divinity student as the favoured suitor (Jimmy Baum, as we have learned, took a different view when he testified.) Looks on the whole family as (being) fearfully nervous and high strung – the mother and Flossie in particular. Did not seem anxious to talk much about the mother.

It is evident that a strong bond of sympathy exists between the nurse and the patient and the latter did not take her eyes off Nurse Walker for a single moment during the interview. Nurse W. feels that all the family are telling the truth and not concealing anything.

Clarke had learned little from his interview with Nurse Walker – except that she had been completely suborned into, and had become a valuable support of, the Kinrade version of events. Now the two psychiatrists waited with interest to see what Thomas Kinrade had to tell them. Clarke describes him as,

... an old gentleman of sixty-odd years, affable and inclined to be garrulous – is evidently somewhat vain and interested in his own appearance – had his vest collar carefully pinned back to reveal an unusual amount of shirt-front. Little fingers constructed in a remarkable way, says it is an inherited peculiarity, (it) has descended from former generations and has been transmitted to some of his children. Thinks it is an 'acquired characteristic' following an injury to some of the original Kinrades.

His family history reveals the fact that tuberculosis has developed in several of the Kinrades – one brother faded away and was evidently depressed. Has had a good many ups and downs, but has weathered the storm, and is now wealthy – income exclusive of ($1,500 per annum) salary as a teacher, $400 or $500 per month. Has defective ears, much like those of his daughter, and is abnormally talkative.

Drs. Clarke and Smith then note that Thomas Kinrade answers questions about his wife, Isabelle.

(Thomas) says his wife has no family history to reveal as she was an adopted child. Knows nothing of her antecedents though they learned from fortune tellers at Chautaqua that she has influential relatives. Just who they were, Mr. K. says, they never found out, thinking that some things are best not followed up as you might learn something you did not want to know. His wife is of the most high-strung type and is so nervous that she can rarely be induced to enter a boat. When she has done so, she becomes so upset that she becomes unconscious and has remained unconscious for more than half an hour at a time…. Told us that before the tragedy, for several days they had gone through many tramp scares and on the day of the tragedy apparently someone had tried to force the window. Both Nurse Walker and others impressed on our minds that Mrs. Kinrade knew nothing of the cause of her daughter's death until after coming to the Arlington Hotel in Toronto.

Mrs. K's examination has been left until tomorrow as I feel convinced that here rests the solution of the puzzle. Whether we can unravel it is the problem. Mrs. K. is a dull, stupid-looking woman of apparently defective type. Her facial expressions would suggest… possible epilepsis (epilepsy?) and the many accounts of her fainting attacks would make me suspect that she may really turn out to be epileptic.

"If this is the case," says Clarke with what might be a touch of professional arrogance, "the problem may be worked out without much trouble." He jots down his conclusions in note form:

> At all events, this much is certain:
>
> We are dealing with an extremely neurotic family.
>
> Secondly, a crime for which no adequate motive exists – a crime so indicative and brutal that it at once suggests insanity.
>
> Incoherent and inconsistent accounts of the crime, accounts absolutely incompatible with the surroundings and statements given as facts and which leave a period of at least three-quarters of an hour (unaccounted for).
>
> The mother kept in the background and said to be ignorant of the true nature of the crime.
>
> The incredible appearance of the mother at the police station to complain of tramps at a time that must have been subsequent to the tragedy.
>
> The possibility of epilepsy in both mother and daughter.
>
> The possibility that the mother knows the whole facts and is deliberately concealing them to shield the daughter.

Against this, writes Clarke,

> … is the statement by the daughter, who said to Mrs. Hickey that the tramp had shot Ethel six times, the actual number of shots fired (In fact, it was seven). Flossie has stated that the man fired innumerable shots at her, both inside and outside of the house – no such shots were fired.

"Bright, Merry, and Gay"

Dr. Clarke's next entry is headed, "Toronto, Mar. 8, 1909 – a time when Florence was still in that city with her parents waiting for the inquest proper to begin in Hamilton." He writes,

> Today, had a second interview with Miss Kinrade and gave her a second series of (word) association tests, the words printed in red being regarded as danger words

as each had a special significance in connection with the tragedy. Again Miss K. seemed self-possessed, full of fun, and not in any way showing stress of mind. In shaking hands it is noticeable that her hand is cold and clammy. As observed yesterday, she seems to depend absolutely on the nurse for coaching, and rarely takes her eyes off the nurse's face. In the two days I have not succeeded in getting a direct look at Miss K.'s eyes. Evidently, some of the test words held most unpleasant associations, if we might judge by the expressions of the girl, especially the word, 'froth.' It took her only a single second though to associate 'smoke' with 'from a firearm.'

Clark continues,

We also interviewed Mrs. K. (Florence's mother) and had a chat with the son (Earl). He is not a strong type, has an asymmetrical face with unusual features (another example of Clarke's preoccupation with physical characteristics). Mrs. K. is short, stout and asthmatic, self-possessed and much more alert than her appearance would suggest. If she knows anything of the crime, she conceals it well, and her self-control is very different from what newspaper accounts would have led us to believe.

She gave a definitive history of many fainting attacks, which have developed when she has been run down and excited. Many of these attacks last for half an hour and more, and during them she is completely unconscious and had no recollection of what occurred. Is also a great sufferer from headaches. In fact, the whole family has neuritis written in every feature.

"It is quite evident—" writes a frustrated Clarke,

… that no satisfactory examination of the daughter can be made while the nurse is present. It will be interesting to see how she will behave when left to the (illegible) before as clever and astute a lawyer as G.T. Blackstock. From one of the boarders at the Arlington (where the Kinrades were staying) we learned that Miss K. is not in any way cast down, but is bright, merry and gay, even singing cheerful songs at times.

Three days later, after attending the first full session of the inquest, we find Clarke more baffled than ever:

> Last night went up at the request of the Attorney General's Department to watch the cause of proceedings in the Kinrade case which becomes a greater mystery as time goes on. The more one hears and sees, the more complicated does the psychological analysis of Florence Kinrade become. It is so evident that the family are linked together to support each other's stories as far as possible, and it is so clear that they are not dealing frankly with the Crown that it was deemed advisable to get the two principal witnesses to tell their stories last night so that discrepancies, if any, might be discovered.

(Here is the explanation for Blackstock's insistence on hearing evidence into the early hours of the morning – so the Kinrades would have less chance to adjust their stories.)

"The evidence of Thomas Kinrade—" records Clarke,

> … must be regarded as decidedly unsatisfactory, and such statements as those he made about the absolute harmony of the family relations do not bear the impress of truth, as was demonstrated in his admission when cornered that Ernest (his eldest son) and he had not always agreed in the settlement of business transactions. When cornered too, he could not possibly deny that he had asserted, 'I knew this was bound to come, long ago,' when he found his daughter dead. It was painfully evident that Mr. K. was covering up a great deal that should be known. His statements too regarding his wife's antecedents are peculiar. It is more than strange that he should not attempt to discover when or what she was before he married her.

(We see here Clark's tendency to ascribe mental abnormalities to bad breeding.)

The greatest interest attached to the examination of Florence Kinrade, and a more startling and complex psychological study has rarely been offered. I must freely confess that at the end of three hours she had not made clear just what her true medical condition is, or where we are to place her. At one moment she seemed to be in a dream state, at the next moment fencing cleverly and offering shrewd explanations. Her lapses of memory – such events, for example, as those connected with her erratic wanderings with the mysterious Miss Elliott – are not to be explained on any other ground than that of a desire to conceal the truth.

Her account of the tragedy and its incidents differs in many particulars from the four other accounts given, and in many particulars is an absolutely impossible story. Either she was so agitated or confused by the shock or the whole thing is a fabrication of the most colossal order. Her behaviour during the tragedy, if she is to be believed, is simply incomprehensible and will not fit in with anything which may be believed.

If Miss Florence is a mental defective… the fabrications, but not the tragedy, would be explained. She stood the fearful strain for three hours (of) nerve-wracking cross-examination with composure and great coolness, and at the end, when it was stated she collapsed, was really in a condition to have gone on. I think she was less exhausted than the counsel (Blackstock), and five minutes afterwards when I saw her and chatted with her she was bright, merry and apparently happy over the way in which she had carried off the honours of the battle.

That she lied, and lied monumentally at different stages of the game is admitted on all sides. Did she do so, first to cover a crime of her own, second, to cover a crime of her own family, or third, simply because she is trying to piece together the patches of a confused recollection? She appeared in the box self-possessed and beautiful – suggesting a Spanish or Creole beauty. Has

she Negro or Spanish blood in her veins? (In view of the rac-
ist views Clarke expressed later in his career, one wonders if
this was idle speculation or a hint at what he might have considered degeneracy). Her little mannerisms of slowly shaking
her head as a negative and pursing her lips when bothered
were very interesting. Again it was strikingly noticeable that
not once did she look at her cross-examiner.

Notes on Florence and the Firearms

On Saturday, March 13, Dr. Clarke caught up with his notes on the inquest
session of the night before, recording that Florence's brother, Earl, "evidently a weakling of a marked type," had "trifled with the truth very mark-
edly, but not as successfully as some of the other members of the family."
At the same time he utterly discredited the statements made to the effect
that Florence was ignorant of the use of firearms. It came out that she had
written regarding the practice of pistol shooting preparatory to a visit to
Savannah, where the coloured people were supposed to be particularly
dangerous. "Earl reluctantly admitted too that he had been involved in a
shooting scrape, although his account of this is said not to accord with the
actual facts."

His chief interest though, admits Clarke, was centred on the recall of
Florence,

> … especially as we are gradually learning that her life has
> been a most erratic one during the last two years. Some of
> her most important statements are not consistent with what
> we learn to be the truth, and the air of glamour she throws
> about such incidents as the Goderich trip take on another
> air when analyzed. Either she was cruelly deceived regarding
> the people she met or she is simply lying without the slightest
> reason. The mysterious Miss Elliott, who seems to have been
> her evil adviser, must have been a woman of strange type and
> unwholesome in the influence on this poor girl.

He noted that Florence looked in good physical health as she took the
stand – a remarkable fact considering the ordeal she had been through –
"cool, self-possessed, and, in her own peculiar way, resourceful in time of
trouble, as illustrated in the opening of the examination."

Earlier, she had told Drs. Smith and Clarke she had never slept so well
as since the time of the tragedy.

When asked (by Blackstock) if that was so, she quietly drifted on with her mass of inconsistencies, sliding over the difficult spots without any appearance of anxiety.... When convenient, her memory failed her, when she regarded it as useful, it proved to be stored with a mass of detail, real or manufactured, even to what her friends were dressed in.

For instance, wrote the doctor,

she recalled that the mysterious Mrs. Kenneth Brown had worn black satin when she attended a musicale in Toronto with Florence – even though no trace of such a person had been found, and Florence had been unable to name the person giving the musicale or the part of Spadina Avenue where it was held.

But now, as he listened to Florence answering and improvising for nearly four hours – "never worried, never at a loss for what she regarded as a suitable reply" – Clarke recognized a type familiar to him in his work with the mentally ill. "The suggestion of the half-dream state so much in evidence the first day no longer hampered me in forming a conclusion regarding her true mental condition. Twice," the doctor claims, "Florence revealed herself through her eyes" although, regrettably, he does not elaborate.

The impression that she was endeavoring to piece together verbally dreams of a horrible picture no longer came to my mind. But (Florence's) whole reaction was the childish one of the moral imbecile, cunningly trying to gloss over a disagreeable situation.

'Moral imbecile' was the term used in that era for a psychopath or, to use more current language, anti-social personality disorder. Clarke continues:

To those not familiar with such exhibitions, it was marvelous that a woman could stand hour after hour of such an inquisition. To those of us who know the type, it is just what we come to expect, or would expect. Her story, inconsistent before, became three times more so under the guidance of the counsel, but no sign of real mental stress appeared. Her facts were often impossible, as Mr. Blackstock showed her.

Now Clarke gave his devastating opinion on the most galvanizing moment of the inquest, a moment intended to evoke profound public sympathy for the young singer. The climax, he noted, occurred when, at the close of his examination, Blackstock purposely eliminated the 'tramp' from her account, leaving only the two girls in the house, suggesting that only Florence could have killed Ethel. Wrote Clarke the next morning,

> She closed her eyes, and pretended to faint. I was within four feet of her. There was no blanching, still the same good colour. Her lover (Montrose Wright) rushed forward and attempted to carry her out of the court assisted by the nurse. She screamed and shouted while this was done, but it was palpably shamming and when we got her in the anteroom, felt her pulse, which was normal, and asked her quietly to straighten up, she did so, and seemed childishly happy over the whole performance. There can be but one conclusion from what we know – no matter who committed the murder, Florence Kinrade is a moral imbecile… cunning, childish and impulsive.

The psychiatrist was exasperated with the whole Kinrade family.

> Her people have not told us all they know, have not been as frank as they should have been for, no matter how dreadful their loss and grief, nothing has been gained by glossing over the truth. Florence Kinrade's sexual history would be more than interesting, her loafing in bed every day until late, her erratic life under the influence of her evil genius, Miss Elliott, her strange companionships, all point to sexual aberrations. If this is so, and the mother proves to be an epileptic psychic or otherwise, it will not be difficult to work out the evolution of such a tragedy.

Not difficult for Clarke in the light of psychological theory of that time, perhaps, but harder for a contemporary researcher.

For Clarke, as for many in his profession at that time, breeding explained everything. Look at the antecedents and everything was clear. In the case of the Kinrades, and relying on what must have largely been scurrilous gossip, he was prepared to take the darkest view of the whole clan, ignoring, for instance, Thomas Kinrade's distinguished career as an educator and businessman.

Thomas Kinrade's sister, recorded Clarke, had married her cousin, Hiram Kipp,

> … and the Kipps were known as the terrors of the neighborhood, a bad lot in every respect. Mrs. Kipp a most peculiar woman, eccentric, full of grandiose ideas, for ever preaching about the greatness of the 'Kean-rade' family, as she called them. Although well up in years, had a most unenviable reputation among young men, and was simply regarded as a common prostitute by them – for reasons best known to themselves.
>
> Husband was jealous of her, and beat her regularly – both drank and, to use the words of my informant who knew them both very well indeed, there was hell to pay regularly in the little household. Their first child was deaf and dumb – this child fell into a well and drowned. The second son, who must now be thirty-seven or thirty-eight years of age, is a drunkard, thief and moral degenerate, lived for some years quite openly with a prostitute. The third child is a liar and a thief and crooked in business – very shrewd. The next son is of degenerate appearance, but is the best of the bunch – was brilliant in mathematics when at school, became a teacher, and is regarded as decent. The next son is a moral pervert, is without much sense, could not do right if he tried, of degenerate appearance, is an absolute incorrigible and spent three years in penitentiary for counterfeiting. Lucy (daughter) was fifteen when got into trouble with a man of forty-five (a baker). This man was forced to marry her. She bore a striking resemblance to Ethel Kinrade. Lucy had the same characteristics as her mother, was full of grandiose ideas. The next girl is a degenerate – when a child at school a persistent thief and incorrigible. The youngest child deaf and dumb.

> To sum up the family history: two children deaf and dumb,
> two girls degenerate and immoral, four sons, three degener-
> ate are markedly criminal, one son normal or nearly so. That
> is, in a family of ten, only one can measure up to the normal.

Well, nobody's perfect! Clarke's characterization of the family seems unjust and arbitrary, and even if it were true, what possible connection could it have to the Kinrade family who were, on the whole, hardworking and respectable?

The passage shows the 'father of Canadian psychiatry' to have had feet of clay. Yet, if there was one thing he was famous for, it was his uncanny ability to diagnose the different forms of mental illness. So as I left the Clarke Institute archives, I knew that I would need to discover what exactly the famous doctor had meant in describing Florence as 'a moral imbecile' and what modern psychiatrists would have to say about his diagnosis.

⚜

Chapter Sixteen

Western Days

The Sunalta (now Beltline) neighbourhood of Calgary where Monty and Florence Wright eventually built their home, with Senator Lougheed's home 'Beaulieu' in the foreground.

The Kinrades in Calgary

As the CPR transcontinental train carried the newly wedded couple to their new Calgary home in the late summer of 1909, Montrose Wright could feel that events had turned out better than expected. Florence, after all, had not been charged with Ethel's murder and Tom Kinrade had skillfully steered the couple's way past the persistent police and press, right up to the altar in Manhattan. Acting on the advice of friends, Monty looked forward to a quiet and prosperous future in the law profession far away from the crime in Hamilton. The shocks and surprises were over.

Florence, perhaps gazing out of the window at ranchers harvesting their hay crops, may have had other thoughts. We can be fairly sure she did not shed tears for friends and family left behind. The Florence we have come to know was all ambition with little room for sentiment. How did she feel about her more or less forced exile to what many people in that era would have regarded as a cow town? No doubt her mind was already full of schemes and possibilities. And quite soon Monty would be in for more surprises.

On arrival, the couple emerged from the railway station into a city that was in the midst of a real estate boom. Construction sites were everywhere, Calgary's distinctive sandstone structures were rising all around (but only for a few years – the sandstone supply soon ran out) and the climbing population had reached 40,000, a tenfold increase in ten years. By 1911, two years later, Calgary was counted the fastest-growing burg in North America after Chicago.

Monty, perhaps guided by his real estate-savvy father-in-law, was awake to their opportunities: Records show that C. Montrose and Florence B. Wright, likely as an investment, purchased a lot in posh Elbow Park from the CPR for $200 (plus another lot) and built a two-storey house that still stands although, in keeping with his status as a lawyer, they were soon living in a large bungalow at 1135 - 13 Avenue W., not far from 'Beaulieu', Senator Lougheed's mansion.

That's not to say Calgary was not still very much a frontier town with its raunchy side. Cowboys from ranch bunkhouses outside town, workers from the tent city near the railway station, and even recruits from the police barracks were regular customers of the dozen or more bordellos in town, and by far the most colourful character in the trade was Diamond Dolly, blousy and boastful with a Mac West gusto. (The police, finally goaded by the city's gentler folk, carried out a raid on Dolly's establishment and discovered a man in bed with a woman who was not his wife. A charge against him was overturned though when he explained the woman was sick and he was nursing her.)

Tackling Calgary's wooden sidewalks and the plank paths across its alternately muddy or dusty streets, Florence would have been particularly interested in one large project under construction – the seven-story sandstone and brick Lougheed Building. For nestled within it would be the 1,500-seat Sherman Grand Theatre, described by *The Morning Albertan* as: "Canada's grandest theatre." Bob Blakey, a retired *Calgary Herald* writer and history enthusiast has described it as "a cultural jewel." And when it opened in 1912 it took its place as Calgary's primary home of vaudeville, hosting in its twenty-five years as a live theatre, stars like the Marx Brothers, Paul Robeson, Ethel Barrymore, and Sarah Bernhardt.

The first Calgary Stampede in 1912 was concurrent with the opening of Calgary's vaudeville theatre venue, The Grand Sherman, around the corner from this parade scene.

No doubt the well-to-do young couple were found frequently in the stalls or dress circle at the Sherman Grand enjoying what was the primary source of public entertainment of the era. The magnificent theatre eventually became a cinema, was, ignominiously for a while, an indoor golf range, and is once again a live theatre venue.

Concurrent with the 1912 opening of the Sherman Grand Theatre, there arrived in town a remarkable manifestation of the 'Wild West' that would forever put its mark on the city. That would be The Calgary Stampede, still known for its chuckwagon races and world-famous rodeo. There is no record of what Florence and Monty thought of that.

But returning to 1909, the momentous year of the Kinrade murder, even as Florence and Monty had headed west, important changes may have been occurring back in Hamilton behind the elegant casements of 105 Herkimer Street. A December 15, 1909 newspaper report from Hamilton suggests that T.L. Kinrade is disposing of his real estate holdings and household furnishings in Hamilton and moving the whole clan to Calgary. But did it really happen? A search of Calgary phone directories for the period shows Monty (and presumably Florence) were definitely there, but there are no listings for Thomas or Ernest. We do know that, after retirement, Tom Kinrade moved with Bella to Florida and when Ernie turns up later in the story, he is living in Hamilton. Like so much else in the Kinrade saga, the truth is shrouded in mystery.

A Lethbridge surprise

So the curtain falls on the Kinrade drama no doubt with a properly chastened Florence assuming a domestic role. A year later the couple receive the joyful news that Florence is pregnant. Joyful news? Maybe. Because in the February 9, 1911, issue of the *Daily Herald*, published in Lethbridge, a small city some 200 kilometers south of Calgary, we learn that Miss Florence Wright (the name which Florence would use on the stage henceforth) would appear in an 'overture' at the Eureka vaudeville and movie theatre in Lethbridge. Then, on March 1, there's a mention that an illustrated song (meaning a song accompanied by lantern slides) would be performed that evening at the Eureka by Miss Wright. The song title: "Sister."

But why would Florence pick for her comeback Lethbridge, a coal mining town, an often-bleak spot in the very heart of Chinook country where 120 kilometer hurricane force winds sweep from the Rockies on 30 to 35 days a year making travel, then as now, difficult and even dangerous? We're talking a city roughly a quarter of the size of Calgary from which it is over two hours away by train. Part of the answer is that Lethbridge was a sort of Broadway of the Prairies. Theatre seemed in the town's blood.

There is even an authoratative history, *Theatre Lethbridge*, by George Mann documenting the twenty-nine theatres built here at various times. And 1910 and, especially 1911, when Florence was placing a cautious toe in this city's theatrical waters, were among the crowning years of Lethbridge's unlikely theatrical boom. Five theatres served a population of 8,000 (which had tripled since the previous census); two of these, the Lyceum and the Eureka (which attracted 3,000 people a week) had opened on the same day, October 12, 1908. "Lethbridge is exceptional," says Dawn Leite, who conducts walking tours along Round Street where theatres once lined the north side of the street. Even the churches had their makeshift stages and put on performances. "This is what you did in Lethbridge," says Leite, "you went to the theatre."

The Eureka, she says, where Florence performed 'Sister,' was the most successful Lethbridge theatre of the period, boasting a 'water curtain' that would set off on-stage sprinklers in the case of a fire. (In the event, no theatre ever burned down in Lethbridge, although the walls of one theatre collapsed.)

In 1911 too, the vital mile-long CPR viaduct over the Oldman River

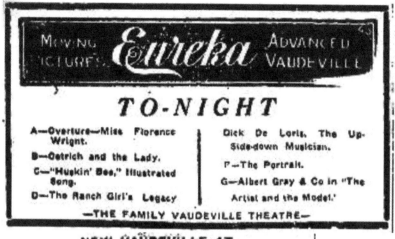

An ad for "Advanced Vaudeville" at the Eureka Theatre , featuring Florence Wright
from *The Lethbridge Herald*, February/March 1911.

was completed, providing the settlers flooding into southern Alberta
with a link to Lethbridge's business district as well as its theatres.

Capturing the spirit of those lively times, a contemporary photograph shows a band marching past the Lyceum, the sidewalks jammed
with spectators. Other days, clowns and elephants filled the street as the
circus came to town and there were even several grand opera presen-
tations. Touring theatre companies from the U.S. and Britain arrived
regularly, sometimes only for 'one-night-stands,' and eventually the
ever-popular Chautauquas – festivals of music and drama – made annual
appearances. Touring companies though were eventually replaced in the
early 1920s by the Little Theatre movement – plays put on by local amateurs. Lethbridge's prosperity too went into decline: in 1913 there was an
economic downturn followed by the 1914-18 Great War, a wrenching
emotional experience which brought Lethbridge's helter-skelter urban
growth to a standstill. The worldwide Spanish flu epidemic that followed
cast a pall over Lethbridge's progress and, as we shall see, dealt Florence
a sad blow.

But long before that, while Florence prepared to return to the stage in Lethbridge, the question left hanging is how on earth did she get her family on side?

Somehow, less than two years after the sensational inquiry into Ethel's murder, she had convinced Montrose – a bit of a pushover – as well as her father that she should return to vaudeville. For Monty, a young man preparing for a career as a lawyer it seems like a serious misstep that would draw attention to Florence's sensational past. For Tom Kinrade, who had made such a huge effort to extract and relocate his family far from the scene of the crime, it was flirting with the danger of further exposure.

The fact is, Florence could always win over her father. And the rest of the family, including her mother? They simply pretended it hadn't happened. As we shall see, they and Florence clung to the tramp theory as if their lives depended on it and ignored all those weeks of contradictory evidence presented at the inquest.

As for how Florence returned to vaudeville, that may be easy to answer. The Eureka Theatre in Lethbridge was part of the Orpheum vaudeville circuit which also included the Orpheum Theatre in Portsmouth, Virginia – where Florence had been taught the elements of vaudeville by Jimmy Baum.

Was Florence still in correspondence with Jimmy? Or had she simply contacted the Orpheum circuit to inquire about their theatres in Western Canada? More than that, the title of the song, 'Sister', suggests she was willing to exploit her fame in order to relaunch her stage career. The words of the song are now lost, but the audience would have recognized the singer as the notorious woman at the centre of the Kinrade murder inquiry and would have been titillated by the subject matter. What wouldn't I give to have witnessed that coy performance!

And if Florence was exploiting her notoriety, she was not the first woman to do so in the wake of a dramatic murder. Clara Ford, 33, a black Toronto woman charged with murder, had also, like Florence, led a double life. She had passed herself off as a man after discovering that this subterfuge secured her better jobs and greater respect.

On a mild October evening in 1894, she rang at the front door of wealthy Benjamin Westwood's west-end Toronto mansion and, when it was answered by the eighteen-year-old son of the house, Frank, she shot him. The boy lingered a few days before dying, his last utterance: "Mum's

Geraldine and Montrose Wright, she in Calgary, he in Trinidad. Montrose took the
bar in Calgary and was partner in the law firm "Ford, Wright & Miller."

the word!" Clara was eventually arrested on good evidence. In the witness
box though she delivered a virtuoso three-hour performance, denying
involvement in the shooting, describing her difficult life and winning
acquittal from a sympathetic all-white jury that may have suspected Clara
had been sexually wronged by young Westwood. Huge crowds cheered
her as she left the courtroom.

Soon after, Clara went into vaudeville – gaining fame and applause
in Canadian and American theatres re-enacting her shooting of Frank
Westwood.

Florence's vaudeville interlude was once again only brief. For on
July 19, 1911, her only child, Geraldine Wright was born – a photograph
shows a fond and obviously involved Montrose dandling her on his knee.
The following year, Montrose was admitted to the bar and eventually
helped found the law firm, Ford, Wright & Miller, achieving the prosperity he had sought by coming West. And what do we know of the couple's
Calgary years with their growing daughter? A good deal.

A first response to the letters page

AUGUST 6, 1987: The woman who greeted me at the door of her eleventh-floor Toronto apartment was tall and impressively erect for her eighty years. She insisted that I take the rocker – "more comfortable" – while she sat with the light behind her. Jeanne Wright had left a telephone message for me in response to a letter I had placed in the letters page of *The Toronto Sunday Star* on July 26, 1987. In it, I appealed to anyone who knew the whereabouts of Florence Kinrade's daughter, whose name I had learned while doing research in Los Angeles was probably Joan, to get in touch with me. Jeanne's message was the first response; there would be another.

My first thought, seeing the name 'Wright' was that she was a relative of Montrose. She was no relative, but no matter: Jeanne, whose maiden name was Sutherland, had known Florence in Calgary and later in Toronto during Florence's vaudeville career, and was a friend growing up of Florence and Monty's daughter whose name, she told me, was not Joan, a name I had heard in the course of research in Los Angeles, but Geraldine.

"I was four years old when we moved to Calgary (from Toronto)," she said. She didn't know how her parents came to know Monty and Florence, but remembered well visiting them in their Elbow Park bungalow with its large rooms, the living room dominated by a grand piano.

"We used to go to their place on Sundays, and they came over to our place with another couple. Monty—" she said, "was a very handsome man with dark hair, and he wore heavy glasses. He was fairly tall, like Florence. I thought I would like to have him for a father – he was so very nice, and my father was so strict."

Jeanne brought out tiny photographs of herself with a rather younger Geraldine looking plain and pudgy, wearing a satin dress and with a tentative eager-to-please smile on her face. "My mother would say, 'Go out for a walk with Geraldine,' but I was afraid to leave in case Florence would sing. She would play the piano and sing, and she had the most beautiful voice in the world." At the Wrights' home Jeanne met Gitz Rice, the famous Canadian World War I songwriter whose melody, 'Dear Old Pal of Mine', became tenor John McCormack's signature tune.

Even as a young girl, Jeanne could sense that Florence was at odds with her surroundings. "I don't think she was—" she searched for the right word, "satisfied. I used to wonder if she had a secret life. She was not like anyone else I knew, that's for sure. She was…fascinating." Jeanne's face still showed some of the enchantment she had felt in Florence's presence.

"When I would go over to her place, she would be all dressed up, as if she was just going out. All the other mothers I knew wore house dresses. I would ask my mother, "Why don't you get dressed up?" She would say, 'Because I have things to do.' I never saw Florence wash dishes. She always had someone there to make the meals. She was very different."

Meanwhile, Florence's determination to defy the norms expected of married women in that day was making an impression on young Jeanne: "I felt a kind of kinship with her because I was not satisfied with an ordinary life." Jeanne told me she married twice, and even now would leave her quite ordinary Toronto apartment to go to the fancy Sutton Place Hotel for breakfast – "just to be different."

When Jeanne was thirteen, her father, William Alexander Sutherland, was transferred back to Toronto by the Japanese firm he represented. It was 1918 – the year Monty Wright would die, one of the early victims of the worldwide influenza epidemic. The Sutherlands, with two sons and two daughters, settled in a house at 358 Clendenan Avenue, two blocks from High Park. It was there that Florence, having resumed her career in vaudeville, would stay while performing at the Pantages Theatre. Geraldine came too, like a spare piece of luggage. Jeanne recalled that

> (Geraldine) was a sweet little girl, very, very quiet. I felt sorry for her – she seemed so lonely. I went to see her in St. Mildred's girls' school on Walmer Road where she boarded (while Florence was travelling). Until they found out about her mother. Kids can be cruel. Perhaps they had taunted her about it (the murder).

After that, Florence took Geraldine with her to California. Later the singer sent Mrs. Sutherland a brooch. "I wear it all the time," said Jeanne, showing me a yellow and green lacquer pin with a floral design.

In Toronto, Florence was more glamorous than ever. "She was beautiful, she had a lovely speaking voice, and she liked fruit – that is what I remember," said Jeanne. "And she dressed very dramatically."

Her father, she recalled, never went to church, but one Sunday, Florence insisted she wanted to go, so her father accompanied her. "She wore a black cape with a white satin lining and my father said everyone looked at them. It was unforgettable. It was the only time he went to church, and the impression lasted him a lifetime."

Jeanne's biggest treat though was going with her mother to see Florence perform at the new Pantages Theatre, also billed Canada's grandest, built in 1920 with 3,375 seats, a dramatic oval mezzanine and glorious banisters. "I remember there was a parrot on the rotunda and Florence's picture was outside the theatre. It was a semi-classical program, and her big number was a song called 'Beautiful Lady.' A male chorus danced gracefully to the music," said Jeanne, still seeing the tableau in her mind's eye. "Then you would hear Florence's voice before she came out on the stage wearing a delicate pastel-shade crinoline." She was silent a moment, remembering. "I only had eyes for her."

"People went mainly to see her (because of her local notoriety) and it was written up in the paper." A *Toronto Daily Star* photographer came to their home to take Florence's picture, and Jeanne remembered the thick makeup, "almost like plaster" she wore for the pose. Sometimes Florence would rehearse in their home, and Jeanne, unable to tear herself away, would be late for school. "The kids at school were always asking me all about her."

Jeanne had heard people talk about the crime. "I asked my aunt what had happened, and she told me." But if she asked her mother about it, she would be told, "Now don't mention anything."

With all the glamour, Florence still seemed withdrawn, said Jeanne. But one time she met Florence's father, evidently visiting Toronto from his home in Florida, and he said, "It's a wonderful girl I have."

Jeanne felt that knowing Florence had bred a certain discontent in her. She never knew what she wanted. "I still don't," said Jeanne, who died in 1996. She had felt there was something more to life, if she could only put her finger on it. "I admired Florence so much. She was so gracious," said Jeanne.

Two weeks later she phoned with exciting news. Her son Bill, who had been in hospital when I visited her, was out and it was his first day home. Bill, a music teacher, had discovered four pieces of music that had belonged to Florence, and Jeanne said would be happy to lend them to me. The sheaf of sheet music sits on my desk now – four songs from around 1920, purchased at the time in Hamilton, New York, and Chicago. There was 'Just That One Hour', 'Starlight Love', 'The Garden of Dreams', and 'The Angel's Serenade.' The music, as the elegant signature on the front page of each one confirmed, belonged to Florence. Only the name was varied each time, as if she were trying out different identities. One was simply, 'Florence Kinrade,' another 'Florence B. Kinrade,' a third,

After Monty's death from the Spanish Flu, Florence would
eventually return to the vaudeville circuit.

'Florence B. Wright,' and, grandest of all, 'Florence Biltmore Wright.'

As for 'Beautiful Lady,' the music section of the New York Public Library confirmed for me later that 'Beautiful Lady, Tell Me' came from *The Rainbow Girl*, a 1918 musical by Rennold Wolf and Louis A. Hirsch. Sample lines:

> *Lady enshrined in perpetual state,*
> *Were you then always so prim and sedate,*
> *Grand and serene in the long, long ago?*

A second response to the letters page

The second response to my 1987 *Toronto Sunday Star* newspaper query arrived in the form of a hand-delivered letter addressed in a bold and distinctive handwriting.

"Dear Mr. Jones," began the letter, typed on notepaper featuring a small etching of a house in the historic Cabbagetown district,

> I am the nephew of Clare Montrose Wright, who married Florence Kinrade, and I am in semi-annual correspondence with their daughter, Geraldine, who is my only cousin on that side of the family. She has changed her name to Joan, and is about seventy-five years old.

Thus began a thirty-year connection with the Rev. Graham Cotter, a retired Anglican clergyman, who has given me unfailing cooperation and encouragement, not to mention the odd prod, in hopes of seeing the story of Florence, his wayward aunt, and his uncle, Montrose, published in book form.

"Gerry," as he called his cousin, had told him she was fifty years old before her mother told her about her Aunt Ethel's murder, so "you and I will have to discuss the delicate question of how much Gerry knows about what was said in the papers about her mother." Gerry, he added, was living in the U.S. on Social Security. He was due to send her a birthday letter, and would ask her permission to pass on her name and address to me.

Graham and his wife, Evelyn, had immediately gone on vacation, so it was a couple of weeks before I received a call from him inviting me over. Their home was in a secret and idyllic corner of downtown

Toronto that hardly anybody knows about. I came across it in the 1960s while researching a series of articles called, 'Who Owns the Slums?' Cabbagetown then was a jungle of rooming houses, drunks, addicts – and exploitive landlords. Today it is one of the most sought-after neighborhoods in the city. Graham and Evelyn bought their house on Hillcrest Park as an idealistic couple moving into a working class neighborhood. But even then it had its charms – a row of handsome old houses fronting right on to the park's green lawns, overlooking the leafy Don Valley, and with cars sensibly consigned to the back lane. Their house was easily recognizable by the bold red Lion of St. Mark shield on the porch, a reference to Graham's last church before his retirement.

We sat in a comfortable living room, the walls lined with family portraits, including a childhood picture of 'Rosy,' as Montrose was known in the family, with a bubbly head of curls. A self-admitted magpie who saves every photograph and scrap of paper, Graham showed me letters and diaries revealing the anguish that gripped the Wright family with the advent of this strange and mercurial young woman, Florence Kinrade. It was a family devoted to the ministry, unusually devout even for those times and the closest the Wrights generally came to sin was a game of croquet on the manse lawn. In the early years of the century though, their faith was sorely tested.

The Rev. Walter Wright, a farmer's son who had studied theology by correspondence at the Chautauqua school of theology was Methodist minister at Palmerston, in south west Ontario. The oldest son, Graham, born in 1881, was studying theology at Victoria College at the University, in Toronto, when, on December 5, 1905, he died of peritonitis following an appendix operation. 'He grew up in the church,' according to one obituary. Montrose, Graham's younger brother, who had been preparing for a career in law, would, after completing his arts degree at Vic in 1908, take up postgraduate studies in theology in order to fulfill the family destiny.

Walter Wright's diary from that time is full of family visits and excursions, illnesses, and adventures and his anticipation of moving to a church in Dartmouth, Nova Scotia the following year. "Past my fifty-sixth birthday, getting old," he comments wryly (He would live another twenty-seven years). Then, suddenly, in early 1909, a note of alarm: "Much concern over M (Montrose) in Hamilton affair."

His parents were hardly helpful to 'Rosy' in his crisis. On March 5

1909, Montrose writes from the Hotel Royal in Hamilton to his sisters, Eleonore and Norma, just as the inquest is getting under way. "Dear girls," he writes in a spider-thin horizontal handwriting,

> Here we are, have a few minutes this morning so will endeavor to catch up on my neglected correspondence. As you can no doubt imagine, I have been going some lately and therefore my silence. Today is the inquest, and we are all nerved up for it. I am confident that it will be all over shortly and Florence vindicated.
>
> The hardest thing I have to bear has been the fact that father and mother have gone back on me, and will persist in writing letters that nearly drive me insane. I'm glad that you at least have confidence in me and I know, girls, that everything is alright, and if I were to leave her (Florence) I should so despise myself I would never show my face again. Every day she grows more dear to me, and I realize more and more the purity of her character. Just trust a little longer and you will see it all clear.
>
> We came up here (from Toronto) last night and arrived without any commotion. Florence is feeling well but her father and mother did not arrive in as good condition. I feel like the fag end of a misspent life. The war will be over and 'we shall rest and aye, we shall need it.'
>
> Yours as ever, Montrose.

But the war would not be over, and things did not brighten up. When, in the years to come, I would call on Graham and Evelyn at their country house near Warkworth, Ontario. Graham would show me the very wicker chair in which his Irish-born grandmother, Emily, is sitting in a photograph from that time taken with Montrose. At first glance Emily, who was a singer when she met Walter, and who sang at her own wedding, seems to be smiling. Closer examination shows her lips pursed, and behind her wire-rimmed glasses there is no laughter in her eyes. Montrose, who is often smiling and sometimes even laughing uproariously in pictures, sits beside her on the lawn, his hand on the family Labrador, his expression uncharacteristically sad as he gazes away from the camera. Family legend has it that he had just told his mother of his plans to marry Florence.

In his diary that day Walter Wright comments tersely, "A sad blow."

Montrose' marriage to Florence created a serious rift in the family. His mother, very much the boss of the family, was unforgiving, her husband less so.

In a short account Graham Cotter's mother Norma had written for him, she relates how, following the wedding and with his hopes for a career in the church dashed, college friends persuaded Montrose to go to Calgary to join a law firm and work towards being a barrister. "We were all rather heartbroken because we seemed to have lost our brother," she wrote. "Father kept in touch with him, and later on (Montrose) would come to Toronto briefly on business." The loss was all the greater because Rosy was charming, always full of fun, his letters often illustrated with little cartoons quite skillfully drawn; he was very much the family favourite. But while he would visit very occasionally, Florence never came east.

In June 1918, with the end of World War One only months away, Montrose travelled east on a choice assignment: he was to go to Trinidad to represent a British oil company, and would be away for several weeks. He visited his parents (his father notes in his diary that Montrose had missed the funeral for his Aunt Carrie, who 'dropped dead in the vestibule of Howard Park Methodist Church after entering for morning service') then left for Trinidad about the first of August.

On September 24, 1918, Florence wrote a determinedly cheerful letter from Calgary to Montrose's younger sister, Norma, the only member of the family with whom she got on. She notes that Montrose has returned to New York from Trinidad,

> … and everything appears to be alright, but he says he is tired out. I was sorry to hear it as I had hoped this trip would do him worlds of good. It appears he has been worrying about me. Imagine!
>
> Now I expect him home Thursday – but will never be sure of his appearance until he walks in the door. He didn't say anything of stopping off at Toronto on his return, but of course, he may do so – only don't keep him too long. I need him! This being without one's husband is not the least bit nice (especially being without mine).

In Monty's absence, she's enjoyed learning to drive the family car, "and I am quite at my ease. Am intending driving down with it to meet Monty – even if he does arrive at the awful hour of 5:30 a.m." A friend of hers is also learning to drive, "but alas!" she comments smugly, "she ran into something right off – and lost her nerve."

There is chatter about babies, and she expresses regret at losing her gold wristwatch, a Christmas gift from Monty.

> (The wristwatch) slipped over my glove while I was pulling them off to go into a store for ice cream one night while out with the Sutherlands (Jeanne Wright's family). Of course it was picked up at once, all inside ten minutes. Oh, I hate to think of it.

Monty though has written telling her not to worry because he will get her another. "I don't deserve it," she writes. Geraldine has started school "and loves it," and their dog, Brownie, "is gone."

"Monty has written that, with his dog gone (which he used to say was his best friend) and his daughter going to school, he sees where he will just have to sit in the corner and smoke his pipe. Poor man!"

Florence promises that, if Monty doesn't call in Toronto, she'll have him write them as soon as he gets home. "Babe (Geraldine) sends a kiss and I my love, Florence."

But there was a sudden change of plan. Montrose had been offered a job in England. For Florence it may have seemed a joyful prospect leaving Calgary for the cultural delights of London, perhaps a chance to sing, and, best of all, leaving behind the snide remarks, the whispers behind gloved hands that followed her everywhere in Canada. It wasn't to be. News came that Montrose lay ill in the Knickerbocker Hotel, in New York. Florence and Geraldine caught the first train.

In his diary, Montrose's father, Walter recorded,

> On the fourth (of October) had a telegram from New York that Montrose was seriously ill with pneumonia at the Knickerbocker Hotel. We wired asking about him and saying we would come if necessary. The second wire said he was very low, to take the first train.
>
> John (Westley, Eleonore's husband) and I started the next morning, got there about 10 o'clock *p.m.* to

find that he had died at 5:30 that morning. Florence and
Geraldine had arrived (the previous day).

In fact, Montrose was an early victim of the Spanish flu epidemic
that ravaged the post-war world.

Florence, likely wanting to avoid the Wright family as well as the
press attention burial in the Wright family plot in Burlington, next-
door to Hamilton, would bring, opted to have the body returned to
Calgary. But by the time she and Geraldine left on the long trek west
(accompanied by Walter), both were ill and a nurse accompanied them.
Walter writes nothing in his diary of the misery of that four-day trip
via Chicago, St. Paul, and Moose Jaw. When they arrived, with the
Spanish influenza now raging, the authorities immediately quarantined
them all at home, and at Montrose's funeral a few days later, Walter and
Florence joined the procession in a closed carriage and waited close by
the cemetery.

If Walter had seen little or nothing of Florence in the nine years
since she married Montrose, they were now in the most intimate contact, as she and Geraldine joined him on another long train journey back
to Toronto. But Emily was unbending: Florence and Geraldine, neither
of them particularly popular, would stay in Toronto with Eleonore and
John Westley. Emily, according to Graham Cotter, was outraged at the
expense of taking Montrose' body all the way to Calgary when there
was still room in the plot in Burlington.

While the natural assumption would be that Tom Kinrade financed
the couple in buying a house in Calgary, Montrose, in his will, signed
shortly before he left for Trinidad, leaves the family home in Calgary,
"and my Strathmore property, only to the extent of $4,500" to his father.
He bequeaths the residue of his estate to Florence.

"What an eventful and strange period," Walter observed in his
diary. "God moves in mysterious ways."

In November, Florence, no doubt hugely relieved to say goodbye to
her hostile in-laws, set out with Geraldine for Palm Beach, Florida, to
stay with her parents.

I sensed that Graham was stalling. We had not discussed the main
reason for my being there – the letter he had sent to his cousin, Gerry.
Finally he took out an envelope. I could see it was addressed in a distinctive handwriting, not unlike his own. "I'll read it to you," he said.

Joan (or Geraldine) was not keen for a meeting. She didn't know anything about the murder, so she really felt she would have nothing to add, she wrote. A door had opened – and now it had closed again.

I sensed that Graham's disappointment was almost as great as my own. I never had a more supportive collaborator. What Joan didn't understand, I said, was that, of course, I didn't expect her to know anything about the murder. What I wanted to talk to her about was her mother's life, something that only she would now know about. Graham agreed. If I wrote a letter to Joan explaining this, would he be willing to forward it? He agreed without hesitation, although I admit I had meager hopes for the enterprise. It would be easier for Joan, who I guessed probably lived in California, to say no than to say yes to someone so far away and from whom she stood to gain nothing.

That night I wrote and rewrote the letter, trying to keep it plain and straightforward, and next day I dropped it off to Graham. Two weeks went by. We were out of the city for the birth of our second grandson when our daughter, Fazia, called from home. Yes, she said, there was a pile of mail. And, yes, there was a letter with an American stamp. It was post-marked Las Vegas.

Chapter Seventeen

NO LADY NEEDS ALGEBRA

Hazel Geraldine (Joan) Wright. The photo, likely styled
by her mother Florence, seems to foreshadow her career as a show dancer.

Sᴇᴘᴛᴇᴍʙᴇʀ 29, 1987: I had breakfast at The Dunes hotel on the Strip, all the time wondering if Joan White (nee Wright) was having second thoughts. My plane from Toronto had been three hours late arriving in Las Vegas the day before, and by the time I phoned her she had friends coming and it was too late to see her. I arranged to see her the following morning; she said not to come too early because she still keeps late hours, a result of having worked the four-to-twelve shift in the gift shop at the Silver Slipper casino for years. Was she stalling, I wondered. I killed time cruising the casinos until nearly eleven *a.m.* and then caught a cab that took me from the bright lights of the Strip to a poorer section of Vegas that few visitors see.

But no, as my cab draws up there she is, waiting in the blistering ninety-six degree heat out front of the nondescript apartment complex on East

Desert Inn Road. She is a small woman, desiccated by the sun, the skin wrinkled and loose on her arms, wearing polyester pants and a floral top and with large eyes peering from behind huge television screen-sized glasses. "They never did give us the grass," she says as she leads me across the bare ground and up to her second floor apartment. Dooley, her overweight bull-dog – one of fifteen she has owned and whose photographs decorate the living room – heaves himself up and greets me, stubby tail wagging.

For the first hour, Joan interviews me, having me go over everything I have discovered about her family, her mother's early life, and the murder. "Oh," she says, with an intake of breath when I bring out a photograph of her mother when she was a young woman, "She was beautiful – even if she was my mother."

She in turn shows me a photograph of herself, tall and attractive in a dance costume. She was in her teens then, she says, in the throaty voice familiar to me from our phone conversations, and already performing in the water ballet at Grauman's Chinese Theatre in Hollywood. "We had to do everything – tap-dancing, roller skating, ice-skating."

She shows me her July 19, 1911 birth certificate naming her as Hazel Geraldine Wright. Hazel was the name of a girl her father had known at university, Geraldine for a famous opera singer of the day. She hated the name Geraldine, which was why she later changed it to Joan, although she didn't mind her cousin Graham Cotter and others still calling her 'Gerry.'

Her mother told her afterwards that it was a difficult birth, and that Joan's head bore forceps marks for some time. "She said she rubbed my head with Vaseline every night. My mother—" she looks down and strokes Dooley's squat head, "she told them, 'Take it back,' something like that."

Before she was born, says Joan, her mother had a miscarriage. "I don't know much about it" – the crucial admission comes early – "because we weren't close. Even when my dad was living." Joan laughs a little, embarrassed, and lights a cigarette:

> I didn't pay much attention to my mother, even when I was five or six years old. She would say, 'Babe, get my hairbrush,' and I wouldn't pay any attention. But my dad would say, 'Babe, did you hear your mother?' And I would go and get it. When my dad said something I really did it."

(Florence should not have been surprised: she too was her father's favourite.)

"I was his girl. I guess she (my mother) had a hard time when my dad was working because I wouldn't pay attention to her. She let the house-keeper look after me. She was from England, a regular nanny type, and she always wore a hat."

Her mother too wore hats all her life. In her mother's last years, Joan recalled getting a phone call from the police. They had picked up a woman wandering the streets. She had no ID and they thought it might be her mother. "The only reason I knew it was my mom, it was because she had a hat on."

There is still a mine of bitterness: "She never did any of the cooking, she never did anything. I guess she sat at her piano and sang – and I would cover my ears."

Her father, she says, wanted a boy, and so, as a little girl, she often wore boyish clothes, sometimes kilts, though some of the photographs she gives me later show her in extremely feminine and expensive clothes bought or made for her by her father's Aunt Carrie (who had taken Monty and Florence's side in the family feud).

Joan must sometimes have been her parents' despair. Montrose's sister, Norma (Graham's mother) came to Calgary once, and had to sleep with Joan. "Oh, I was fit to be tied!" Joan remembers. "I kicked her out of bed. It was my room and my bed. And then we got to be friends."

She remembers,

> My father, he was gentle and nice. I never saw him mad. I know I had everything – tricycle, wagon, everything I hollered for. I was spoilt. He wanted a tomboy, and I was that. I never played with dolls or my teddy bear. Mother didn't bother if I got dirty – she didn't bother with me at all.

She would have been seven years old when her father went to Trinidad on that fatal business trip. "He got the fever. My mother and I came from Calgary, and he was in the Knickerbocker Hotel (in New York)." She remembers how her father, always trying to please, got out of his sick bed to show them the jewelry and gifts he'd brought them from Trinidad. She remembers too her mother telling her they would be moving to London, England, where her father had been offered a job. She laughs at herself: "And I might have been a millionaire instead of a no-good nothing! And then he died. I remember that real well." Years later, she would always think about it when she passed the Knickerbocker Hotel.

"Then she (her mother) took his body back to Calgary. Why did she do that? There was nobody (in the family) left in Calgary." She could not remember her mother showing grief.

Now, her champion gone, Joan was a waif adrift. She remembers being lodged in Toronto with her Aunt Leonore (Eleonore) in the Westley house near High Park. "She was never friendly; she would watch you all the time when you sat down. She didn't care for my mother either." Later she boarded at St. Mildred's, a high Anglican girls' school in Toronto. "The sisters were nice, but I didn't like it. I ran away twice – to Leonore's house."

She has happier memories of staying with her Kinrade grandparents in West Palm Beach, Florida. "He was a millionaire, real estate was booming, but then he lost everything. I liked my little grandma, she was such a tiny thing." She shows me a little flexible gold bracelet with a ruby that had belonged to her grandmother.

"They lived in a big building called 'The Arches' and—" a thing a child would remember, "they had a big tarantula in the corner of the hallway. My grandfather said, 'Now don't you be afraid of that, it's not going to go anywhere, it eats all the bugs.' It did too."

Meanwhile, Florence voyaged to Europe three times, once on the Mauritania, taking musical training in Paris. Was she seeking escape from her grief? Joan laughed merrily: "She was young and beautiful and queen of the ball on those ocean liners, dancing with the officers, always sitting at the captain's table because she was on her own and often sang. She loved that life; I don't think she worried too much." There is wonderment, even admiration in her voice: "She had guts going over there all by herself, didn't she! I wish she'd found some rich guy. Maybe that's why she went."

Like a shuttlecock, Joan was now shipped off to live in Los Angeles with Florence's younger sister, Gertrude and went to public school there. But she didn't get along with Gertrude, "and I fought every boy in the school. I was terrible."

Stumped what to do with her rebellious little daughter, Florence appealed to the Wrights. Her father, says Joan, had set aside money for her to attend the Ontario Ladies' College at Whitby, east of Toronto (Motto: Truth, Virtue and Loveliness) commencing at age thirteen. She was only eleven, but with Norma having taught art at the college, and Eleonore playing an active role in the school management (both sisters had attended the college as girls), strings were pulled, and, says Joan, she was admitted at age eleven.

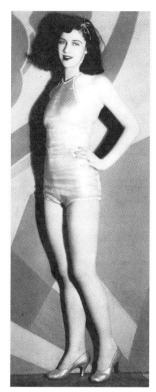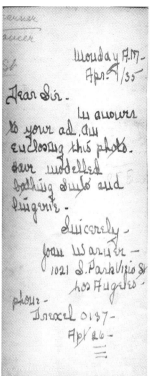

Joan Wright, who changed her professional name to Joan Warner
applies for a modelling job for bathing suits and lingerie.

It was a brilliant decision. "I loved that place," she says. It was the home she was looking for. When the dashing Prince of Wales (later Edward VIII) came to visit, it was Joan, perhaps because she was the school's youngest student, who was chosen to present him with a bouquet of flowers. "They were so good to me there: when I was through at seventeen, I didn't want to leave," she says.

It was a surreal existence: attending school with the proper daughters of clergymen, lawyers and other professionals and then, in the summer, when the other girls went away to the lake with their families or else travelled to Europe, Joan would join her mother on the vaudeville circuit. "I enjoyed that," she says.

> We went all over, Portland, Vancouver, Seattle, Los Angeles.
> She'd leave me in the (hotel) room, tell me if I needed

anything to call downstairs. She did that in San Diego. I remember I used to lean out of the window and listen to the Salvation Army band at the corner. She wasn't ashamed of me. I guess she figured there was nothing for me to do over there (at the theatre). The first time I saw her on the stage, I'd be eleven or twelve years old. Oh, that was great! She sang 'Indian Love Call' and 'Roses of Picardy' and a lot of operettas. I thought, 'That's what I'm going to do,' but only I ended up dancing.

Later at the Pantages Theatre, in Los Angeles, she saw her mother's picture in the lobby alongside those of Alexander Pantages' other stars. She could admire her mother – but the war between mother and daughter continued.

She never came near the school, never, and I used to lose all my privileges because I wouldn't write my mother. We had a man principal and a lady principal, and she would get me cornered in her sitting room and make me sit down and write a letter to my mother. I never would because she didn't bother with me, see.

(Of course, it's possible Eleonore had laid down the law, insisting that Joan would simply be better off if her notorious mother did not visit the school.)

Joan became good friends with Grace Moody, daughter of a wealthy Hamilton family. But when Grace invited her to stay for a holiday weekend, her mother, Joan remembers, "was having a fit. She didn't want me to go there." Eventually Florence gave in, paying for an expensive outfit for Joan for the visit. Only years later, when she learned about Ethel's murder, did she realize the reason for her mother's reluctance. "She was praying, I suppose, that no one would bring up the tragedy. But no one ever did – then or later."

Florence was not entirely oblivious to her daughter's needs. Algebra was a constant torment for the girl, and not even the principal could teach her. She must have mentioned the problem in a letter to her mother because Florence wrote the principal saying, "No lady needs algebra." After that Joan was excused.

Joan was never a singer, although she learned to play the piano (A visiting music examiner at Whitby told her he had once graded her mother in singing in Hamilton, "so they knew who I was"). She decided though that there was more money in dancing than playing piano, and switched.

And it was her mother, she says, who put the idea in her head of going into show business. As she got older and joined her mother on the circuit during summer breaks, Florence allowed her to perform as an acrobatic dancer with her performing group. When it came to the singing,

> She (Florence) was the star! She had crinolines and lots of feathers and fans. I would just mouth the words. I was so excited to be there. I thought it was something else! The stories I was able to tell when I went back to school! In vaudeville, it was just continual, you might do seven shows a day, holidays and Saturdays too. The money was good too – nothing taken out of your check.

Bitten by the showbiz bug, she says that when she left school, she moved to New York without telling her mother, and stayed with a former Ontario Ladies College music teacher, Mary-Jane Merchant and her doctor husband (Joan would remain lifelong friends with two other former teachers at the college). Somehow she found money for a year's dancing lessons, and when a dancer in the Ziegfeld Follies was killed in a boating accident, Joan filled in for her, although the job only lasted a few months. Moving on to Los Angeles ("Gertrude was not especially glad to see me"), she got a job as a nightclub hat check girl, answered an ad for a job at Grauman's Chinese Theatre, and performed there for forty weeks. Like her mother, she says, she was rarely 'resting' – without stage work.

Mother and daughter were so busy with their careers, in fact, that they lost touch with each other. When they both ended up performing in New York, the only way they found each other was through a regular feature in *Billboard*, the show business newspaper, through which performers kept in touch with their friends. (One wonders if, on the vaudeville circuit, Florence ever encountered Jimmy Baum again and what they said!)

Joan performed under the name 'Joan Warner.' She knew that the ultra-respectable Wrights disapproved of her mother being a vaudeville performer. "That's why I changed my name – because I didn't want to disgrace the Wrights."

And then, in the 1940s, vaudeville's day was over. The movies reigned supreme as the popular entertainment and Florence and Joan gravitated to Los Angeles where for periods they lived together.

Florence, says Joan, always had acting ambitions, and worked for a while as a straight woman with William Demerest, an actor and comedian who, over a lengthy career, appeared in no fewer than 137 movies. It might have led to a movie career for her – "when she got older she could have played one of those society women real well. But you needed an agent and you needed the breaks." Instead, while Joan got a job in a bank, Florence for a time worked four hours every night in a department store selling gloves. Once she sold a pair to the actress Joan Crawford, "and (gossip columnist) Louella Parsons was always coming in for gloves."

There was still occasional friction between mother and daughter: "She told me she didn't like me because I didn't put on for people. 'You are not going to have any friends.' Well, I said, I don't need any of that kind. That used to bother her, that I didn't care whether they liked me or not."

But as Joan talks, the image of that younger Florence – the schemer and prevaricator, the resentful, cold mother, the ambitious woman who, having dodged a murder charge, couldn't wait to escape from her provincial life in Calgary – begins to fade. Professional fulfillment in the theatre made her, in her daughter's eyes, someone to admire. And when hard times came, Florence showed courage and a certain gameness of spirit.

"We got real poor there for a while," says Joan. She and Florence were living in an apartment building owned by Tom Kinrade (who had moved to LA from Florida with Bella in the Depression) on Central Avenue, in a poor part of town.

There was a grocery store downstairs owned by an Italian named Al Fagaldi. Even in poverty, says Joan, Florence wore her hat and was smartly turned out. When she'd call by for items, Al was obviously impressed.

> Well we hadn't got any money, and Al used to bring us food. So she married him. I liked Al. For some reason or other it didn't work. Al rented a piano, and she accompanied herself. But when Al left, the piano went back. He was a heavy-set man and he was getting sick. He went up to 'Frisco (where his sister lived) and died up there.

Another time, another apartment,

> … and we couldn't pay the rent. So there was a back window on the alley and my husband, Harold – he was my boyfriend then – he came along with the truck and we moved all the

stuff out of the window. We didn't have any money, but it never seemed to bother my mother. Something always turned up."

But through the failed marriage to Al and hardship, Joan says she never heard her mother raise her voice – "except once – with Gertrude." Gertrude, she recalls, was executor of their father's estate.

> The money went – she (Florence) never saw it. She got fed up with Gertrude wasting all the money, and she blew her top that time. Gertrude didn't care if we had a place to live or not. She wanted to be boss. Gertrude had a terrible temper. She had a red-haired temper, as we call it. I had it too.

If relations between Florence and Gertrude were sometimes stormy, she was close to her brother, Ernie, who once came visiting.

> He was a gambler. He went to the racetrack a few times. We had only one room, and a Murphy bed came down from the wall. So he must have stayed in a little hotel. With Ernie my mother used to talk about Maggie (his first wife) all the time. She had all those children, then they lost the only girl they had. Everybody liked Maggie, and she liked Maggie too.

One day, Florence asked Joan, "How would you like to go to school and your father was the principal?" She must have been thinking of her own experience when her father was teaching in Hamilton. But it was likely no great hardship: "She liked her father best. She spoke up to him. All the rest liked their mother."

In 1944, Joan met and married Harold White, who was driving a truck, delivering lunches to the studios. Harold had a two-year-old daughter, Diane who, since her own mother took no interest, Joan brought up. And perhaps Florence finally had time for a daughter, because she got on famously with little Diane. "She and my mother had a lot of fun together. Diane called her, 'Flossie-Bell.' She liked that."

With age, Florence mellowed. She was less intense, and ambition no longer drove her. She responded well to life's vicissitudes. She got on well with Harold, and the four of them, Harold, Joan, Florence, and Dianne, even went camping together, though, says Joan, her mother was not the outdoor type. In the city, when Joan had to work until nine *p.m.*, Florence and Harold would cook up chicken or chili and bring it to a park for a late-night picnic. Sometimes in September it would get so hot in the apartment they all shared that they would go and sleep on the beach, Florence too.

Eventually, because the LA smog affected Joan, she and Harold moved to Las Vegas. She got a job within a couple of weeks, "but there was no work for him, and that was a lot of the problem. Later he got work driving an ice cream truck."

Florence even came to live in Las Vegas for several months, but didn't like it – "No sidewalks," she sniffed. Alcohol was an increasing problem for Harold and in 1964, after they had been married twenty years, he returned to Los Angeles to live with his now-grown daughter. He died within a couple of months of returning.

Harold's mother, who had never liked Joan, would not tell her where and when the funeral was to take place. "My mother said, 'I'll find out where it is.' And she did, the time and everything." Joan and Florence, who had always liked Harold, went to the funeral and sat in the front row. "I was still his wife! His mother looked daggers at me," says Joan.

It was after the funeral that Joan finally heard a version of the truth about Ethel.

> About three o'clock the funeral was over and I had to wait until seven or something for my plane (back to Las Vegas). So we went up to her apartment and we were having a cup of tea. We were closer then than we had ever been. We were just sitting there and she started to tell me (about Ethel). I still think about it. Maybe because of the funeral she was thinking about death. She told me Ethel was upstairs and she was downstairs, just the two of them were home, and somebody came in the front door and went half way up the stairs and then she heard a shot.

Then Florence looked at Joan and asked, "Do you think I did it?" Joan goes out to the kitchen to put the kettle on. On her return:

> I don't know why she told me. I see her sitting there now. I borrowed a black dress and I had a little black beanie that was my hat. Mother would have had the right hat. 'Do you think I did it?' I thought about it going home on the plane. Isn't that silly, I say to myself. Why did she bother (to tell me)? I didn't know her sister. It didn't really change anything.'

Florence in 1960 in California – always wearing a hat.

And then she contradicts herself: "After the funeral, when she told me about Ethel, I thought about her in a different way – because I was figuring she did it. Otherwise," says Joan, "why did she wait so long before telling me?" Was she afraid to tell her? "But I wouldn't ask her outright either" – even though, she admits, she wanted to.

Florence never mentioned the murder again. She would come to Las Vegas, "and have a ball. My mother was the life of any party. Her favourite was playing bingo at the Showboat casino. When she was older, she would put on all kinds of necklaces and bracelets. I'd have to tell her to leave some off." But a photograph of Florence taken in her eighties shows a woman who could have passed easily for sixties, as smartly turned out as ever, her neat little floral hat still perched on her head. Even though they were closer in later years, Florence never told Joan much about her early life, about collecting rents for her father in Hamilton, or even about her adventures in Virginia or her romance with Jimmy Baum.

"Then, the last time I saw her, I took her to the airport and she said, 'I'm not coming here any more. If you want to see me, you'll have to come down.' There was no way I could go to see her: I had two dogs. I did have a car, but I wouldn't drive all by myself."

After she was found wandering the streets, Florence was taken first to a general hospital and then placed in a nursing home.

> I used to phone the home, and they would say not to come because she wouldn't recognize me. She said she had no daughter. They said there was a man with a guitar who came every Wednesday to entertain, and my mother would go along and sing with him. She was happy, see. She could still do that.

When her mother died, the telegram went to the wrong address. It was a week before Joan learned the news, and by then the funeral had taken place.

This evening after I leave Joan, I am standing in line at the restaurant in the Silver Slipper Casino, chatting to a man from Nigeria, when I see Florence – or think I do. She is a tall, erect woman, perhaps in her eighties, her silk dress of royal blue complementing her dove-grey hair. She passes within a couple of feet of me with that benign, self-assured air that only a person of an earlier generation can carry off. It isn't her, of course, but in her I can see an older Florence, a Florence who has faced down life's vicissitudes, who has survived widowhood, poverty, a vanished career - and a long-ago crime she very rarely thinks about any more. Putting it all behind her as she strides into her favourite casino to give the dice another throw.

The following day, before returning home, I phone Joan to say goodbye. She asks me to give her address to Jeanne Wright, her long-ago friend from Calgary and Toronto, and ask her to drop her a line. "I really enjoyed talking to you," she says. "I get a bit lonely sometimes."

Afterwards we wrote each other from time to time. In April the following year, she sent me a card: "Every time I think of all you found out (about her mother), I have different feelings – for some reason why I never loved my mother right from the start." On a brighter note: "I have a new puppy, a little Boston terrier. Poor old Dooley got too strong for me."

A week before Christmas that year she wrote that the new dog, 'Lil Guy' "is driving me crazy. I am not having any Christmas – they raised my rent. So can hardly manage it now… Wish you luck. Do have a happy holiday, Love 'Jo.'" Three years later Joan died.

Chapter Eighteen

OF SCARLETT AND MADNESS

Florence Kinrade and Scarlett O'Hara (played by Vivian Leigh).
Their similar personalities were both ruthlessly flirtatious and deceitful.

M ARCH 1, 1988: Snow covered the grounds of the Penetanguishine Mental Health Centre near the shores of Ontario's Georgian Bay as I pulled into the visitors' parking. It was a tranquil and sunny late winter scene, yet behind the barred windows of its Oak Ridge unit for the criminally insane reside some of Canada's most dangerous individuals. Russell Johnson, for example, a handsome body-builder who terrorized London, Ontario, in the 1970s by his knack for scaling high-rise apartment balconies and strangling young women in their beds.

I opened an elegant Georgian door only to be confronted by bars in the waiting room. After a while, two psychiatrists, Dr. Morton N. Menuck, a roly-poly man with wire-rimmed glasses, and Dr. Russ Fleming, thinner, bearded, ushered me into Menuck's office which was brightened with a Toronto Blue Jays poster on the wall. Both men, by the nature of their jobs, are experts in the mental disturbances that lead to murder, while, in addition, Menuck has an interest in the history of psychiatry.

I had decided to approach four psychiatrists making up as it were an

223

informal panel to review Dr. C.K. Clarke's diagnosis of Florence Kinrade as a 'moral imbecile.' Fleming and Menuck were intrigued by Clarke's case notes, copies of which I had sent them, and wanted to hear how I had come across them. "It's like opening a window into the past," said Menuck.

Society, he said, has wrestled with the concept of evil going back to Ancient Greece. "Once they got over the idea it was caused by devils – Jesus driving the devils into the sea, for example – they had two basic theories which still exist to some extent – that people who do crazy things are either mad or bad."

The notion of a 'moral imbecile,' he said, developed in the nineteenth century. "It's a fuzzy concept that does not really relate to 'moral' in the modern sense. It referred to a lack of human feeling for other people."

Fleming put in:

> It helped to explain outlandish acts without associated craziness. Causing people to do things about which one should feel anxiety, but which they did not. It was as if the imbecility was part of the person's development that stayed at an infantile level. Clarke was not really attaching blame to these people: he was seeing this incapacity as a real illness. It is a very modern concept.

On the other hand, there was an unfortunate tendency in nineteenth century psychiatry to look for physical or racial clues to mental illness. "There is a decided tone of snobbishness to it," said Menuck. "A really unacceptable flavour of ethnocentricity." In this, Clarke's notes "reflect the medicine bag of nineteenth century psychiatry."

Menuck identified a list of symptoms, some dubious, that Clark identified as suggesting Florence's possible 'moral imbecility.' They included: lies and confabulations, feigned fainting and forgetfulness, impulsivity, Spanish, Creole, or Negro blood and family traits such as asymmetrical fingers, ill-formed ears, and general degeneracy. Looking for clues to a possible epileptic personality, Clarke mentions dream states, memory lapses, fainting spells, episodes of incoherence, vasomotor disturbances, headaches, head and mouth mannerisms and maternal epilepsy.

Many of these approaches would, of course, be scorned today. But, said Menuck, "It's not that he was a creep; it's that psychiatry was a creepy practice – still is," he said with a laugh. He continued to say,

> … but they were not entirely off base: some criminality is inherited. A recent study involving twins found that four fifths of psychopathic traits in children could be ascribed to genetic or inherited factors. Also they were not completely wrong in suspecting epilepsy was linked (to psychopathy). It's a fact that epileptics – and schizophrenics – are over-represented in the prison population. The point is there was this constellation of quasi-psychiatric beliefs abroad at the time, and people with little odds and ends of mental problems and people who did outrageous things were all whomped together as some sort of problem of degeneracy.

Menuck also remarked on Clarke's reference to Florence's 'dissociative states.' In fact, a German psychiatrist, Dr. S. J. Ganser, in an 1897 paper entitled 'A Peculiar Hysterical Twilight State,' identified symptoms similar to those Florence displayed in the witness box. Subjects with this rare condition, observed Ganser, "were unable to answer the most simple questions put to them, although they acknowledged by the way they answered that they had grasped the sense of the question."

Menuck said of Ganser's patients.

> They seem to be between feigning illness and being legitimately ill. Many of these things fit into Florence's picture. We are not allowed to use the term 'hysterical' any more, but studies of criminal families show the sons become criminal and the daughters hysterics.

The assumption, he said, is that people acquire Ganser's symptoms as an escape mechanism. "They can bring on weird and wonderful symptoms; Florence has that sort of hysterical personality – she could behave like that on the stand because that was her basic personality. The other possibility," he said with a grin, "is that she was basically a liar."

She could, agreed Fleming, "have been an out-and-out con artist with no conscience, a pathological liar, one of those mixed forms of disorders, like Ganser's. But there was no evidence," he said, "that she was either epileptic or schizophrenic." Both doctors, however, remarked on Florence's tendency to narcissism.

On the other hand, said Fleming, "I have seen it repeatedly – murder doesn't have to result from craziness. It could have been an impulsive act, with no motive needed. Many people have killed over minor things," he said. He cited Dr. Jeffrey MacDonald, the American military doctor who killed his pregnant wife and two small daughters in 1979, and then rigged the murder scene to make it appear that drugged hippies were responsible. MacDonald, a pathological liar, often seemed to be deceiving himself about the truth as much as those asking the questions.

It was tempting, Menuck said, to be critical of Clarke who made his deductions on the basis of often-faulty nineteenth century psychological concepts, "but it was probably a capable assessment."

Was Florence then a moral imbecile, a psychopath, or possessed of an antisocial personality disorder – chose your terminology? "In part—" offered Fleming, "but I think she was more of a mixed bag. If she had been (a psychopath), this is a lifelong condition." And Florence Kinrade had gone on to a successful vaudeville career.

"What we have here," concluded Menuck, "are overlapping terms – hysteric, narcissistic, anti-social personality. We are talking about very closely related variants of a super syndrome."

Historically, where the male psychopath might have ended up in prison, women, said Menuck, could "escape into the respectability of marriage."

Dr. Basil Orchard, a well-known forensic psychiatrist I talked to, was inclined perhaps to give more credence to Clarke's diagnosis. "C.K. Clarke was a very perceptive and careful diagnostician," he said. "The diagnosis of moral imbecility or psychopathy is not easily made. But he didn't just see Florence – he saw the whole family." Orchard read Clarke's notes with obvious pleasure:

> It's wonderfully clear. You get a very good picture of what's going on. He does not jump to conclusions rapidly. He's starting off considering all sorts of things, and gradually comes to his conclusion – which was like him. I would lean pretty heavily on Dr. Clarke's diagnosis.

The diagnosis, he believed, explained a good deal of Florence's behavior.

> She was breaking the mold, not behaving as society expected her to. She was somewhat grandiose, trying to give an impression of fame and glamour. Being merry and bright after Ethel's death was typical behaviour (for a psychopath).

Also, being able to withstand Blackstock's cross-examination
was natural.

"As a psychopath," said Orchard, "she would feel no anxiety unless she
was cornered. And she didn't feel she was cornered."

As for a reason to kill her sister, "If she was truly a psychopath, she
doesn't need the kind of motive that ordinary people do. She only needs
someone getting a little close to her or threatening her plans and making
her anxious. She can't tolerate that – she will do extraordinary things."

He lit another cigarette and looked out of his office window at the fea-
tureless highway landscape. For psychopaths, he mused, "achieving their
desires is the ultimate good, and anything blocking those desires is the
ultimate bad."

And whatever Florence did, it was only natural, he suggested, that her
family would have rallied around her. "The loss of her good name, for a
woman then, was the loss of her future. Families were closer in those days.
You didn't wash your dirty linen in public. If you had a retarded child,
you put them in the attic." Could that also mean Florence's mother being,
as Clarke suspected, a co-conspirator, helping to cover up the murder
by going to the police station to complain about tramps? "Oh yes," said
Orchard. "To keep it in the family. She'd lost one daughter – she didn't want
to lose another."

As a psychopath, Florence would have been able to carry on after the
murder, "because they learn." If, as sometimes happens, the condition had
burned out after a few years, "she would have been able to carry on quite
well. And if she had symptoms, her husband would likely have been blind
to them."

But another Toronto psychiatrist with whom I discussed the case, Dr.
Sandford Fleming (no relation of Russell Fleming), firmly rejected Clarke's
diagnosis of Florence as a moral imbecile or psychopath. "Up to that point,"
he said, "her behaviour had been too rational – she had performed (as a
singer) in public, she had returned home (from Virginia) when requested
to by her parents." Evidence of 'moral imbecility' would have emerged
much earlier, he suggested.

Fleming, then an assistant professor of psychiatry at the University of
Toronto, believed the traits

> are more consistent with her being a hysteric. They have a lot
> in common with psychopaths – an emotional shallowness,

an apparent emotionality which, on closer examination it is revealed there is no depth of feeling. They are apparently sexual and seductive, but are in fact timid of sex. Hysterics were the terrain of Sigmund Freud. The great psychoanalyst used to say these are the women who can disassociate. A hysteric in 1909 you would expect would disassociate herself from unpleasant things around her by, for example, fainting, having no conscious access to her own behaviour. She would not have remembered the crime.

"The term 'hysteric' is no longer fashionable," said Fleming.

When we see it, we are reluctant to see it the way Freud saw it – as an Oedipal problem. What we are finding is that people who disassociate and show emotional shallowness are far more primitive in their emotional structure. Basic elements have not fallen into place. They are borderline or, its first cousin, narcissistic. A borderline (Borderline Personality Disorder) will show minor distortions, poor control, sometimes intense rage. They have a fear of being alone, a fear of death and of forming long-term friendships.

If Borderline Personality Disorder describes Florence, what made her like that? "A certain kind of deprivation in the first year or two of life," he said with certainty. "Poor mothering." Her brother Ernie's antisocial tendencies too may have emanated from his mother's shortcomings. And Mrs. Kinrade, as an adopted child, may also have had a deprived upbringing.

And the rage which may have led to murder? Fleming describes Florence's rage

... a tremendous sibling rivalry between Florence and Ethel. Maybe Ethel was the one who squealed on Florence being on the stage. Maybe Florence saw Ethel destroying all her chances. The two sisters might have been at each other from infancy, especially if there was not enough love to go around. Ethel didn't have a boyfriend, she was not beautiful, she did not sing (as well as Florence) – so she may have set out to queer things for Florence. This would all set itself up nicely for the Oedipal rivalry – both wanted to be the apple of daddy's eye.

And then Dr. Fleming delighted me by drawing a literary parallel that had already occurred to me: in an uncanny way, Florence Kinrade's life parallels that of Scarlett O'Hara, the heroine of Margaret Mitchell's book, *Gone With the Wind* and the unforgettable 1939 movie starring Clark Gable and Vivien Leigh.

Scarlett, self-centred, ruthless, flirtatious yet emotionally distant and sexually timid, is the archetypal Southern belle, much studied and written about in Southern feminist writing. In her 1936 best seller, "Mitchell set out to create a portrait of the 'decorous deviousness' required of the southern belle," writes Betina Entzminger, professor of English at Bloomsbury University. Scarlett, she suggests, incorporates the belle's worst qualities, "her deceitfulness, shrewdness, manipulativeness, and superficiality."

Interestingly, Entzminger notes that the belles of Southern fiction, like Scarlett, are generally raven-haired, often of dark complexion, reflecting the unspoken side of Southern sexuality – slavery and miscegenation (in fact, Margaret Mitchell's first, unpublished, novel deals with miscegenation).

Scarlett O'Hara rebels too against the straitjacket of decorum that governs her life, complaining:

> I'm tired of everlastingly being unnatural and never doing anything I want to do. I'm tired of acting like I don't eat more than a bird, and walking when I want to run and saying I feel faint after a waltz, when I could dance for two days and never get tired. I'm tired of saying, 'How wonderful you are!' to fool men who haven't got one-half the sense I've got, and I'm tired of pretending I don't know anything, so men can tell me things and feel important while they're doing it.

The parallels with Florence Kinrade are startling. When we read Florence's self-absorbed words, inscribed on the back of a quite pleasant portrait: "18 years old – how could anyone fall for me???" we could be hearing a young Scarlett. Florence rebelled spectacularly against the constraints put upon her as the daughter of a middle-class family in early twentieth century Canada: she lied to her family, inventing stories and characters to allow her to roam free, even prevaricating when there was little to gain, as when she told Southern friends her father was a professor, her uncle a judge.

The men in her life too seem to foreshadow the characters in *Gone With the Wind*. Florence, like Scarlett, is closely attached to her father;

Scarlett is in love with the gentlemanly Ashley Wilkes, and hates the saintly Melanie Hamilton, who wins him. In the end, of course, she realizes she really loves the unobtainable Rhett Butler and, as he walks out of her life, famously declares, "Tomorrow is another day."

In Florence's life, Montrose Wright, gentlemanly and devout, was her Ashley Wilkes and, considering Montrose at one time accompanied both Florence and Ethel on outings, we can assume Ethel was Melanie, the other rival for his heart. Only, in this scenario, Florence won 'Ashley' hands down and ultimately disposed of 'Melanie.'

In Florence's story, it was the actor Jimmy Baum who was the romantic and dangerous Rhett Butler character, threatening her family and her future, and tempting her to throw over convention and join him, not just as a wife, but as a vaudeville performer. Jimmy was jolly, even comic, and neither as handsome nor as alluring as Clark Gable, who played Rhett Butler. Yet, if the murder of Ethel had not intervened, there is at least the possibility that a frustrated Florence would have thrown restraint to the wind, rejected Montrose and a life in the manse, and chosen Jimmy and vaudeville's bright lights.

The parallels continue to surprise: Florence, like many of the Southern belles of nineteenth century fiction, was described by Dr. Clarke as Latin or Creole in appearance. And whatever it was that originally drew her from starchy Ontario to Richmond, the one-time capital of the Confederacy, we can only wonder at yet another coincidence. It was not Atlanta, the setting for much of *Gone With the Wind*, but it was not so different, and we can imagine Florence, so willful, so flirtatious, feeling completely at home in an environment where Southern belles deceived to please. The perceived danger from the former slave population – that indeed resulted in occasional riotous outbreaks – and the need for a respectable young white woman to carry a gun and know how to use it, would only have added to the romantic excitement of living in the post-bellum South.

So many theories! And then as I was making the final revisions to this manuscript in late 2018, I heard from Dr. J. Thomas Dalby, a leading forensic psychologist who, after reading his colleagues comments on the case, swept most of the Kinrade theories aside like so many cobwebs.

> I agree with Sandford (Fleming) that psychopathy is very unlikely given the 'symptoms' – they are really just behaviours someone is trying to ram into a box. Pathologizing is what

mental health professionals sometimes do – if you only have
a hammer then everything is a nail.

When he is reconstructing a past case, even a historic one, he said, he
looks for simple evidence. "And there seems little (evidence) that Florence
actually perpetuated the crime. When you assume she did, then the theories flow. The absence of the gun is telling," he suggests. "And it was never
found."

A random murder by a tramp? "Overkill – as when Ethel was shot
seven times – is often attributed to strong emotions where victim and perpetrator are connected," said Dr. Dalby, "but I can draw on cases where an
absolute stranger did the same thing to victims he had never met before."
Did she lie? "If she did, she joins the rest of the human race who lie probably at least once a day. But the Kinrade case and this telling of it," he said,
"provides a window on an era when perceptions and actions were different
– but human behaviour remains constant since the beginning."

Florence innocent of the crime? Dr. Dalby's doubts echo those that
would have been expressed in the cabinet room when the Whitney cabinet decided not to lay a murder charge. Where was the gun? What was
the motive? And, finally, what chance was there of securing a conviction
against such an impressive accused?

Chapter Nineteen

A MURDER FOR AMBITION

THE FASCINATION of the Kinrade murder case lies in the fact that, today as I write about it more than a hundred years on, it is still a mystery – as complete a mystery as the Lizzie Borden case of 1892 ever was. The comparisons are intriguing: it was a sweltering hot August morning in Fall River, Massachusetts, when Lizzie called up the stairs to the maid, Bridget Sullivan, saying someone had killed her father, wealthy Andrew J. Borden. The body of her stepmother, Abby, was found shortly after. Snow though blanketed the city of Hamilton, Ontario, that February day in 1909 when Florence Kinrade ran across Herkimer Street crying, "Ethel is shot," leading to the discovery of her sister's body in the family dining room.

Both Lizzie and Florence were immediately suspected. Yet in both cases no murder weapon was ever discovered (although a hatchet found in the Borden basement was dubiously put forward as a possible weapon) and no bloodied clothing was seized by the police (although Lizzie tore up and burned a blue dress in the kitchen stove a few days after the murder, claiming she had brushed against wet paint).

If anything, Lizzie had a clearer motive for killing her father and stepmother: She and her sister Emma were at odds with their father over his decision to divide his fortune between his daughters and his wife's relatives. Lizzie had attempted to purchase cyanide from the local druggist; the whole family had fallen ill a few days before the murders, and Abby feared they were being poisoned.

Florence Kinrade's motives – and, as I shall explain shortly, it is difficult not to believe she murdered Ethel – are altogether subtler and more unusual.

Both women escaped conviction, Florence not even being charged with her sister's killing. The chivalry of the Victorian and Edwardian eras may have played an important role. As historian Mary S. Hartman writes in her classic study of thirteen French and English women accused of murder, "It is possible to conclude that it was wise to be female and respectable if one intended to dispose of someone in the nineteenth century. Middle-class women were literally getting away with murder."

A century later, getting away with murder is not the main issue. What interests us now is what these murders reveal of women's lives then. The nineteenth-century code of behaviour, which sociologist Jane Synge confirmed, was still largely in place in turn-of-the-century Hamilton, "defined the proper young woman as a frail but appealing, intellectually inferior but morally superior being, whose duty it was to be passive, decorative, and sexually pure." Ethel Kinrade, from all we know of her, nicely fitted the stereotype. Florence, never.

In that age of decorum, murder cases like nothing else threw the doors wide open on the inner lives of middle-class women, capturing whole households by surprise. Breaking the greatest of all taboos, they revealed women as sexual creatures, caught up in issues of pre-marital sex, masturbation, abortion, lack of sexual satisfaction in marriage and, most explosive of all, adultery. These women were neither freaks nor victims, but women who found extreme solutions to ordinary problems, suggests Hartman. It would be a mistake, she says, to regard them as "rebels, even proto-feminists, using murderous schemes to challenge outmoded codes of behaviour." They were "neither reformers nor public defenders of their sex." Yet, as the nineteenth century ended, middle-class women, Hartman argues, commit murder "not merely to escape what they perceive as hopeless or desperate circumstances, but also to achieve or retrieve some imagined happier state."

Lizzie took up her axe to protect the family fortune, preserve the way of life to which she and her sister were accustomed, and wreak horrible vengeance on her stepmother and even her beloved father for threatening that idyll. Florence, I will argue, had experienced a real, not an imagined happier state when she went into vaudeville and fell in love with charming but forbidden Jimmy Baum, and now believed, rightly or wrongly, that her sister Ethel, had destroyed it.

It would be wrong too to regard Florence as an early feminist. Yet to a modern audience her motives are completely understandable. She would have murdered mainly for ambition. In wanting to strike out on her own, leaving the family home, independent and unchaperoned, in order to build a career on the stage, she was simply ahead of her time. But it was not to be: her father may have been indulgent, but her mother and her sister were adamant: vaudeville was simply not an acceptable choice for a well-brought-up young woman. Especially one engaged to be married to a young minister.

But how on earth could she think that murdering her sister would allow her to return to the stage and marry Jimmy! It would be tempting to say that Florence, no moral imbecile, simply killed Ethel impulsively in a fit of anger. Psychiatrist Dr. Sandford Fleming had told me: "I have seen it repeatedly – murder doesn't have to result from craziness. It could have been an impulsive act, with no motive needed. Many people have killed over minor things." I don't believe that is plausible. The evidence suggests to me that Florence had planned the murder for several weeks at least and had a fairly clear notion of how she would proceed afterwards.

For Florence, unbearable tension had been building up since the summer of 1908 when she returned to Hamilton from Virginia. The excuse given by the family for her return, of course, was that she had symptoms of malaria and was advised to go north to escape the heat. But it is not hard to imagine the shock at the house on Herkimer Street when it was discovered that Florence had been deceiving them and had gone on the stage. In her father's eyes, it seems, she could do little wrong. But her mother and sister must have been like tigers. Not only had she lied repeatedly, but she had put her engagement to Monty at risk, and, by threatening the family's respectability, possibly blasted Ethel's chances of making a decent match.

It says a lot for Florence's persuasive powers – and her hold on her father – that in the course of a few months she won his approval to return to the South and even resume her stage career. We can surmise that relations between the sisters during their trip with their father to Chautauqua, in upstate New York, for the arts festival in August must have been strained. Florence would have used that musical occasion to remind her father of her own musical potential; Ethel would have simmered.

Florence returned to Portsmouth in October over her mother's strenuous objections. Then news arrived at 105 Herkimer, either in a letter from Florence or from another source, of the attentions Jimmy Baum – 'an actor without means' – was paying her, and she was ordered home before Christmas.

At that point the clock started ticking down on the tragedy. Florence was not prepared to give Jimmy up. Love letters were sent but inter-cepted – likely by Ethel. A brooch from Jimmy was also intercepted and returned to him by Bella, doubtless with Ethel at her shoulder. Florence would have been frantic. She told Jimmy to write to her under her stage name, Mildred Dale, care of the Hamilton post office, and he did so. In one of those letters she told him she thought she would go crazy over her troubles. Again, her subterfuge was discovered. Her mother and sister had had enough. This time they persuaded Tom Kinrade to put down his foot.

On February 10, 1909 we find Florence staying at the sumptu-ous King Edward Hotel in Toronto. Her parents were perhaps trying to bribe her to ditch Jimmy by offering her a stay at the King Edward, conveniently close to where Montrose was continuing his studies. If so, they succeeded. On that day she wrote what must have been the hardest letter of her life, dumping Jimmy.

She concluded it: "Our correspondence must end. I hope you will forgive and forget, which will not be hard for me to do. Yours sincerely, Mildred Dale." The casual words were meant for other eyes – her par-ents', perhaps Monty's. The signature, Mildred Dale, is the clue. It was like a code to Jimmy – "I won't forget." The letter was written and mailed just fifteen days before Ethel was shot.

The easiest question to answer is: who killed her? Florence did, of course. There was plainly no tramp-murderer. It is inconceivable that a tramp would shoot her in the head then wait around for fifteen or twenty minutes before delivering the *coup de grace*. No other mem-ber of the family, including Bella Kinrade, had either the motive or the opportunity. Florence's remarkable performance during her days on the witness stand was all about covering-up her crime. And when, in 1965, she asked her daughter, Joan, "Do you think I did it?" she was telling us quite plainly that she did. Why else, after relating a family tragedy, would she impute blame to herself? As Joan realized instinctively later on, her mother's odd question was inviting another: "Well, did you?" The daughter wished later that she had asked it, because it is quite possi-ble she would have found her mother in a mood to confide. The harder question to answer is, if Florence planned the murder, what could she possibly hope to gain from it?

We speak of those who would do violence to others as having an 'irrational hatred' of their victim. In this case it could be called a rational hatred. Every avenue had been closed off to Florence. There would be no more travelling alone. It was not likely she could use the Marion Elliott ruse again. Plainly she had been told she must wait meekly until such time as she and Montrose could marry, and then, like thousands of women of her era, she would be expected to swallow the bitter pill of her ambitions, smile bravely walking down the aisle on her father's arm, and resign herself to a life of children and duty. Her singing would be confined to solos with the church choir and the odd community concert. There would be no more jokes and pranks with Jimmy and fellow performers at the Orpheum. No more would she be the woman of mystery, receiving gifts from dangerous admirers. No more playing the willful and seductive Southern belle teasing gentlemen admirers. No more fun!

That was not her way. Almost before the letter was in the mailbox, she must have regretted it. No doubt Monty was charming, agreeable and had shown incredible patience during Florence's escapades in the South. But he was not offering her the life she wanted. Writing and mailing the letter must have made Florence realize that, in the course of her adventures in Virginia, she had found her destiny.

She seethed with resentment and sought for some escape. Her father could no longer be relied upon to save her; her mother was implacable. And standing as the guardian and enforcer of the new regimen she identified her sister, Ethel.

But how would the removal of Ethel restore her freedom? Florence probably had no clear idea. But, like dynamite freeing up a logjam, Ethel's removal would make change possible. Her mother was weak and sickly and inclined to throw up her hands at family crises. With Ethel out of the picture, Florence would once again hold sway over her father. She would have had no clear idea how events would work out, but she had escaped the domestic trap before and was confident she could do it again. Anyway that, I suspect, is the direction Florence's thoughts were taking in the hours and days after she was forced to write that wrenching letter to Jimmy.

And one vital part of her plan was already in place: the gun. In his evidence at the inquest, Tom Kinrade was quite definite – in fact, suspiciously emphatic – in saying no member of his family ever had anything to do with guns, had even handled a gun. He knew quite well that his second son, Earl, had been in a couple of scrapes with a gun he had borrowed from the bank where he worked. Why would the father be so determined to deny any gunplay had ever taken place? Because he knew by then that Florence had brought a gun back with her from the South, and he wanted to put a full stop to any questions about guns in the Kinrade home. Neither he nor Florence could have dreamed that the amusing gun incidents at the Orpheum, or a suggestion that she had practiced with a gun before going to Savannah would figure in evidence at the inquest. If we accept that Florence shot Ethel, the likeliest source for the gun is Portsmouth. Then as now, American women had far greater access to guns than their Canadian counterparts, and given the racial tensions in the South then, females were far more likely to carry them.

For Florence, owning a gun would have been part of the aura of the Southern belle that she was cultivating, with the hint of danger and fearlessness that it suggested. When she was ordered home, she was not going to give the weapon away – she would have slipped it into her valise. It would be stretching probability to imagine she had any thought then of shooting Ethel. She just took the gun along – because you never knew when it would come in handy.

That moment came, I believe, when she was forced to write the letter renouncing Jimmy Baum. The gun, perhaps hidden in a shoe, or a hatbox in her bedroom closet, was central to her plan. In the nineteenth century, women murderers were more likely to use poison than gun or knife – usually to dispose of unwanted husbands. Poison compensated for a woman's weaker physique and, because she was usually in charge of the food, was easy to administer. But Florence had the weapon to hand – she only had to come up with a scheme. The plan she came up with was not at all bad – except that, like so many murder schemes carried out almost inevitably by amateurs lacking any experience, it went awry.

In Hamilton in the depths of winter, it was not hard to find the storyline. The threat – real or imagined – posed by the hundreds of tramps seeking shelter and food in the city was on everyone's lips, and the newspapers played up any reports of tramp delinquency. The murder and rape of a Stratford farmer's wife by the tramp, Frank Roughmond, five months earlier was still well-remembered. With tramps frequently coming to the Kinrades' door to have meal tickets signed, the story of a tramp-murderer would naturally have suggested itself to her.

In her many idle hours, Florence, all the while playing the part of the newly submissive daughter and fiancée, worked on the details. Some days before the murder she began playing up the tramp danger, claiming to have seen a tramp peeping in the window. The gouge discovered in the windowsill beside the front door conforms in no way with the small marks tramps left on houses to indicate a good touch or otherwise: could it have been made by Florence using a chisel while other family members were out? And then, on the night before the murder, she claimed to have been woken in the night by a scraping sound at the door.

So we come to the day of the murder. It might have gone like this: Florence waits until she hears the front door close as Gertrude and her father leave for school. Her mother and Ethel are downstairs, her sister likely clearing away and washing the breakfast dishes. She looks out of the window at the snow gently falling on Herkimer Street. Checking to make sure she has locked the door to her room, she places a chair in front of her closet and reaches for a shoe box she keeps on the top shelf.

She places it on her bed and unties the string. She has the gun wrapped in a hand towel along with the small wooden box of bullets. In her hand the .38 calibre weapon feels heavier than she remembers when she practiced with it in Portsmouth. She checks to see the chambers are empty then takes a practice aim at the window. There might not be time later, so she loads five of the stubby bullets into the gun then, not wanting to risk an accident, wraps it up again and returns the box to the closet.

Sitting in her still-warm bed again, Florence steels herself for what is to come, rehearsing in her mind her grudges against Ethel, the insults she has received at Ethel's instigation, the future that will be possible for her in just a few hours when her busybody sister has been removed forever. She needs this time on her own to go over step by step what she has to do and the story she must afterwards tell the police. The hardest thing will be telling her father. It does not seem enough to tell him that a tramp killed Ethel. Somehow she must divert his sympathy to herself. Because she knows that, with her father on her side and no Ethel to interfere, she can do exactly what she wants. Then it comes to her – what she must say. And Florence, pulls down the pillows, snuggles between the sheets, and smiles to herself.

At noon, Tom Kinrade and Gertrude return home, and Florence emerges for the main meal. She must at all costs ensure that her mother is out of the house this afternoon. At dinner, she can speak of nothing besides the tramp alarms of recent days, the gouge in the front windowsill, and it is at her prompting that her father suggests Bella make a trip to the police station and the tramp mission to complain. From George Blackstock's line of questioning at the inquest – constantly querying what time she had left the house – it was obvious the authorities suspected Bella Kinrade was still in the house when Florence shot Ethel and had then proceeded to the police station to bolster the tramp theory. I don't believe it: When Bella Kinrade on returning home saw an ambulance outside the house, her first thought was that her younger son, Earl, had died and been brought home from Montreal. It was altogether too natural a mother's reaction to have been concocted. And it is too much to believe that Mrs. Kinrade, so prone to upset and fainting, would have been able to carry off the visits to the police station and the hostel in a calm manner after seeing her daughter shot.

So we see Florence waiting impatiently for her mother to leave. What can she be doing! Finally, bundled up in her fur coat, Bella Kinrade sets out.

The two sisters have been preparing to go out for a walk. Ethel is already downstairs and has on her coat and hat and veil; her muff sits ready on the dining room table. On some excuse – maybe going back for forgotten gloves or some other item – Florence returns to her room. Perhaps Ethel calls up the back stairs for her to hurry up. Florence has got herself up for this. She comes down the back stairs, the gun concealed perhaps in her muff or behind her back. Ethel is sitting in a chair near the door. If she sees the gun at all, it must be puzzlement that registers on her face. Is this another of Florence's games? The next moment there is an explosion. Ethel still sits there. Panicked, Florence fires three more times. Two of the bullets are to the mouth. Is Florence in some subliminal fashion stopping Ethel from ever again saying words that can hurt her? With relief, she observes Ethel crumple forward and fall heavily to the floor.

To her surprise and dismay, the room is filled with acrid smoke. Florence throws up the sash in the dining room bay window then dashes around the house opening more windows and letting in the cold. In her room, she returns the gun to the shoe box then stands at her bedroom window listening. Everything is still: no one seems to have heard anything. All she sees is a horse plodding up and down pulling a carriage, the driver hunched against the cold.

She knows now what she must do to corroborate the tramp story. She goes downstairs and climbs out of the dining room window. Standing on the building's sill, she remembers she has neglected to bring the items she needs – a pair of men's winter overshoes.

She climbs back in, finds a pair in the kitchen, and puts them on over her much smaller winter boots. She may have read of the trick in some detective story: opening the door, she walks across the yard, dragging the overshoes as if they were being worn by a man. At the back fence she takes off the boots and minces back to the house, stepping in her earlier footprints.

She has been so busy, she has hardly looked at Ethel, now a heap on the floor. To her horror, the 'corpse' is making noises. Gurgles and groans are coming from Ethel's shattered mouth.

This was not part of the plan. This she had never anticipated. It comes to her that, if Ethel lives, she is finished. It is no time for compassion or regret. She retrieves the gun from upstairs, pushing four more bullets into the chambers. Hurrying downstairs, she pushes the dining room table to one side to give herself room, and then tugs and pulls, rolling Ethel over on to her back. In doing so, Ethel's body now conceals the pool of blood that had collected from her head wounds. Her sister is still showing signs of life. Her eyes may have opened. Florence pulls open her sister's topcoat. The heart is on the left, she remembers. She presses the muzzle of the gun against Ethel's breast and fires, once, twice, three times. The noise again seems to her deafening, but only because she is in a confined space. There is a strong smell of smouldering wool where the bullets have ignited the clothing. Now Ethel is still, there is no life in her eyes. Looking at her own hands, Florence sees they are blackened with powder, and goes to the kitchen to wash them. She examines her winter coat for any signs of blood. If they are there, they are too small to attract attention. And the police, in the event, will never examine the coat.

Time is getting short. Her mother might come home at any minute, or her younger sister, Gertrude, might come home from school early. Florence puts the gun back in its hiding place, studies her face in the mirror to detect any telltale signs of blood, and puts on her hat. She looks around the dining room once more to make sure everything is as it should be for the police investigators. She stands inside the front door for a moment, and perhaps smiles. Everything has not gone exactly to plan, but she has, she feels, coped well with the little difficulties. She looks up Herkimer Street and, observing the streetcar approaching at a slow pace, she times herself carefully. Throwing open the inner and outer doors, she rushes down the steps and, as if demented, dashes across the tracks bringing the car to a squealing standstill.

"Mrs. Hickey, Mrs. Hickey," she cries, throwing herself on to the neighbour's stairs a moment later, "Ethel is shot. Ethel is shot six times."

There is the trip to raise the alarm at the butcher's, and her mother's arrival at the scene of the tragedy. Tom Kinrade is just leaving his school when he is called back for an urgent phone call. Someone from the butcher/grocery store on Herkimer Street tells him, as he recalls, "A tramp has got into your house and shot your daughter and she is dead."

As he testified, he feared that Florence's Portsmouth paramour had come north and shot her. His mind would have been in turmoil as he drove home in a hackney carriage from the school. At the house, his first words to Detective Bleakley are: "I have just expected something like this to happen." That could refer to the fears over tramps. And then the oil cloth covering is pulled back and to his surprise, it is Ethel. It is the crucial moment. A rejected lover would hardly shoot the wrong sister. The tramp story does not seem to have figured in the father's thinking. And, watching as the ambulance attendants cart away Ethel's body so unceremoniously, the truth dawns on him: it is Florence who has shot Ethel. And he knows the reason very well.

Tom Kinrade is a senior educator as well as a businessman. As school principal he is used to making decisions. His experience serves him well at this terrible point in his life. He decides in an instant that his priority must be to protect Florence. This is the age of capital punishment. He has lost one daughter: he resolves he will not lose another. From this moment Tom Kinrade takes charge. He and he alone will determine how the script is written. Of one thing he is certain too: he will never ask Florence what happened.

Crossing the street to Mrs. Hickey's, he is met by Florence who, not realizing he now knows the truth, throws her arms around him, making her big play for his sympathy: "Oh, Papa, you must keep up. I will keep up if you will, Papa. And you know, it could have been worse, He said he would shoot me too!"

When Detectives Bleakley and Coulter had arrived at the house, it was within their power to solve the crime in a matter of minutes. The gun was almost certainly still in the house, concealed in Florence's room along with any bloody clothing she may have discarded. Bleakley mentions later searching the house with Coulter looking for the intruder and the weapon, but a proper search would have taken several officers and some considerable time. Bleakley also loses his chance when, still distracted by the tramp story, he allows Tom Kinrade to put a stop to his interrogation of Florence. Within a couple of hours, the Kinrade family move back into their home, and the disposal of any evidence is now within their control. The police have been thwarted, and will continue to be.

Tom Kinrade proves a master at protecting his family from their questions – first by removing them from Hamilton and then by employing the best legal counsel available to challenge the investigating authorities. For her part, Florence quickly learns that hysteria is her best defence: during questioning by police and then at Ethel's funeral she distracts attention by rolling her eyes, screaming and declaring that she can see Ethel's murderer. It proves the best sort of rehearsal for her performance later in the witness box.

And the weapon? The one sibling Florence remained close to throughout her life was her brother Ernest. It seems entirely likely that the roguish Ernie helped her get rid of the weapon. Where? Historian John Weaver tells me getting rid of a body or a weapon has always been a relatively easy matter in Hamilton: they either ended up on Hamilton Mountain or in the bottom of the harbour. In this case, the harbour seems the likeliest destination for the weapon, and its disposal may have been the secret Ernie's wife, Maggie, told her son, Ken, she would take to the grave with her.

Where did the murder start? Possibly decades earlier. So we start with Ethel and Florence as children and Dr. Sandford Fleming's theory of "a tremendous sibling rivalry. The two sisters," he said, "might have been at each other from infancy, especially if there was not enough love to go around." And Ethel, even though she was the eldest sister and entitled to special consideration, was always losing out. She was plain and had no boyfriend while Florence, much more attractive and personable, had two presentable men vying for her hand. Florence was a talented singer while Ethel was merely a choir member. Florence was even physically taller than her older sister. Most hurtful, Florence was her father's favourite. Ethel would have had to be less than human not to be jealous of her younger sister.

Up to this point, though, Ethel may have concealed any envy or resentment. Being Florence's sister could be great fun! In March 1907, two years before the murder, we find the two young women leading on the poor sap, Harold, who had advertised in a matrimonial column. It must have seemed a great lark! But as Florence developed her great scheme of deception, involving Marion Elliott, Marion's brother, Claude, Colonel Warburton, Mrs. Kenneth Brown and other characters, Ethel, I suspect, was kept as much in the dark as her parents. While Florence chatted gaily about her wonderful new friends, especially the glamorous, wealthy Miss Elliott, and her travels and the parties she attended and the homes where they stayed, Ethel must have felt very much the outsider.

Where the idea for the Richmond scheme came from, there's no telling. Perhaps on her trips to Syracuse or Toronto she indeed met someone from the Old Dominion and, listening to descriptions of life in the South, had been intrigued. She had earlier travelled with her parents to Atlantic City, and perhaps had the urge to go further south. Certainly, as she made her plans in freezing Hamilton in the winter of 1907-8, Richmond's warmer climate would have appealed to her.

But it was still a brave undertaking. No Miss Elliott would be there to meet her at Philadelphia or anywhere else. She was going to a strange city in a different country and when she emerged from the railway station at Richmond all she had to offer were her charm and her remarkable singing voice. It may have been enough: she would have been a social catch for any Richmond hostess, and in the few weeks she was there, she made several trips to surrounding areas, suggesting she had friends and a social life. She may too have passed the time visiting vaudeville theatres feeding an ambition she had likely acquired attending theatres in Toronto and Hamilton. She made regular trips by streetcar across the James River to Manchester to collect her mail because, after all, she had told her family that she was to be a soloist at the Manchester Presbyterian Church.

But why, after three weeks or so, did she leave Richmond? If there is a single moment when, by projecting ourselves back a century, we could witness and understand what really happened, I suspect it would be the events of April 6th to 8th when, by her own admission, Florence stayed two nights at the Queen's Hotel, in Toronto. Why on earth would she endure three or four days of train travel and go to considerable expense to return secretly to Canada without her family's knowledge after going to all the trouble of setting herself up in Virginia? It could hardly be, as she suggested, to see Montrose. He was putty in her hands. A letter would have convinced him of anything. Was there already another man – who paid her way? The detectives found nothing incriminating in the registers of the Queen's Hotel or the hotel where Florence stayed briefly in Fortress Monroe on her return to Virginia.

But by the time she arrived at the Hotel Virginia Beach she was emotionally shattered and in tears for days. Something must have happened on that trip home, something now beyond the reach of guesswork or clues.

This of course is only one of many missing pieces to the puzzle. What was the pile of mail waiting for her when she arrived in Portsmouth – responses from lovelorn columns to which she had responded? Did she really go to Savannah, as she claimed? Much of what she did while she was in the South is a mystery.

Clearly, getting into vaudeville was now her main concern. But she was deadly afraid her parents would hear about it and order her home, so she used the 'Violet Kensington' ploy to make it appear it was not her at all who was seeking work at the Orpheum Theatre in Portsmouth. We can sympathize with Florence: she was a talented young woman, forced into deception in order to get her chance in front of the footlights. But without knowing it she had also brought herself another step closer to the tragedy on Herkimer Street.

The Orpheum Theatre was small time, part of a chain of vaudeville theatres. Yet as 'Mildred Dale,' Florence made a good start and, tutored by Jimmy Baum, quickly established herself as a favourite. She was on her way: she could expect eventually to be picked up by one of the major chains. At that point, she could come clean, presenting her parents with the fait accompli of a glamorous offer and, relying on support from her indulgent father, launch herself as a singer using her real name.

But her behaviour was as bizarre as ever. She made daily mysterious trips on the ferry to Norfolk, she would cry for no apparent reason in her dressing room, talk of threats made against her by her 'ex-husband' and others and went into a flap over flowers and a letter she received from an admirer. It all seems now like a cry for attention, yet in her social bearing she could not have been more demure, sitting quietly in company and going to bed as soon as she got home from the theatre.

And then, around June 1908, came the letter home telling them she had left her employ as a church soloist and was appearing at the Orpheum. Whether or not we believe the 'malaria' story, it is likely that Florence was ordered home post haste.

In Tom Kinrade's evidence, it is always his wife who is adamantly opposed to Florence going on the stage. Only when Blackstock asks specifically about Ethel's views does the father respond, "Oh, I don't think she liked it. She, being the eldest girl, was more in touch with the mother during the time Florence was away; I don't think she liked it at all."

By Kinrade's account, all was harmony and serenity the summer of '08 at the time of that Chautauqua trip. But had Ethel really been taken in by Florence's grand deceptions? What, we wonder, were the older sister's thoughts as she listened as Florence read aloud the letter she claimed to have received from Marion Elliott, apologizing for failing once again to make it to Hamilton, and making elaborate plans for Florence to travel from Buffalo with the fictitious Mrs. Goldsmith? From the time they were little girls, Ethel must have known her sister was a little sneak: lies and invented stories are not a habit suddenly acquired in the twenties.

Around this time, I suspect, Ethel figured out that her sister was engaged on a wholesale scheme of deception. Florence did not destroy the phony Elliott letter, and it is quite possible Ethel saw it and recognized the handwriting as her sister's. Regardless though of Ethel's possible suspicions, Florence had triumphed again, setting out on another journey to resume her glamorous life.

Florence, if we are to believe Dr. Clarke's diagnosis, was of a personality type incapable of loving another human being wholeheartedly. As when she married the greengrocer years later in California, marriage was a means to an end. In Jimmy's case, he would be her ticket out of a provincial Canadian city and into a life in vaudeville.

It may have been at this point that Ethel, acting on long-held suspicions, threatened to tell their parents about Florence's whole bogus scheme. There could though have been an even bigger secret – one that would make her made-up stories and her actor-boyfriend seem of little consequence. The clue lies in an incident when Florence is being interviewed by Dr. Clarke. He notes that she is alarmed when he proposes to examine her patellar reflexes, and hurriedly leaves the room with the nurse. She returns only after the nurse has explained that the doctor merely wants to check her 'knee-jerk' reflexes – a normal and uncontroversial procedure. Does Florence though believe he is about to give her an internal examination to determine if she is still a virgin? From her extreme reaction it seems plausible. If so, what was she afraid of? It raises the possibility that Florence's adventures in the South were of a sexual nature. Dr. Clarke mentions 'sexual aberrations,' and in that time aberrations could simply mean having sex outside marriage. For a middle-class family of the period, nothing could possibly be worse than having a wayward and promiscuous daughter. And if Ethel had even an inkling of this, and was inclined to tell her parents, we need look no further for a motive for her murder.

Whatever Ethel knew, Florence now regarded her as her mortal enemy and the author of her troubles and convinced herself that, if Ethel were removed from the picture, she would be free once again to lead her own life. Of course, that is not logical thinking, but as Dr. Basil Orchard, the forensic psychiatrist, explained, "If she was a psychopath, all you need is for someone trying to get too close to her or threatening her plans for behaviour quite extreme and impossible to explain to occur." The whole story of psychopathic murder is of people resorting to illogical and extreme measures to solve their immediate problems.

An obvious question is whether it is even credible that a well-brought-up young woman in a genteel neighbourhood would, in broad daylight, shoot her sister, not once but seven times simply over disagreements about whom she should marry and how she should live. The answer is: absolutely. The only unique feature about the Kinrade murder is the novelty of sister shooting sister. It is unheard of. A search of the true crime literature produces no parallel. The closest comparison would be a 1997 California case in which Gina Han, 22, was convicted of conspiring to murder her twin sister, Sunny, by hiring two thugs who bungled the job. Gina, a petty criminal, believed Sunny had reported her to the police.

In just about every other sense though, Florence Kinrade is an entirely typical female murderer. As Patrick Wilson writes: "Women do not kill as often as men, and the vast majority of murders by women spring from circumstances within their family lives."

At the time of the Kinrade crime, women were regarded as the weaker sex possessed of finer feelings than men. Yet even then there were murders that challenged this common view.

When Lizzie Borden slashed her hated stepmother to death with an axe, and then, ninety minutes later, dispatched her beloved father in the same way, she caused thoughtful people in North America to revise their view of what a well-brought up lady was capable of. Lizzie was certainly not Florence, yet we hear echoes in the descriptions of Victoria Lincoln, who grew up in Fall River, and, as a girl, knew Lizzie Borden:

> Lizzie longed for a place in the sun. But she was obsessed with self-image, and her longing for popularity was self-defeating; she was always suing for favour, wounding without intent, and withdrawing into her shell... she never learned the secret of being a friendly equal.

Such crimes may have inspired F. Tennyson Jesse, a woman who edited many of the Notable British Trials volumes, to write in 1924 of the woman murderer:

> It is not only that she has by nature fewer inhibitions than men – it is also that she has the quality of excess. Hence she can be more cruel in revenge, more relentless in pursuit, and more utterly conscienceless.

Rather than being random acts of violence, she suggests, "women's crimes nearly always have a story."

Yet, Florence, like most other 'respectable' women accused of murder in that era, could, like Clara Ford, have expected a generous and sympathetic hearing from judge and jury. Middle-class female murderers, says Mary S. Hartman, had the effect of mesmerizing judges.

In the context of Hartman's study of middle-class French and English women accused of murder, Florence Kinrade's elaborate inventions are not at all surprising. "All the women here lied," she says of her thirteen subjects. Hartman goes on to say that:

> It is tempting, of course, to regard the murderesses as extraordinarily gifted in deceit, but nineteenth century middle-class conditions were so favourable for developing female skills in mendacity that the judgment would be hasty. The reputation for lying has admittedly always belonged to women, and it is deserved to the extent that, like any other group with limited control over decisions which affect their lives, they have resorted to deceit as a survival technique. But in the Victorian age (which could

be said to be still alive in 1909 Hamilton), deceit in matters large and small was elevated as a socially prescribed
form of female behaviour. Women were encouraged to
hide their affections, conceal their bodies (as well as the
bodily functions of menstruation and pregnancy), and,
depending on the advice they followed, either hide or
feign sexual pleasure with their husbands.

While the thirteen women in her study should not be regarded
as social rebels, even proto-feminists, it is possible to identify among
them some women whose more 'positive' motives suggest a growing
consciousness of struggle against constricting social roles. Especially in
the later period (of the nineteenth century), women murder not merely
to escape what they perceive as hopeless or desperate circumstances –
but also to achieve or retrieve some imagined happier state.

Here, finally, we are approaching the mainspring of Florence
Kinrade's crime. Certainly as a woman who murdered another woman
and she her sister, she could not be regarded as an early feminist.
Equally, it is difficult to ascribe her brutal act to any single motive.

The psychiatrist, Michael H. Stone, using true crime accounts of
notorious murder cases, has compiled a list of no fewer than twenty-two
categories of murder, everything from self-defence to psychopathic tor-
ture murders. Only one of his definitions comes close to Florence's possible motivation: the psychopathic murder of elimination. Men, almost
invariably, are the perpetrators, usually getting rid of spouses in order
to pursue their romantic adventures. "Glib, egocentric, and skillful at
lying, these men often try to make it appear as though the crime were
an accident or as though someone else were responsible," writes Dr.
Stone. "They bank on their good reputation and appearance to gull the
authorities. Almost never do they admit their guilt, even in the face
of overwhelming evidence. Many naïve people are taken in, unable to
believe that 'such a nice looking man could have…'"

F. Tennyson Jesse, in *Murder and its Motives*, devotes a chapter
to the 'murder for revenge,' using as her example the famous British
Constance Kent case. Following the death of her mother, Kent's
father married the family governess whom Constance detested. On a
June night in 1860, she abducted her four-year-old stepbrother from
his bed, and the child's body was discovered in the garden, his head
nearly severed from his body. Suspicion fell upon her father and upon

a nursemaid and it was only five years later that Constance, having under-gone a religious conversion, confessed, and was eventually condemned to penal servitude for life. (It is interesting, though perhaps not central, that Lizzie Borden, Constance Kent, and Florence Kinrade all identified with their fathers.)

There was certainly an element of revenge in Ethel's murder: For Florence, it was payback time for the indignities she felt she had suffered in having her mail interfered with, and her future destroyed by her sis-ter. But again, the single motive of revenge does not quite cover the facts. And then, reading Anne Jones' landmark study, *Women Who Kill*, I came across, not an explanation for the Kinrade case, but a phrase that resonates.

Jones believes that, of all the latter-day theorists about Lizzie Borden, "Agnes DeMille came closest to the bone of Lizzie Borden's existence when she created her ballet, *Fall River Legend*. Lizzie's life," she wrote, "consisted mainly in things… that didn't happen."

Murder for a life that didn't happen. That is as close, I believe, as we can come to accounting for the shooting of Ethel Kinrade. Florence, in her months in Virginia, had tasted a larger, more exciting life. It was not the stultifying world of Herkimer Street, encompassing boring afternoon walks with Ethel, at home days when no one visited, and where the only prospect of escape was marriage to Montrose Wright and being eternally under the social microscope as the wife of a clergyman. Rather, it was freedom – travel, a glamorous life behind the footlights, the applause of audiences, and life with the easy-going and humorous Jimmy Baum.

Even when Florence first went south to Virginia, time was running out if she hoped for a career in vaudeville. Many stars of vaudeville, coming from show business families, had begun as child performers, while others, emerging from a lower stratum of society, were treading the boards in their teens. At twenty-two, Florence was already running to catch up. But now the door had slammed shut. Her parents, egged on by Ethel, had put their foot down. There would be no more travelling on her own, no more show business, and no more Jimmy. Naïvely, she thought the removal of the one person she now regarded as her real enemy would turn back the clock and make all her dreams possible. In an age when middle-class women's lives were still largely confined to matrimony and child-bearing, you could call Florence's crime a murder of ambition.

But killing was not as easy as she thought it would be. It all went wrong that February day in the dining room. It was only Florence's calculating ruthlessness – what Dr. C.K. Clarke would call her moral imbecility – which allowed her to complete her fatal plan. And it was that same crazy fortitude – as well as the rock-like support of her father – which allowed her to survive those brutal weeks of investigation and interrogation. She endured – at the cost of compromising her ambition. She would make a show of humility, perhaps even gratitude, in marrying Montrose and embracing obscurity. In doing so, she demonstrated that, although murdering her sister seemed like an act of madness, Florence was quite capable of making logical decisions in her own interest. And in spite of the labels Dr. Clarke and modern day psychiatrists have pinned on her, just like most of the women murderers Hartman writes about, she went on to lead a successful life, achieving many of her ambitions.

As for Montrose – dear, innocent, naïve Monty – he never seems to have doubted Florence's innocence for a moment. In October 1909, when a man who eventually proved to be mentally unhinged made a false confession to the police in London, England, that he had been paid $500 to murder Ethel Kinrade, a reporter once again called on Florence and Monty in Calgary for their response. "Thank God for that, old man," gushed an excited Montrose. "You have brought us the best news we have had for many a long day. Shake! My God, I only hope (the confession) is true. We will both be awfully glad if it's true. I knew it would come at last, but hardly hoped it would come so soon."

If there were any more dispatches, he told the reporter, "don't worry about the time – bring them right along." When the reporter called by later, Florence was present, but "she preferred to let her husband do the talking and never even turned to look at the reporter, even when questions regarding her were put."

She continued to play her role as the wife of a Calgary lawyer even though, as little Jeanne Wright noticed, she always seemed to be dressed up ready to go out. She wasn't to know that the world would turn again and that, within a decade, as Florence B. Wright, she would get another chance to become a vaudeville star. She would never make it into the top ranks of musical stardom, but few in her audiences, listening to her sing the roles of Violetta in *La Traviata* or *Carmen*, realized that Florence Kinrade's own story was every bit as passionate, as mysterious and dramatic as of anything encountered in opera.

That was her secret.

Florence Kinrade went on to lead a successful life, achieving many of her ambitions.
Only *she* knew the answer to her secret.

Afterword

105 Herkimer Street

Demolition in 1967 of the Kinrade home at 105 Herkimer Street.

ʔⵊⵊ

DECEMBER, 1987: I check my watch as I pass Hamilton Cemetery, where Ethel's twice-buried remains lie in the Kinrade plot under a stone that says simply, "Ethel Caroline." I am already a few minutes late for my appointment with Joe Varga. I hope he waits.

Herkimer Street, as I turn off Caroline, still retains an air of comfortable gentility, and some of the remaining Victorian residences have even been gentrified. It's not surprising that a comic strip running in the local newspaper, *The Hamilton Spectator*, is titled 'The Herkimers' and is about an upwardly mobile yuppie family.

I park across the street from where the Kinrade family home once stood. The site is now occupied by a nine-story, red brick apartment building. A red GMC pickup belonging to Varga Bros. Wrecking Ltd. pulls up behind me, and a middle-aged man in a blue parka gets out. A blast of cold air rushes in as he opens the passenger door of the Volvo and gets in, extending one very large, warm hand.

"How ya doin'?" growls Joe Varga. No, I'm not taking him away from his work: The demolition business is kind of slack in the winter. Yeah, he remembers, it was the spring of 1967 he got the contract to tear down an old rooming house at 105. By then the house had lost all sign of its former elegance. The little, second-floor gingerbread balcony from which, Florence said, she thought of giving the alarm – and then thought better of it – was gone, the broad wrap-around verandah where the Kinrades once posed for family photographs had not seen a coat of paint in years, and Bella Kindrade's tasteful Edwardian wallpaper had been replaced by layers and layers of tawdry pink and bilious green paint.

"It was awful," a neighbour complained of the house's last days as a rooming house, "Fights, drunks, naked women running around."

That wasn't how Nathalie Webb Carnachan, who would write me in 1988 from Sonoma, California, with her reminiscences of growing up at 105, remembered it. Her father, Malcolm McNeil Webb, like Thomas Kinrade, was a contractor building houses in Hamilton, and he too has a street named after him on which he built most of the houses. He bought the old Kinrade house in 1910 or 1911, wrote Mrs. Carnachan, when she would have been two or three,

> … and it was our home until we left Canada in 1923. It was a beautiful house… there were eight children in our family… the house had polished hardwood floors throughout. The front entryway had double doors, the upper parts plate glass. The vestibule had a marble floor and then two more doors of plate glass. The 'parlour' had a marble fireplace, the formal dining room behind it had a bay window of glass from ceiling to floor.

Behind that, she wrote, was the large family dining room where Ethel was killed. "We also used it as a family room, and my father built a big brick fireplace in it beside which our Christmas tree always stood." Her father, she said, in building a larger new kitchen on the back of the house, tore down the back servants' stairs that also played a part in the murder. She concluded her letter: "I will be eighty years old in November, and 105 Herkimer Street is still among my dearest memories. When I was a child, I

Detail of verandah photo of the Kinrade home. (Full photo on page 23.)
Left to right. Ernie, Gertrude, Earl, Ethel, Bella, and Thomas. Florence was absent, in Virginia.

became used to people saying, 'Oh, you live in the Kinrade house!'"

It had been nearly sixty years since the murder when Varga's men set up their construction fence around 105, but Hamilton had not forgotten. The day it went up, a police cruiser came by, the officers demanding to see the contractor.

"Those detectives," says Joe, thirty years away from Hungary and still speaking his own brand of English,

> They say to me, 'You want to work with us, fine. And we be able to find something.' And I say, 'I promise to tell my men, whatever you find, hidden underneath the floors, blood on it or something, keep it.' I am very interested, be honest with you. We'll look for that gun very hard, and if we find it – that's what I tell my men – we never touch it. Policeman come down, and he's got experience, can take finger mark off gun.

For the week it took to tear down the house, Joe Varga was a minor celebrity. A photographer from *The Hamilton Spectator* took his picture, passers-by stopped and told him what they remembered of the murder, and even at night people would gaze up at the gaping windows. But whatever the walls could tell, they remained silent. Ripping up the floorboards, smashing the lath and plaster, Joe and his men found nothing. Until the last day when he was bulldozing the site level. "I found bones under where back porch was," he says, his intense blue eyes alight. "I called the detectives. They smelled it, but they said it animal, dog, something like that." Joe got back on the bulldozer and soon the site was level, only a few pieces of splintered wood and broken bricks marking where the house had stood.

I thank him for his memories of that twenty-year-ago demolition job, his hand engulfs mine, and he walks back to his truck, the snow drifting in ropes down Herkimer Street. From my bag I pull the remarkably clear photograph I have, taken on a fine summer's day, likely in 1908, of the Kinrade family on the verandah of number 105. The upper floor is partly concealed by the broad leaves of the chestnut trees, but the figures on the verandah stand out sharply.

Thomas L. Kinrade lounges in a rocker in front of the double front door, silver hair shining magisterially, a white handkerchief peeping from his top pocket. His wife, Bella, plump and self-conscious, stands beside him while, as far away from his father as he can possibly be at the other end of the verandah, Ernie, his tie askew, a straw boater on the back of his head, squints roguishly at the camera. His younger brother Earl, soon to depart for Montreal to work in a bank, perches on the rail, his sister, Gertrude, still at school, sits demurely in the background. But it is the oldest daughter, Ethel, then likely twenty-four, who occupies the centre of the picture. She is neither engaging nor glamorous like her sister, Florence, who would have been twenty-two at the time. Ethel, wearing a high lace collar, a necklace and with a wide buckled belt crimping her waist, is plain goods. For once though she is at the centre of the picture, enjoying the attention normally claimed by her younger sister, who is nowhere to be seen. For, by then, Florence had flown the coop and was likely charming audiences in far away Virginia.

Acknowledgments

A FRIEND WHO DIED ONLY RECENTLY AT 104... his son, a retired English professor now teaching in China... a former Las Vegas showgirl... a retired Anglican clergyman... a brave Calgary publisher: I owe gratitude to these and many more people, some of whom helped me originally trace Florence Kinrade's strange story and some who more recently, assisted in the rejuvenation of a story that has been more than thirty years in the telling.

Without the Rev. Graham Cotter the heart of the story – what happened to his relation, Florence, after the sensational investigation into her sister Ethel's murder – would have gone missing. Without the willingness of Florence's daughter Joan, to remember her often painful relationship with her mother, much insight into Florence's character would have been lost. Joan and her girlhood Calgary and Toronto friend, Jeanne Wright, are gone now but they were wonderful observers and willing sharers and Joan especially, became a friend. Gone too is Florence's nephew, Ken Kinrade who revealed some of the darker aspects of that 'most affectionate' Edwardian family.

I was helped by a number of psychiatrists and psychologists, Dr. Morton N. Menuck, Dr. Russ Fleming, Dr. Basil Orchard, Dr. Sandford Fleming and Dr. J. Thomas Dalby, of Calgary, although in some cases I think they were just as grateful to me for bringing them the notes of the pioneer psychiatrist, Dr. C.K. Clarke which I had discovered in the Clarke Institute archives.

As always I owe thanks to many librarians — especially in Richmond, Virginia, and Hamilton, Ontario.

And then there are the people responsible for the second life granted to this manuscript lost to time. My neighbour, George Edward Hart, well after he passed a hundred years old, was fascinated when I told him Florence's story. His son, Jonathan Locke Hart, a writer and teacher, had contacts in the publishing business and, shortly I received an email from Lorene Shyba, whose firm, Durvile Publications, specializes in law themes and is publishing a 'True Cases' series. We sealed the deal for the Florence book over a bowl of brussel sprouts late one evening in a Toronto Japanese restaurant in the midst of a torrential flood on the street outside and since then Lorene has embraced the project with breathtaking skill and enthusiasm. Lorene pointed me in the direction of Western Canada aspects to Florence's story, and to two history enthusiasts, Bob Blakey in Calgary and Dawn Leite, in Lethbridge. My thanks to them both.

I offer my love and gratitude to Ayesha, my wife now of sixty years, who originally suggested that I should write about true crime, and our daughter, Fazia who, with her mother, keeps a wary eye out for the health and wellbeing of this senior writer.

Index

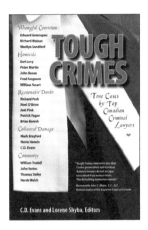

**Tough Crimes: True Cases by
Top Canadian Criminal Lawyers**
By Edward L. Greenspan *et al*
Book 1 in the True Cases Series

*SHRUNK: Crime and
Disorders of the Mind*
True Cases by Forensic Experts
By J. Thomas Dalby *et al*
Book 2 in the True Cases Series

*More Tough Crimes:
True Cases by Canadian Judges
and Criminal Lawyers*
By Donald Bayne *et al*
Book 3 in the True Cases Series

*"Tough Crimes demonstrates that Crown
prosecutors and criminal defence lawyers
do not escape unscathed from serious
trials. The disturbing memories remain."*
— Hon. John C. Major, CC QC,
Justice of the Supreme Court of Canada.

*"The workings of the criminally disordered
minds has always been a fascinating
subject. Does our prison system throw
away the key after incarceration, or is it
worthwhile to rehabilitate?"*
— Earl Levy, QC

*"A revealing, at times searing and
always very human look inside our
criminal courtrooms and the people
who populate them."*
— Sean Fine, Globe and Mail

Tough Crimes is a collection of
thoughtful and insightful essays
from some of Canada's most prominent criminal lawyers. Stories
include wrongful convictions,
reasonable doubt, homicides, and
community spirit.
Edited by C.D. Evans and Lorene Shyba

SHRUNK is a collection of true
cases by eminent Canadian and
international forensic psychologists
and psychiatrists facing the tough
topic of mental illness in the
criminal justice system.
Edited by Lorene Shyba and J. Thomas Dalby
Foreword by Dr. Lisa Ramshaw

The third book in the "True
Cases" series, *More Tough Crimes*
provides readers with a window
into the insightful thinking
of some of Canada's best legal
minds from coast to coast.

Edited by William Trudell & Lorene Shyba
Foreword by Hon. Patrick LeSage

Price: $29.95, 24.95 US *Paperback*
288 pages

Price: $29.95, 24.95 US *Paperback*
272 pages

Price: $29.95, 24.95 US *Paperback*
272 pages

ISBN: 978-0-9689754-6-6 (2014)
E-book: 978-0-9689754-7-3 (2015)
Audio: 978-0-9689754-7-3 (2017)

ISBN: 978-0-9947352-0-1 (2016)
E-book: 978-0-9947352-3-2 (2016)
Audio: 978-0-9952322-7-3 (2017)

ISBN: 978-0-9947352-5-6 (2017)
E-book: 978-0-9952322-2-8 (2017)
Audio: 978-0-9952322 9 7 (2018)

**DURVILE &
UpRoute Books**

DURVILE.COM

DURVILE'S TRUE CASES SERIES

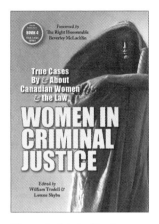

Women in Criminal Justice:
True Cases By and About
Canadian Women and the Law
By Hon. Susan Lang *et al*
Book 4 in the True Cases Series

"The reader emerges with pictures in mind ... women working without respite to achieve just outcomes for the people they deal with often in the face of difficulty."
— Rt. Hon. Beverley McLachlin

Stories in *Women in Criminal Justice* deal with terrorism, drugs, sexual assault, mental disorders, motherhood, child protection, LGBTQ+, Indigenous, and other urgent issues of our time.

Edited by William Trudell & Lorene Shyba
Foreword by Rt. Hon. Beverley McLachlin

Price: $29.95, 24.95 US *Paperback*
272 pages

ISBN: 978-0-9947352-4-9 (2018)
E-book: 978-1-9888241-4-7 (2018)
Audio: 978-1-9888241-4-7 (2018)

Florence Kinrade: Lizzie Borden
of the North
By Frank Jones
Book 5 in the True Cases Series

"Frank Jones has always had a knack for finding the quirkiest and most interesting true crime tales, and relating them with the skill you'd expect from a lifelong, first rate journalist, and this latest is no exception." — Linwood Barclay, Author

In 1909, Florence Kinrade is a dutiful daughter, engaged to the parson's son. She also leads a double life as a vaudeville showgirl in Richmond, Virginia. Florence becomes the central figure in a gruesome crime.

Price: $29.95, 24.95 US *Paperback*
288 pages

ISBN: 9781988824352 (2019)
E-book: 978-0-9952322-8-0 (2019)
Audio: 978-1-988824-31-4 (2019)

TRUE CASES BOXED SET
The First Four Volumes

Eds: William Trudell, C.D. Evans QC,
Lorene Shyba PhD, J. Thomas Dalby PhD

ISBN: 978-1-9888241-7-8 (2018)
Price: $90.00 Canada., $75.00 US
Trade Paperbacks in box set
1350 pages

For media contact:
Lorene Shyba | 403 818-4808 | lorene.shyba@durvile.com

For orders contact:
University of Toronto Press (UTP)
Ph (416) 667-7791/ (800) 565-9523
utpbooks@utpress.utoronto.ca | utppublishing.com

DURVILE &
UpRoute Books

DURVILE.COM

OTHER BOOKS BY FRANK JONES

Paid to Kill

Master and Maid: The Charles Massey Murder

Beyond Suspicion

Murderous Women

True Murder Stories